G000116156

Village Schooling in Somerset

Learn 'em Hard

Village Schooling in Somerset

Learn 'em Hard

Sarah Villiers

First published in Great Britain in 2012

British Library Cataloguing-in-Publication Data
A CIP record for this title is available from the British Library

ISBN 978 1 906551 33 9

Typeset in New Century Schoolbook

RYELANDS
Halsgrove House,
Ryelands Business Park,
Bagley Road, Wellington, Somerset TA21 9PZ
Tel: 01823 653777 Fax: 01823 216796
email: sales@halsgrove.com

Part of the Halsgrove group of companies
Information on all Halsgrove titles is available at: www.halsgrove.com

Printed in China by Everbest Printing Co Ltd

Dedication

To my godmother Joyce Power-Steel, of Donegal
– an educator, who met my mother
at a small school in West Runton, Norfolk
and also taught at the
Universities of Trinity College, Dublin
Queen's, Belfast
Reading, England
and went on teaching all her long life;

and to all inspiring teachers
and aspiring learners
past and present.

Acknowledgements

We would like to thank the Library Services of
Somerset for their helpfulness and support,
in particular the staff of the Somerset Heritage Centre, Taunton
and of the libraries at Street and Somerton.

Contents

List of Plates

Copyright permission to reproduce items was gratefully received from the following:
www.spartacus.schoolnet.co.uk fig ii Hannah More; Enmore School Archive T and J Poole
www.heritagecentre.org.gov (Plates 1,2 Somerset Heritage Centre)
www.allerfordmuseum.org.uk (Plate 7 Victorian Classroom)
www.nationalarchives.gov.uk/doc/open-government-licence (Plate 10, Plowden Report, HMSO 1967)
www.radstockmuseum.co.uk (Plate 11 Handwriting in the Victorian Classroom)
Mr Partridge (Plate 11 Maths Book): Mr D J Wheadon (Plate 12 Egg-Shackling)
and, archivists at N Cheriton (Plate 4), N Curry (Plate 9), W Huntspill (Plate 12)

Prologue

This project began by chance. While browsing in churches in the Quantocks, I found a memorial plaque in Nether Stowey Church, fulsomely dedicated to one Thomas Poole. I was intrigued. Who was this Thomas Poole and how had he made such an impact on his fellow parishioners? It soon led me to his more modest cousin, Rev John Poole, Rector of nearby Enmore, who had established an important school in 1810. Thus began a three year journey around the village schools of Somerset, visits to the County Archives and meetings with many helpful, obliging, knowledgeable and patient people that I met on my forays into the unknown.

Which schools would be the focus of this study?
Not the already well-researched ancient foundation schools, usually in larger towns and often grammar schools. It was the small, unassuming rural schools in which I was more interested, those which are often overlooked (except at times of anniversaries and Jubilees, by the families whose children attend them). So it was to the villages that I turned.

First, what counts as a village?
For my purposes 'a village' meant any settlement that supported only one school for any one age group or gender, unless of a different religious denomination. Thus, small-town Somerton was included, for it had three separate schools for children of elementary age: one for Boys, one for Girls (and Infants), and one for Infants only, all of which were Church of England schools. A few settlements had both a British (non-conformist) as well as a National (Anglican) School: thus, Long Sutton had both a National and Quaker school, Oakhill had a British and National School, West Pennard had a National and Wesleyan School, while Lullington only had a British school. In several villages with both kinds of school it appears that the British school often came to accept a closer relationship with government (and its grant opportunities) and became the Board school post-1870. Thus it came to be managed by a locally elected body, while the National school continued to maintain greater independence from government and local 'politics', under a Diocesan umbrella. Some villages were too small to have had a school: those children had to walk to the next village, or often did not attend at all.

Secondly, what do we mean by 'a school'? Often a school is mentioned, particularly those from the early pre-C19th period, but with no indication of where it was located in the village, or in what kind of accommodation. Thus a 'school' cannot be assumed to be synonymous with a dedicated 'school building'; in addition the date by which a 'school' can be said to exist is sometimes ambiguous as its very existence may not be continuous. Schools are mentioned as being held in diverse places. Many of these were short-lived, but some survived to be re-housed in dedicated buildings when funds became available.

There were also plenty of Sunday Schools, frequently more than one in a single village where there were chapels as well as a church. Sunday schools provided a much more substantial education than we associate with the current version today: in the C18th and C19th Sunday School usually lasted all day and the prime purpose was to teach children to read – so they could read their Bibles. It was often the only means by which poor children might learn to read and write if there was no other school available, or, if their parents could not forgo the earnings their children might bring in during the working week. For this study these schools were discounted as they did not provide the full range of educational opportunities available in the day schools. Sometimes, in addition to the Parish School, there were dame schools, also private day or boarding schools – often for Ladies, from families which did not want their daughters mixing with the rougher elements of the population and who could afford to pay to go elsewhere. These latter schools were also discounted.

Thus, for the purposes of this study, the focus in on the main day school(s) of the parish whether it might be termed Parish or Parochial School, National or British School, a Wesleyan, Baptist, Quaker or Congregational School.

Where are the sources? To determine the existence of a school or master, the first sources are the records of Charities which might specify monies to be used for schooling. **Collinson's History of Somerset in 1791** and the **Reports of the Charities' Commission** between 1818 and 1830s usually give a good summary of these. **Trust documents** and **Indentures** can also shed light on early beginnings. Details are sometimes available about the main benefactors, any participation of the Lord of the Manor, subscriptions from the local community and any existing local rates raised for educational purposes (Ch. 4).

In trying to trace the development of any school we can turn to the local **Trade Directories** which appear irregularly from 1840 to the 1930s. From these we can often find the date of any school build, subsequent enlargements and occasionally, the cost and size of the school buildings. Through these fragments we can make some progress towards determining the geographic distribution of schools and the dates of their spread. To gain an idea of the variety in the appearance of the school buildings, it was necessary to tour the county and photograph the buildings – many now closed and privately owned but often conveniently called *'The Old School'*. Some architect's plans are held in the Heritage Centre but many of these only date from C20th when the County Councils took responsibility for many existing schools (Ch. 5).

The names of the Master and Mistress, sometimes of an Assistant Teacher, are given in the **Trade Directories** – though often no supporting staff, particularly the young monitors and pupil-teachers on whom the Head frequently solely depended. For details about qualifications and training, if any, additional books tracing this development have been used (Ch. 6).

The best source of evidence to gain an insight into the day-to-day life of the school is the **Log Book** kept by each Head in every school from the 1860s or 1870s. The keeping of a Log Book followed from the acceptance of a government grant, since it served as a form of accountability, in addition to the regular inspections from HMI and the Diocesan Inspector. Further, **Managers' Minute Books** – where they are available – provide another dimension, as do the **Punishment Books**. However, one or other or all of these do not always still exist. Some are kept in the Somerset Heritage Centre, some in individual schools (in cupboards or lofts), some have found their way into private homes around the village but many are missing. **HMI Reports** (often copied into the Log Book) also give a fascinating view of changing expectations from the official body responsible for assessing schools and holding them to account.

Registers and Logs had to conform to the guidelines provided, so there is a recognizable format. However, the Logs were often highly personalised: some Heads noting little more than numbers attending and reasons for non-attendance, while others seem to use it to record the highs and lows of leading a small school in often difficult circumstances. We have to recognize that the data is not consistent nor complete (Ch. 7,8,9).

Thanks are due to many people who have assisted in different ways: from chance meetings while out photographing buildings, to local historians who have generously given their time such as John Lamb, Celia Mycock, Norman Voake. Thanks are also due to Katherine Judelson for invaluable comments, as well as the support and encouragement of Jake Tan.

In particular thanks go to the Heads who allowed me access to their Log Books on site – or even to take them home. These, together with Logs from the Heritage Centre, enabled me to read a variety of these remarkable documents from schools (22) across the county. These are:

Village	Hundred	Area of County	Location	Years covered
Blagdon	Winterstoke	1. Mendips (north)	On site	1876-1960s
Enmore	Ansfield	2. Quantocks (west)	On site	1872-1960s
Cutcombe	Carhampton	3. Exmoor (far west)	On site	1876-1960s
Nettlecombe(cls)*	Williton		Heritage Cnt+	1897-1945
Skilgate (cls)	Williton		Heritage Cnt	1875-1939
Isle Brewer (cls)	Abdick	4. Levels (central W)	Heritage Cnt	1877-1912
Westhay+Meare	Glaston	Levels (central N)	Heritage Cnt	1929-1946
Chaffcombe(cls)	Petherton, S	5. South	Heritage Cnt	1878-1959
Chillington (cls)	Petherton, S		Heritage Cnt	1907-1960s
Kingsdon (cls)	Somerton	6. Central	On site	1872-1960s
Charlton Mackrell	Somerton		On site	1863-1919
Keinton Mandeville	Somerton		On site	1889- 1960s
Somerton Boys Free	Somerton	}	On site	1891-1963
Montecliffe Mixed	Somerton	} merged 1963	On site	1867-1960s
West End Infants (cls)	Somerton	}	On site(now private resid)	1875-1916
Horsington	Horthorne	7. South Eastern	Heritage Cnt	1871-1939
West Pennard		8. Eastern (Wesleyan)	Heritage Cnt	1911-1930
Ashwick (cls)	Kilmersdon	(British)	Heritage Cnt	1904-1948
Oakhill		(C of E)	Heritage Cnt	1863-1950
Coleford	Kilmersdon	9. Mining (NE)	On site	1876-1960s
Holcombe (cls)	Kilmersdon	(Wesleyan)	Heritage Cnt	1906-1960s
Writhlington	Kilmersdon	(NE)	On site	1901-1960s

* cls = closed + Cnt= Somerset Heritage Centre

Also, from books containing extracts from Logs and other school documents (area in brackets):

Kingston Seymour	(NW 1)	Fiddington	(Quantocks 2)
Churchill	(Mendips 1)	North Curry	(Central W 4)
East Harptree	(Mendips 1)	Brewham	(East, Bruton 7)

Plus, Sunday Schools: Kingsbury Episcopi (5), Stoke-sub-Hamdon (6), Oakhill (8).

Thus most geographic as well as administrative units have been covered in order to note any variety of regional characteristics. In general, however, whilst the issues of small rural schools were very similar, the individual Head and local context could make a considerable difference.

Overall, these Logs, together with Managers' Minute Books and Admission Registers where available, paint a fascinating picture of rural schooling.

The heart of the study is in Part IV – the teaching and learning inside the classrooms of the C19th schools: how and what teachers taught and what the experience of the pupils was. This kernel is embedded within what we know of the teachers' training, the buildings and funding of schools (Part III). Parts I and II set the scene regarding early efforts and the influences of Somerset's two important contributors to education – philanthropist Hannah More and education pioneer John Poole. Finally, Part V completes the story in modern times.

Part I

The Framework of Development of Schooling in Somerset.

The turbulent years of the mid-C17 saw many individual efforts to bring schooling to some of the villages. The religious upheavals, even in this period, began to exert what became long-lasting influences. The geographic pattern of the early distribution of schooling continued to influence the development during the next 200 hundred years.

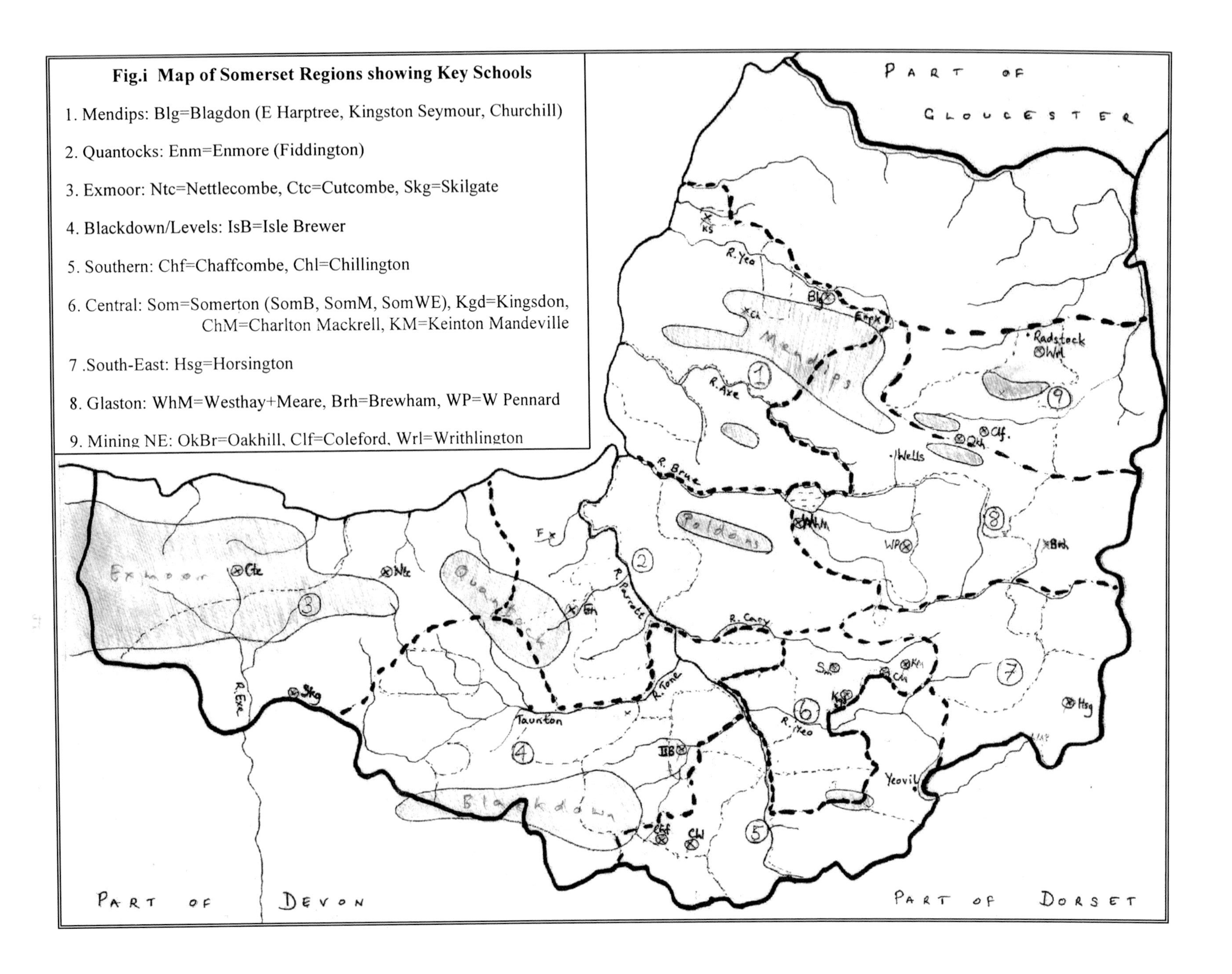
1. Mendips: Blg=Blagdon (E Harptree, Kingston Seymour, Churchill)
2. Quantocks: Enm=Enmore (Fiddington)
3. Exmoor: Ntc=Nettlecombe, Ctc=Cutcombe, Skg=Skilgate
4. Blackdown/Levels: IsB=Isle Brewer
5. Southern: Chf=Chaffcombe, Chl=Chillington
6. Central: Som=Somerton (SomB, SomM, SomWE), Kgd=Kingsdon, ChM=Charlton Mackrell, KM=Keinton Mandeville
7 .South-East: Hsg=Horsington
8. Glaston: WhM=Westhay+Meare, Brh=Brewham, WP=W Pennard
9. Mining NE: OkBr=Oakhill, Clf=Coleford, Wrl=Writhlington
PART OF GLOUCESTER
PART OF DEVON
PART OF DORSET
Mendips
Poldens
Quantock
Blackdown
Exmoor
R. Yeo
R. Axe
R. Brue
R. Parrett
R. Cary
R. Tone
R. Yeo
R. Exe
Taunton
Yeovil
Wells
Radstock

Fig.i Map of Somerset Regions showing Key Schools

Chapter 1
From the Dissolution to the late C18th

i. Beginnings of Secular Education: Tudor and Stuart Developments.

The Tudors may be said to have liberated education from the near monopoly of the Church, so that many new schools became 'free' schools – free of exclusive ecclesiastical control. Yet religious battles continued between Catholic and Protestant groups. The Stuarts, on the other hand, released education into still wider sections of society where there was a rapid spread of charity schools and 'English' schools – schools which no longer taught in Latin but in the vernacular. Many of these were free to those children supported by the terms of a charity or by a sponsor, while others had to pay. Yet again battles raged, this time between different Protestant groups, mainly the Anglican and nonconformist, or Dissident, groups. Thus Religion continued to dominate the debate on education throughout the C19th, sometimes inspiring greater competition between the different groups thereby dividing scarce resources, to the potential pupils' disadvantage. It continues to pose a challenge now, concerning the treatment of all the religions professed in England and Wales. The repercussions of these national conflicts played out in Somerset, a county reputedly with some areas of high numbers of Dissidents, often thought reformist and even radical in outlook.

The Dissolution of the Monasteries, which began in the 1530s and gradually spread across the country over a period of several years, had profound repercussions, especially in rural areas where monks and nuns had often been depended upon for employment, medical help and, also, for schooling. It was, possibly, the girls who particularly suffered, as there were so few alternatives to what some of the nuns had offered. Somerset had several monasteries, priories, friaries and chantries, in particular, the monastery of Glastonbury as well as smaller ecclesiastical houses, for example, at Cleeve, Muchelney, Withiam and elsewhere.

From the 1540s Tudor bureaucracy moved into secular education. Ex-monastic and cathedral schools were often reconstituted as Edward VI Schools. This was followed in 1547 by the Chantries Act which caused a second wave of re-organisation. These schools, however, were often allowed to continue, with a stipend from the Crown paid to the Schoolmaster (who had to be licensed by the local Bishop). In 1559, under Elizabeth I, Bishops had to continue to license teachers, having examined them on the 39 Articles which represented the new core tenets of the Protestant faith which underpinned the recently State-created Church of England. The Crown, having entered the education field, was then able to exert its influence not only through exercising controls over the appointed Masters but also through the books from which they taught. Several textbooks were given royal approval:

1540 a *Royal Grammar* was authorised by Henry VIII
1543 *The Ground of Arts* by Robert Record – on numbering, to show '*it was not vile and contemptible as some assert but useful for summing wages, victualling and casting ground for encampment*'

1546 *The Well Spring of Sciences* by Humphrey Baker, *'which teacheth the perfect work and practice of Arithmetic'*
1571 *A Book of Divers Hands* by John Baildon and de Beauchaesne which proposed several clear 'hands' so scholars could develop a readable handwriting-style for record-keeping and accounting, both much needed in a government bureaucracy
1596 *A course of Mathematics*, at Gresham College, City of London, with strong links to mercantile needs and interests.

We can see how closely mathematics was drawn in for State purposes, as was science and the art of navigation. Yet these subjects were still regarded as *'too mechanical and not academic, and therefore not appropriate for gentlemen'* (Lawson and Silver, 1973). It seems the aversion to maths is both old and strong. It was neglected in the dominant educational establishments for the (Anglican) elite, who preferred the Classics as being a more gentlemanly pursuit. Those young Etonians and Harrovians who were later to go out and rule vast tracts of India did so with copies of Pliny's letters to Emperor Trajan together with Virgil's speeches in one hand and a rifle in the other. It was often left to the C17th nonconformist Dissidents, in their separate Academies (whose scholars were denied access to mainstream English Universities) to fly the banner for more practical subjects, to develop industrial machinery for manufacturing ventures, go out to new colonies and plant estates, build railways, start mining operations, all of which underpinned the success and creativity in both trade and industry and came to express the new wealth of Empire.

For Somerset, two particular Oxford Colleges became havens for west-countrymen: **Wadham College** which was founded through the Will of **Nicholas Wadham** and his wife **Dorothy** of Ilminster, in 1610**;** and **Exeter College**, founded in 1315 by a Devonian (then expanded in the C16th by another). The ferment of ideas that spurred this growth in education was further stirred from other sources: the criticisms by Francis Bacon (1561-1626) of Aristotelian scholasticism who, instead, urged *'observation, experiment, induction and the pursuit of Science in the service of Society'*; the Czech pastor, Comenius (1592-1670), who visited England in 1641 and spread his ideas of education for young children to be based on sensory experience; and later Milton's *Of Education* in 1644 in which he urged schools to spread *'knowledge, civility and godliness throughout the land'* (Lawson and Silver 1973).

The mid-C16th to mid-C17th was the period of the fastest growth in education until we come to compulsory education in the late C19th. To help meet the pressures from the increasing number of schoolmasters, the early C17th also saw a number of books addressed to meet the needs of these new schoolmasters:

1596 *The English Schoolmaster*, Edmond Cooke
1616 *Ludicas Literarius*, John Brindley
1642 *The Good Schoolmaster: The Holy and Profane State*, Thomas Fuller
1660 *A New Discovery of the Old Art of Teaching School*, Charles Hoole
1673 *An Essay to revive the Ancient Education of Gentlewomen*, Bathusa Makin (tutor to Elizabeth, daughter of Charles I)

These often served as handbooks for the hard-pressed schoolmaster, including those known as *'abcdarians'* – the masters working with the youngest children to teach them their *abcd* (from a horn book), to use a basic primer and to acquire knowledge of the Catechism. However, in many schools, it was expected that children would start school at around seven years of age, having already learned their *abcd* and become at least basic readers.

A major change was taking place resulting in greater diversity of the types of schooling. So far the new Grammar schools served the middle-classes and provided a Classical education, in Latin, in imitation of the gentry who attended the major ancient establishments. Now the Pettys emerged, for the little children, *les petites*. Hoole describes these schools as *'For children for whom the Latin tongue is thought unnecessary. They should have more time to read religious books and other delightful books of English History and Poetry... I conceive that 40 boys would be enough to thoroughly employ one man, to hear everyone so often as is required without making use of any of his scholars'* (Seaborne, 1971). Here, the notion of any kind of monitorial approach – later, so popular – was rejected. These schools could make greater claim to be the precursors of the small, English, village school.

The turbulent times, during the Civil Wars and Commonwealth, were good years for education. We find that between 1600 and 1640 numbers of scholars at Oxford increased dramatically and, for the first time, *'plebians outnumbered gentry'*. It was a period of great investment in education, particularly among the new Puritan groups who saw the teaching of reading as essential for all to be able to read their Bible, in English. The lands and money confiscated from Bishops' estates by Cromwell between1646 and 1649 raised £20,000 – much of which was paid to schoolmasters, teachers and preachers. The Cromwellian Reforms of 1651-57 yielded *'a harvest of extraordinary good and sound knowledge'* (Lawson and Silver 1973). It was a time when Wren and Locke were at Oxford. In addition, while John Wilkins (Cromwell's brother-in-law) was Warden at Wadham College, he helped form the **Wadham College Club for Science and Maths** which later became the Royal Society for the Study of Science in 1660.

After the Restoration and Religious Settlement of 1660 it was necessary for everyone holding office to subscribe to the 39 Articles of Faith. Thus, following the 1662 Act of Uniformity, at least 150 schoolmasters were 'deprived' and many clergy also. Some of these casualties can be identified in the following table showing teachers in Somerset during the C16th and C17th.

These figures include a handful of very early examples of schooling: 1372 an unlicensed school in Shapwick was taught by an 'unfree tenant of the lord of the Manor' and there was a Master teaching 'in the vernacular'; in the C14th a Chantry Priest was teaching in Woolavington, and another in mid-C16th Martock.

Table 1.1: Distribution of pre-C19th village teaching and schooling by Regions

	Teachers					Subjects			Types				
Area No	**License**	**Un-licensed**	**Un-specified**	**Women+**	**Church Officials^**	***Unspec***	***3Rs***	***Lat/ Gram***	*Parish /Corp**	*Eng*	*Gram*	*Chrty*	*Diss*
1	8						02			01			
2*	30	11	15	2L 2U 1r	3R 3C	24	07	06	07	14	03	01	01
3	04						03	01		04			01
4	06					04				01	01		
5	03	01	07	1r	2R 1C	11		01	02	01			
6*	04	02	05	2U	2R	11		01	02				01
7*	11	04	07	2U	2R			02		05	03		04
8	04		06	1U		03	01			01	01		03
9	04									02	02		

+ L = licensed, U = unlicensed, r = resuscant [who refuses to attend CoE Church]
^ R = religious posts (vicar, rector etc), C = civil / parish posts (sexton, clerk, churchwarden etc)
* Corporation, as in Axbridge and Ilchester.

Note: For the map of regions, see p10. Reading the table from left to right we find that areas 2, 6 and 7, (8) show higher numbers of teachers. Data for each area are not always accessible. The totals in each of the three main categories (teachers, subjects, type of school) are not equal as information is incomplete, categories are not mutually exclusive and several teachers may be listed but without further details. Some C17th examples show the results of the political and religious upheavals of the mid-century Civil War and Interregnum, before the Restoration of Charles II in 1662. Throughout the period, most schooling resulted from individual personal efforts – often the Lord of the Manor – though some were recognised by local post-holders in the Church Vestry, or Parish Overseer.

Area 2: Quantocks *Women*: one *Prudence Poole in 1630s*, another identified as a *recusant*
Church officials: one vicar is described as 'deprived during interregnum'
Subjects taught: this is commonly unspecified, sometimes given as reading, writing, casting accounts/arithmetic, while one is identified as licensed to teach grammar, or Latin.
Area 4: **Levels/Taunton** Four of these six were from the same Levels village (Meare)
Area 5: South *Women:* one is a *recusant* (who rejected the Anglican orthodoxy) but was nevertheless permitted to live in the Almshouses, perhaps in return for her teaching services.
Church Officials: one is an 'intruded' vicar 1663
Type of School: one is described as a 'farm barton' school at Manor Farm.
Area 6: Central *Women*: 'several women' taught the pauper children in the C18th. By excluding the Grammar schools at Martock and Langport we omit one Vicar 'ejected' in 1646 (who became the first master of Strode's Grammar School 1662), one 'ejected' curate (who became Master of Langport Grammar School also in 1662), two civil teachers (a sexton and a parish clerk) and seven other licensed masters. This leaves one infant teacher at Long Load, and two unlicensed teachers at Long Sutton – possibly at the Quaker school.
Area 7: South East *Women:* a 'very old woman' taught children 'in the Matins'.
Type of School: A Dissident school is reported in Milborne Port in 1717, which later became a British School, while two others were cited at Stoke Trister and at Upton Noble. Finally Wincanton had two Dissident Schools, one of which was an Academy, one a British School.
Area 8: East *Type of school* Dissident schools existed in W. Pennard, Oakhill and Faulkland.

This profile shows wide discrepancies between different geographical areas, discussed later in this chapter, mirroring the table concerning the distribution of early Sunday Schools (App.1), which shows a similar profile where areas 2, 6 and 7 seem dominant.

In the Tudor-Stuart period more evidence of schooling is found: in 1565 the curate at Misterton is 'teaching the ABC book', Somerton had teachers in 1577 and 1593, Shepton Beauchamp in 1575 and 1586, Martock in 1583, Ashcott in 1586, and in 1599 the Rector left money for a teacher in High Ham. Finally, Quakers, imprisoned in Ilchester in the C17th, held a school in which several children gained '*more in two weeks than in six months elsewhere'*. The Rector soon put a stop to that. Later, another Quaker school opened in Sidcot and, briefly, in Long Sutton. Each of these places was only a small settlement. Probably very few children were taught and it was likely to be limited to the reading of the Bible. Nevertheless, a start had been made.

In the aftermath of the Restoration, the procedure for appointing staff was carefully controlled. When a Schoolmaster was nominated to the Bishop he had to be supported, in writing, by several local sponsors who could guarantee his conduct and suitability. In order to obtain the License needed to teach, the applicant needed to make many solemn declarations regarding his loyalty to Church and King, rather than demonstrating his qualifications to teach. In these letters there seems to have been an accepted formula of phrases and certain set pieces to be declared and sworn. An example from Midsomer Norton in 1776 will illustrate this. After notice of a vacant position, there is a letter from the applicant, Elijah Bush, and, finally, a letter of support from the sponsors. The two letters are transcribed below.

The Applicant's Loyalty

I Elijah Bush do sincerely promise and swear to bear Faith and true allegiance to his Majesty King George the Third, so help me God. I do swear that from my heart I do abhor and abjure as impious and Heretical that Damnable Doctrine of Sedition that Princes excommunicated by the Pope or any authority of the see of Rome may be deprived or deposed by their subjects or any other whatsoever And I do declare that no foreign Principality or Prelate hath or ought to have Jurisdiction Power Superiority or Authority Ecclesiastical or Spiritual within this Realm.

The Sponsors' Support

We whose names hereunto subscribed have known Elijah Bush for upwards of three years last past, and have known him to be of sober Life and Conversation, and a member of the Church of England, and that he is qualified to Teach Reading, Writing and Arithmetic, Do humbly beseech your Lordship to grant him a License to teach at the Free School in the Parish of Midsummer Norton.

The qualities which a schoolmaster was expected to show included *'being of sound religion, of sober and honest conversation, no tippler, no haunter of ale houses, no puffer of tobacco, an aptitude to teach and severe in governance'* (Lawson and Silver 1973). The training and education of the proposed master was not a primary concern. It seems that it was the possibility of seditious or heretical influence on young minds that was the greater fear.

Given that some of the sponsors were not literate and could only 'make their mark' what were literacy levels like at this time? Such levels, as one possible measure of the extent or effect of education, are extremely difficult to assess and figures vary depending on how they are calculated. It has been estimated that between 1600 and 1660 perhaps 33% of adult males were literate (Lawson and Silver 1973). For women, estimates between 1580 and 1640 show only 5% of women were literate, but between 1660 and 1700 this had risen to 18% (Cressey 1981). Across the population perhaps 98% of gentry were literate, falling to 15% of unskilled workers. Expectations of general literacy were very low: yet a child learning at their mother's (or dame's) knee was expected 'to read' within eleven months and to be able 'to sign' within a further 4-6 months, by the age of 7 or 8 years.

Plate 1

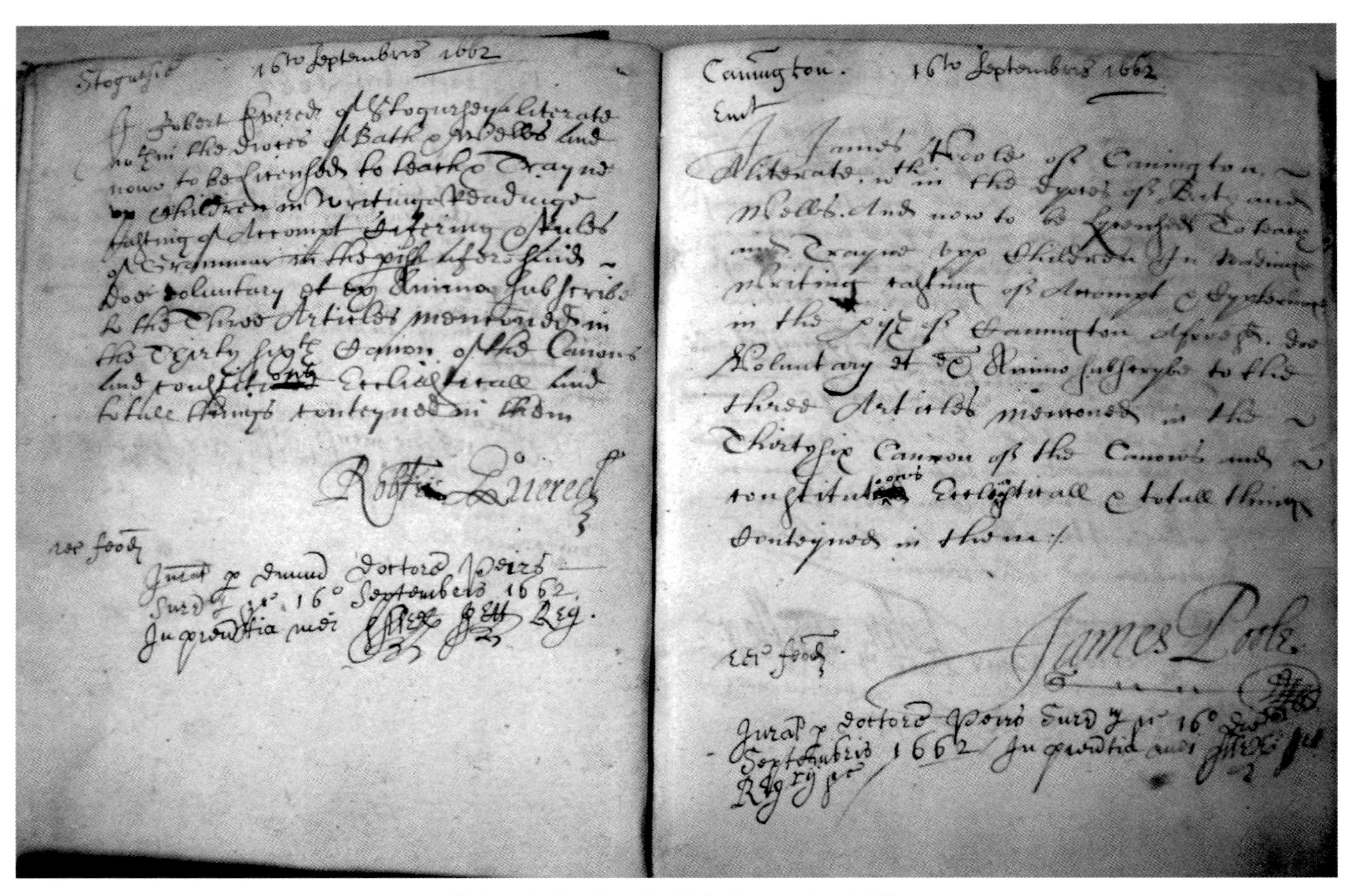

Subscription Book: 16th September 1662

I, James Poole, of Cannington
Aliterate in the diocese of Bath and
Wells. And now to be licensed to teach
and trayne upp children in reading
writing casting of accounts & ciphering
in the Parish of Cannington aforesaid Do
Voluntarily and ex animo subscribe to the
three Articles mentioned in the
Thirty-Sixth Canon of the Canons and
Constitution Ecclesiastical and to all things
contained therein.

James Poole

Plate 2

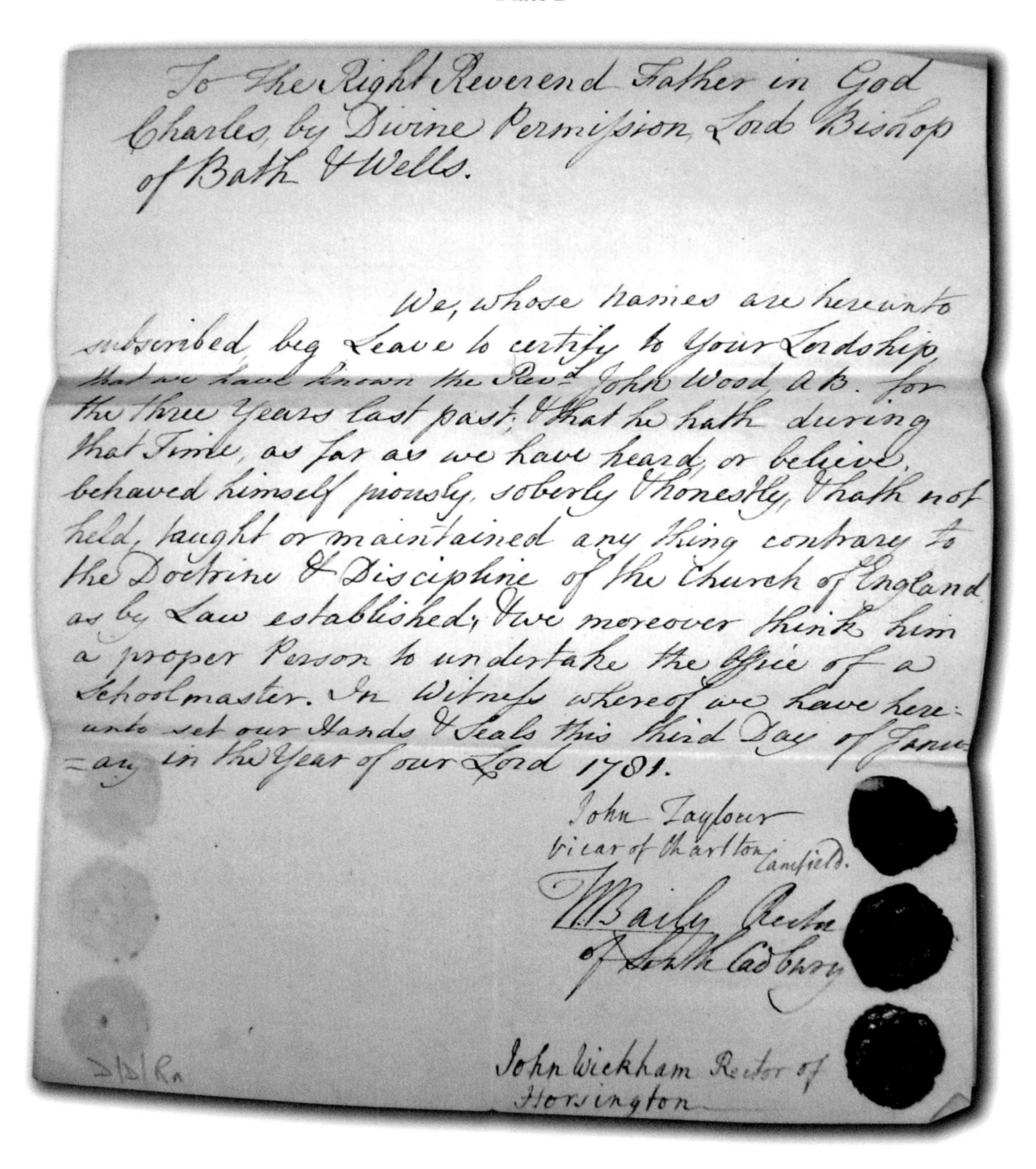

To the Right Reverend Father in God Charles, by Divine Permission, Lord Bishop of Bath & Wells.

We, whose names are hereunto subscribed beg Leave to certify to Your Lordship that we have known the Revd John Wood A.B. for the three Years last past; & that he hath during that Time, as far as we have heard, or believe, behaved himself piously, soberly & honestly, & hath not held, taught or maintained any thing contrary to the Doctrine & Discipline of the Church of England as by Law established; & we moreover think him a proper Person to undertake the Office of a Schoolmaster. In Witness whereof we have hereunto set our Hands & Seals this third Day of January in the Year of our Lord 1701.

John Taylour
Vicar of Charlton Camfield.

W. Baily Rector of South Cadbury

John Wickham Rector of Horsington

D/D/Ra

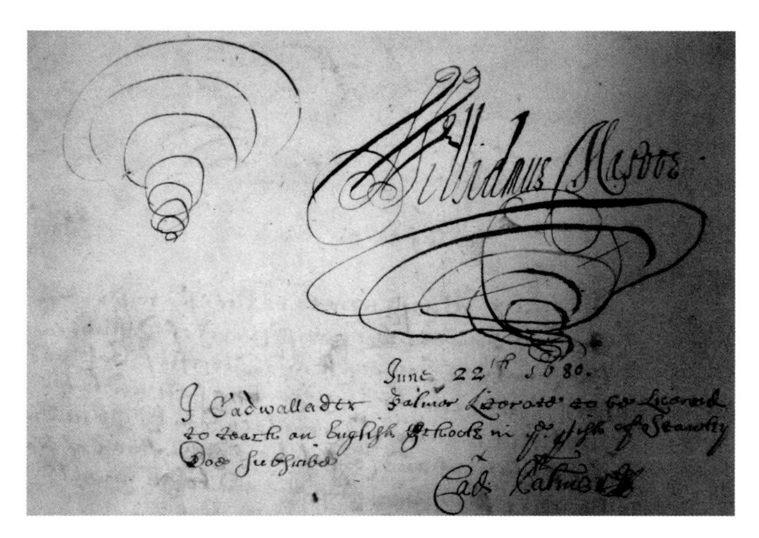

Willielmus [illegible]

June 22th 1680.
I Cadwallader Palmer desire to be Licensed to teach an English Schoole in ye p[ari]sh of [illegible] Doe subscribe
Cad: Palmer

Above: Nomination in support of a License for Rev John Wood, Horsington 1701

Signature of Licensee, 1680

Plate 3

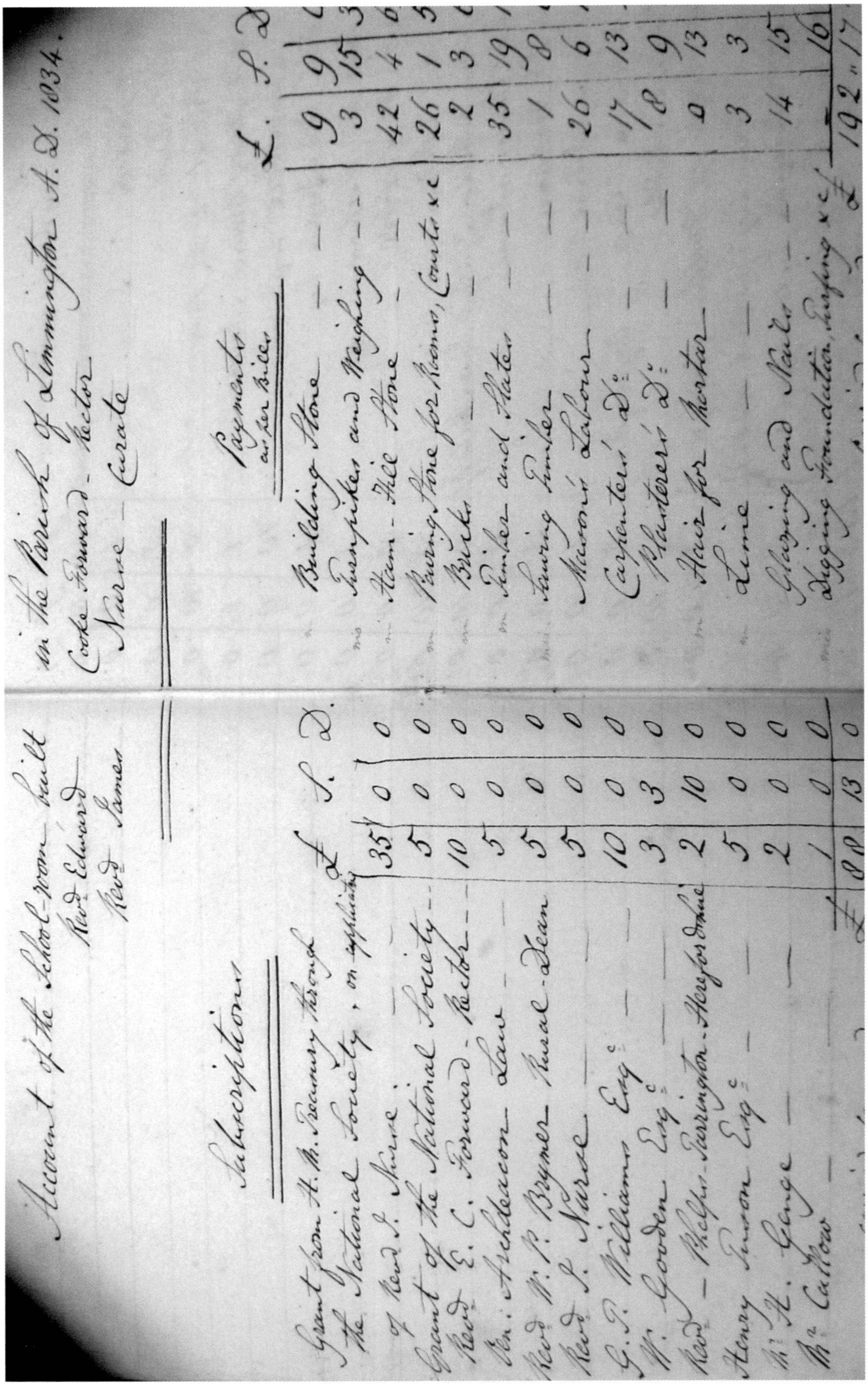

Limington School Building Fund Accounts, 1834: showing range of subscribers + costs

Plate 4

Date.	Article Sold.	Number Sold.	Price Received per Article.	To whom Sold.	Total Amount Received: Needlework	Total Amount Received: Handwork
8-7-40	Knickers	1	8	N Kingdon	8	
3-9-40	Raffia Mats	3	3	B Thorpe J Aitken J Hal[illegible]		9
	Work Box	1	1 6	M Champion		1 6
	Knickers	1	8	N Kingdon	8	
	Small mats (crochet)	3		Infants	9	
14-11-40	Hot bottle Cover	1	6	G Kingdon		6
"	Chair Backs +	2	8	Mrs Jones	1 4	
	arm covers	4	8	"	2 8	
	Table runner	2	6	"	1 -	
	Hot Bottle cover	1		J Aitken	6	
	" " "	1		June Masters	6	
	Raffia mats	1	2½	R Fardwick		2½
	Hot Bottle Cover	1	8	M Champion	8	
	Purse, Hot Bottle Cover	1 ea	6 8	E Higgins	8	6
	Bedsocks	1 pr	6	M Champion	6	
	Hot Bottle cover	1	8	K Penett	8	
	Sewing/Wool bag		1 -		1 -	
	Hot Bottle Cover		8	J Brown	8	
	Feeder		3	M Champion	3	
Jan 1941	Hot Bottle Cover		8	L Holloway		8
15th	" "		6	B Allen	6	
31st	Dolls Clothes		4	Miss Emery	4	
					13 4	4 1
						13 4
						17 5

E. G. Hardy

Date.	Article Sold.	Number Sold.	Price Received per Article.	To whom Sold.	Total Amount Received: Needlework	Total Amount Received: Handwork
25th July	Stool	1	3 -	June Masters Pd		3 -
	Material for frock	1	4 6	Mary Champion Pd	4 6	
	" "	1	4 9	Beryl Blake Pd	4 9	
	" "	1	3 6	Kathleen Penett Pd	3 6	
30th July	Babys Frock	1	3 0	Mrs Street Pd	3 0	
	Frock (material)	1	3 6	B Gamey Pd	3 6	
	Material for overall	1	4 9	June Masters Pd	4 9	
	" frock	1	4 9	Joyce Aitken Pd	4 9	
	" "	1	4 9	Doreen Funk	4 9	
	1 " Petticoat (material)	1	1 9	J. Othen Pd	1 9	
	2 Petticoats	2	9 4	Mrs Jones Pd	18 8	
	Nightdress	1	9 8	Pd	9 8	
	Material for frock	1	4 9	A Whitcombe Pd	4 9	
	" "	1	4 9	Joy " Pd	4 9	
	" "	1	3 6	N Kingdom Pd	3 6	
	Nightdress	1	4 6	~~Pamela Vitney~~ Mrs Jones	4 6.	
					4 1 1	3 -
						4 1 1
	Total		30th August. 1941			4 4 1

Sales of Work Accounts Book: N Cheriton 1920s

Estimating literacy is difficult as many people rarely needed to write and what they did write is often lost. Signatures were required on legal documents such as Depositions (for those who got embroiled in the courts and had to sign as witnesses regarding tithes, probate, local disputes or petty offences), or on Musters (military roll-calls), or Registers (which had to be kept from 1536 for Christenings, Weddings, and Burials for purposes of estimating poll tax, though these did not need to be signed by the participants till 1753). A further source of evidence about 'signing' comes from the 1640 Protestations which had to be declared and signed when acknowledging acceptance of the teachings of the Church of England.

None of these, however, meant that the individual could do more than make a signature. Thus all such estimates must be treated with caution. Nevertheless, it seems these 'good times' for education ended with retrenchment under James II and remained so for almost a century. The next revival in education extending, in particular to the poor, relates to the Charity and Sunday School Movements, both of which played an important part in Somerset.

ii. The new Movements.
Though the C17th had seen evidence of concern for the poor and, in particular for orphans, the motive may well have been practical and monetary. This was because it was believed that by educating such children they would be able to earn their own living and thus not be a burden on the parish. This theme underpinned many education developments for the next two centuries. The new **Charity Schools** were ones in which a schoolmaster, rather than a curate or priest, was appointed to educate the 'scholars', often orphans (Seaborne 1971). They were usually found in towns where the larger size of the target group made such institutions more economically viable than in the villages. Thus, in the town of Bristol, the early C17th saw a charity set up called the **Red Maids' School** in 1634. This was followed by the **Blue Schools** in the urban areas of Frome, Wells, Bath and, later, Bridgwater. However, in the villages, it mostly fell to the curate, Rector or Vicar to undertake the teaching of some of their flock, for whom a few were paid from specific charitable bequests.

It was often the Dissidents who set the pace of educational innovation. The Quaker organisation, Society of Friends, was prompted by member John Bellers in 1695 to seek to create a network of colleges of industry 'of all useful trades and husbandry' to relieve the pressing problems of poverty. In 1699 the newly founded Society for the Promotion of Christian Knowledge (SPCK) supported schools which gave a 'Christian and useful education to the children of the poor' to combat vice and debauchery. Such schools, which were sometimes referred to as 'charity schools', may have simply been linked to and helped by individual endowments or bequests or, later, by national organisations rather than been full, independent charity schools. Although many claims are made for the growth of charity schools during the C18th and C19th, the figures may be misleading. Names ascribed to institutions do not always clearly show what kind of an institution a 'school' might be. Associations are sometimes rather loose and the label or status ascribed may not always represent the true picture (Simon 1968).

The Sunday School Movement was an alternative movement supporting the spread of education into parts of society that other organisations had not yet reached. This was a very different venture. In its most popular form its origin is credited to the West Country evangelist Robert Raikes, though others' efforts with wider aims were tried (fear of which could lead to dangerous outcomes as experienced by the leading chemist, intellectual and Dissident, Joseph Priestley, one of the Lunar Men, whose Sunday School work in Leeds and Birmingham became linked to political reform which culminated in riots in 1791, causing him to flee and eventually emigrate to America a year later). Raikes noted that the children of the poor could not afford to forego wages to be able to attend school. Their only free day was Sunday and therefore Sunday was the only chance to provide them with any education. Appalled by the filth of the factory children on the nearby streets of his home town of Gloucester, he resolved to start a school, in Sooty Alley, in 1780. The aim was attractively simple and therefore attainable: to teach such children to read, write and be clean. Children flocked to attend these 'good conduct' schools. Within twenty years it was claimed by the movement that three quarters of working-class children attended such classes.

Raikes ignored some of the more radical ideas of fellow Dissidents, such as Joseph Spence who advocated the reform of the alphabet to make spelling easier for the 'laborious part of the people', or Horne Tooke who advocated the evolution of language to 'defy divisions between the vulgar and the elite' (Uglow 2002). He also side-stepped the agitation for the repeal of the Test and Corporation Acts which debarred Dissenters from civil office and the Universities (not finally achieved till 1828). Raikes managed to make support for his Sunday Schools something safe and positive: as a form of association which instilled a sense of duty and responsibility, provided an opening to basic literacy for children who would otherwise have remained illiterate and which also provided treats, rewards and local benefits to maintain the children's loyalty. These Sunday Schools seem to have been well-regarded by the respectable and aspiring artisan and by the genteel society which would fund them. These aspects were probably key reasons for their popularity and success.

Sunday Schools were linked to the local Church and, increasingly, local Chapels of many nonconformist groups which each had their own Sunday schools. Such schools were set up to teach the poor to read the Prayer Book and Bible and were thus acceptable activities for the Sabbath. School lasted all day and often provided the only chance children would have of gaining any schooling at all. To support the work of the Sunday Schools several books had been written for children and further books to guide would-be teachers were also becoming available. The SPCK gradually came to focus efforts on publishing books to serve their missions both at home and abroad. Many of these were also used in the Sunday Schools, for example *The Christian Schoolmaster* published in 1707 by the SPCK and written by Rev Dr J Talbot, vicar of Spofforth Yorks (Dent 1977).

Interesting insights can be glimpsed from contemporary accounts, as in the one below relating to the centenary of a local Sunday School and reported in the *Castle Cary Visitor* of September 1897. The writer notes that rewards were given to children who spent from early morning till evening in their school and won the good opinion of the committee and teachers. The school's accounts book lists expenditure on the following items:

	£	s	d
5 boys' hats		8	04
5 pairs boys' stockings		5	10
4 maids' hats		6	02
4 maids' handkerchiefs		2	04
5 boys' shirts		15	06
4 girls' shifts		10	06
5 boys' hats		7	11
5 pairs boys' stockings		7	10
4 girls' hats		6	7 ½
4 girls' handkerchiefs		5	4

The difference in the prices of the first four items and the last four may be differences of size or of quality, perhaps there is a clue in the change from 'maids' to 'girls'?

One difficulty is in determining where the school met: sometimes in the church itself – the vestry, side aisle, gallery or in the small room sometimes found above the porch known as the 'parvis' (from the Latin *parvus* meaning small). Sunday school could be held in the Rectory/Vicarage, in existing school rooms or a day school building. The Sunday school sometimes came first, followed by a day school, but not always. Some villages appear to have had no recorded school of any type till after the Acts of 1870 or even 1891: some were too small ever to have had any school of their own.

In terms of the uneven distribution of sunday schools (App. 1) we find a profile which is repeated in the distribution of day schools as well. The spread can be surmised from a mapping of the schools which can be plotted from the data in the already mentioned sources. The reasons for where and when a school is established are not given but are of equal interest.

a. Geographic: The areas (2, 6,7) represent an arc from the Quantock Hills (hinterland on the west of Bridgwater port), along the Polden Hills (hinterland to the east of Bridgwater), on to Somerton and down towards Milborne Port in the south-east (not a shipping port, but a 'gate' into an established trading post, with a strong manufacturing tradition). These areas are of higher land which may be significant as so much of low-lying Somerset was (and still is) prone to severe winter flooding making travel well-nigh impossible. It also carries the ancient pilgrim route from the northern coast to Glastonbury, and parts of the old Roman road.

b. Economic: The arc links two trading districts: 'port' areas are typically more cosmopolitan and outward looking. It created links by which goods and ideas could spread and where minds were receptive to new ideas. It also stimulated settlements which were certainly in need of a literate and numerate workforce.

c. Networks of significant patrons with money and influence could support and protect new initiatives. We know the names of many of these and we know something of how they operated from supplementary sources, for example, details of life-style from contemporary diarists such as Rev Holland of Over Stowey and Rev Woodforde of Ansfield. Potential patrons might be drawn from the personal networks which criss-crossed the area based on **social class** (the dominant landowners regularly visited and exchanged frequent letters). Thus active support from a local landowner or Lord of the Manor probably made a considerable positive difference and we find several such promoters of schooling in figures such as Lords Egremont, Poulett, Portman and Acland baronets in particular.

d. Religious influences from alternative places of worship and the consequent competition between church and chapel could have had a possible impact on the number of Sunday schools. In addition to the social networks, there were the sometimes parallel, sometimes interwoven but distinct **religious networks** of committed members and itinerant preachers, especially amongst the Quakers and other nonconformists. These latter groups (as they were banned from the prestigious universities with academic studies and linked career opportunities) strongly supported independent education institutions, especially those favouring a more vocational and commercial emphasis. Where such interest in education might already exist and the ground be fertile, it may have been easier to develop additional forms of education. However, areas where Anglican Sunday or day schools were established early had already met a need for education and, if also poor (as in the lowland and central southern regions) one school was probably all that could be afforded.

e. Individual campaigners who were strongly motivated to promote the 'education of the poor, or labouring, classes' and who, from personal philanthropy or by using their contacts to gain sponsorship, donations, endowments or eventually grants, were in a position to inspire communities to provide schools. We will note the number of charities and bequests, and also individuals who gave of their time and money to support their local school, in a later section (Part III). There seem to have been both personal and religious links between Rev Poole in Enmore on the Quantocks to the west, reformist groups in the central Polden Hills and the Quaker Clarks of Street to the east. Such personal, social and religiously-motivated contacts helped to foster a beneficent culture and an interest in developing education facilities. With schools and academies springing up, pride and not a little competition between these philanthropists no doubt boosted their efforts.

In whatever way these possible factors may have combined, there seems to have been a mushrooming of worthy efforts: supporting Sunday Schools became one of the options for social action to which concerned public-minded people could aspire, and which, by the late C18th, was gaining currency. It became popular, especially with women, to support a local Sunday School and, sometimes, a 'school of industry' (which instilled 'industrious' habits, usually through training girls in knitting and spinning). These can mostly be found on the Mendip Hills, perhaps in response to the activities of Hannah More, as we shall see in the next chapter.

Whilst some may argue that Sunday schools were a means of instilling the submission of the poor to their 'betters' they did, nevertheless, often provide the only chance of learning to read before day schools became widespread and children's working hours legally restricted which released them to attend school. As we can see from the expenses listed above, they also provided much needed items of clothing (and sometimes food) – a good reason for attending! Another attraction was that throughout the nineteenth century it was still the Sunday school which was likely to be the sole source of any local entertainment – summer outings, lantern shows given by missionaries on their return from Africa and, between the World Wars, film shows and local dramatics. The School Log Books regularly record poor attendance at school when the local churches and chapels held their Annual Treats.

Having established a general outline of schooling opportunities in the county during the C17th and C18th centuries, we can now turn to examine the particular contribution of a determined philanthropist, Mrs Hannah More, whose work in the villages (at the turn of the century) around the Mendip Hills of Somerset, brought both enlightenment and cast a long shadow.

Part II

Philanthropists and Pioneers: Hannah More, 1745-1833 and Rev John Poole, 1770-1867.

Both these Somerset personalities, in their different ways, made significant contributions to schooling in the county. **Hannah More** was a member of the well-connected Blue Stocking Circle – of which many members were outspoken in their support for education for the poor and several became writers for young children, whose books would be widely used. **Rev John Poole** was directly involved in daily teaching and also in training young women who then went on to set up other schools in the locality. His book, the *Improved Village School*, drew upon and adapted the work of Lancaster and Bell for use in a village context. It was a guide used by many to establish their own schools.

Fig. ii Illustrations of Hannah More and the Poole cousins

Hannah More 1787

The cousins, Tom (left) and John Poole (right) 1797

Chapter 2

Hannah More: Mendip schools, and the Blue Stocking Circle

Women have always played a key role in the upbringing of their children and particularly their education. There is a charming memorial, in what is now a vestry in Axbridge church, to a certain Abigail Prowse, 1683-1763) daughter of the Rev D George Hooper (Bishop of Bath and Wells), which reads:

She was one of the Most Accomplished
Women of her time, admired for her excellent
Understanding, extensive Knowledge and
Agreeable manners...
... The early part of her Life
Was dedicated to the care and Education of her Son.

She must have been remarkably successful as an educator, for her son Thomas was six times chosen as Knight of the shire, where 'he discharged his duties to Parliament'.

Education was a hot topic, particularly among well-born women like Abigail. Had she had a daughter, she would probably have been taught first to read from a horn book and then to stitch her sampler with rows of alphabet letters, various stitch patterns and finally a text, perhaps from **Isaac Watts** (1674-1748) - a minister and writer of many hymns and moral verses, which were collected and published as *Divine and Moral Songs* in 1715. These were hugely popular as texts for young girls to work in their samplers. [One text, *Against Idleness and Mischief,* which begins '*How doth the little busy bee Improve each shining hour...*' was famously parodied by Lewis Carroll in '*How doth the little crocodile...*'.] Watts was also associated with the Stoke Newington Dissident Academy in London which was later attended by Hannah More, William Wilberforce and other reformers.

As an educated and well-read woman she is likely to have been familiar with some of the writings of **John Locke** (1632-1704) the English philosopher, born in nearby Wrington, Somerset. In particular, his *Essay concerning Education* (1690), and *Thoughts concerning Education* (1693) might have provided food for thought – where he asserts that knowledge comes from sensory perception and experience and not merely from reading and recitation. Concerns were echoed by **Mary Wollstonecraft** in *Thoughts on the Education of Daughters* (1787), though 'sensory education' remained rare till after the second world war! Further, Wollstonecraft was revolutionary in her recommendation that girls should be taught '*to compare and combine... to be taught to think*'. She urged girls to '*avoid trifling conversation and exterior accomplishments*'. **Jean-Jacques Rousseau** (1712-1778) may also have been a familiar writer, especially after his flight from France to the safety of England in 1766. This followed the publication, four years earlier, of a description of his own method of educating his child, *Emile,* in which he claimed that, as children are born innocent and later corrupted by society, they should therefore be removed from society as much as possible and brought up freely to allow their 'natural' spirit, to develop unharmed without being forced to become 'adult' too soon. This was famously followed by more revolutionary claims that 'Man is born free but is everywhere in chains'. No wonder he had to flee.

However, such advice seems to have made little impact. Jane Austen, in *Persuasion* (Ch.5), showed scorn for the Musgrove daughters who *'had brought from a school in Exeter all the usual stock of accomplishments .. such as drawing, dancing, singing, at the expense of proper learning'*. The heroine Anne declares that she would *'not have given up her own more elegant and cultivated mind for all their enjoyments'* and, in *Northanger Abbey* (Ch. 14), Catherine, notes, *'A woman, if she should have the misfortune to know anything, should conceal it as well as she can'*. A little later Dickens, in *A Sentiment* (from *Sketches by Boz*), was also disparaging about the education of girls from 9-13 when they acquire a *'smattering of everything and a knowledge of nothing'*, while Hughes in *Tom Brown's Schooldays* expresses what perhaps was a common rural opinion about Ladies' Academies, describing them as places *'where farmers' daughters care more to make bad foreign music than good English cheeses'*. Each of these writers was referring to the mushrooming middle-class establishments for the gentry and not to poor village children who were, as yet, largely left 'natural' (!) and without schooling.

Contemporary fears concerned the immorality, bad conduct, indiscipline and possible rebelliousness amongst the poor, who appeared to be flooding into the towns in pursuit of opportunities for work in the developing factories as England began to industrialise. If this was the fear, what was the solution? More Religion. In order to support the renewal of religious discipline, people should be taught to read *The Good Book*. Hence, attention turned to the need to school them as a means to support the status quo, rather than to change it.

i) Sarah Comer of Cheddar 1678-1752: an example of individual commitment to bettering the poor [1]. Sarah came from a local family. Her parents, Hercules Comer and Joan, were people of modest means whilst another Hercules Comer, probably her grandfather, was a constable, churchwarden and moor warden. Her father was identified as a 'husbandman', a fairly wealthy tenant farmer. He certainly had enough money to leave Sarah and her two unmarried sisters £200 each and also some land for each of them – for Sarah, 'an acre of ground'. A grandson, William, was bequeathed some money to assist him in an apprenticeship. Clearly it was a family in which education and training were deemed important. They were probably also thrifty and hardworking to have accumulated enough to have been so generous.

On February 10th 1684, Sarah and her 5 older siblings were all baptised, when of 'riper years'. In fact they were between the ages of 6 and 16. This is consistent with families of non-conformist inclination who often avoided baptism in the Church of England unless forced to conform. Some not only refused the Anglican sacraments but also withheld tithes to the Church. It would seem that Hercules was certainly a sympathiser, even if not a full member, of such a group. We know that Quakers had been established in the West Country since 1654 and, by 1662/3, are noted in the Bishop's Visitation Reports filed by the local churchwardens. Quakers are reported in Cheddar and had established a base in nearby Sidcot. Hercules' second son, John, was a local Representative of the Cheddar Meeting House and bequeathed £100 to 'the local poor called Quakers, for ever'. Sarah, herself, requested to be buried at Sidcot. This would certainly suggest close involvement with Quakers.

---

[1] I am indebted to John Page for information on Sarah Comer.

We know almost nothing about Sarah's life, where she was educated or how she spent her time. She never married, but was given the title 'Mrs' as were most mature women at this period, as a mark of respect. We have to rely on her Will to glean a few insights into her character, standing, values and beliefs.

Sarah appears to have used her funds to operate as an informal local 'banker' to many of the poorer households in the village. (The first bank only opened in Bristol in 1750 and there were few ways poorer people could raise money for their immediate needs.) By lending out money she could help to alleviate the immediate impact of poverty: over one third of the 200 households of Cheddar owed her between £50-£200 at the time of her death. After her death she set a period of time during which borrowers would be given grace to return the monies owed, so that the hardship of repayment would be reduced.

Through her Will, she tackled the causes of poverty, which she appears to have believed lay in lack of education and therefore reduced employability. She was unusual for her times in supporting both boys and girls and, also, in helping young people escape poverty through education, training and apprenticeships. The final section relating to the Residual Estate, was to be divided into four equal parts. This, in particular, reveals her priorities and values.

One section relates to the distribution of '*corn and apparel*', specifically in February and November, two of the bleaker months. The Trustees later amended this to include '*meat, potatoes, bread or ffuel if it were more convenient*'.

The second focus was education. To this end she directed that a schoolmaster should be appointed to instruct a '*proper number of boys and girls in reading, writing and arithmetick*' (about 30), who should be paid £20 out of which £4 or £5 would be for the rent of a house with a schoolroom, which was also to be provided.

Not only was education clearly important to Sarah, but so too was proper training for work. For this reason, a further amount of money was to be used for '*placing out*' poor boys and girls as apprentices, or advancing them in any business, trade or profession. This could make the difference between a skilled job with prospects for enhancement and betterment, rather than a life of drudgery and unskilled labouring.

The final part of the Residual Estate was to go to '*poor decayed housekeepers*'. This is a very particular and personal concern, probably relating to a friend of Sarah's who had certainly fallen on hard times. The plight of women was very dependent on marriage (where they might keep house as wife or widow), or on employment (where they might also keep house, as an employee). Sarah was clearly aware of the difficulties facing such poor but genteel women and set out to find a way to overcome some of their problems.

However, the good intentions left many difficulties in the interpretation of the key clauses. The Trustees, not wanting to be accused of mishandling the will, left the task of decision-making to the Courts. This resulted in a twenty-three year delay in implementation! Meanwhile, between 1752 and 1756, £60.6s was spent on food and apparel, £15.5s yearly for the Schoolmaster, and £45.10s for apprentices in agriculture and manufacturing. The real problem area was that of the poor decayed housekeepers. Irregular payments continued while the Court took its time to make a ruling.

There are several sites attributed to the Sarah Comer's Charity School, so it would appear that possibly each new master might have lived in a different house and thus the 'school' moved too. The school is of particular interest in that it gave equal weight to boys and girls and, also, in that it required teaching, not just of reading – (usually the Bible) and was thus much more likely to be about moral training and obedience. Sarah Comer also insisted on the teaching of writing, which some – including Hannah More – believed to encourage sedition. It was also quite unusual for girls to be given equal access to arithmetic and casting of accounts – again a task which some believed was too difficult for the female mind. Sarah Comer's conception of education was thus much broader and perhaps more helpful for those in the pursuit of employment.

It was not till 1788 that the first full meeting of Trustees took place. John Ford, one of the Church Wardens was given the task of teaching the children to read and write – no mention was made of arithmetic (perhaps not his strong subject). An allowance was given for books, pens and paper. We know, for example in 1818, the vicar, who kept a supervisory eye on the school, ordered other 'necessaries' for the benefit of the children. These included:

46 spelling books,
46 prayer books,
6 Bibles for the use of the Charity Children

However, there was competition. In late 1789, just 18 months after the Sarah Comer Trust was eventually up and running, Hannah More and her sister Patty, arrived in Cheddar, inspired and financed by William Wilberforce, to take action against the terrible poverty of the area. Hannah and her sisters had been brought up and educated in Bristol with a social life amongst the aristocracy. Their 'mission' and mode of operating were alien to the local people and their focus as much about perceived 'spiritual needs' as physical ones. Their initial Sunday school worked alongside Sarah's reading-writing-arithmetic conception of education but, on her death, Hannah More left £45 towards the building of a permanent school with two large school rooms sufficient for 300 children.

Additional subscriptions came from many prestigious sources: £100 from the Marquess of Bath, a further £25 from the Chapter of Wells Cathedral, £5 from the Princess Sophia Matilda of Gloucester. This school became a National School affiliated to the Church of England Society, whilst Sarah Comer's school – though never discriminating between children from different religious backgrounds – remained true to her more non-conformist upbringing. Much later, in 1872, a British School (also linked to the non-conformist tradition) opened in Cheddar.

Yet once the More's mission steam-rolled into Cheddar, the low profile, unobtrusive work of the local girl, Sarah Comer, was overshadowed by the flamboyance and patronage of the well-connected Mores. Nevertheless, the Trust continues to this day and still supports actions compatible with the original aims of the founder. Although hardly known outside her home town, Sarah Comer is still remembered amongst the established residents of Cheddar.

ii. The Blue Stocking Circle and the More Family of Bristol

At about the same time, there emerged an interesting group of well-connected and well-educated women, who had personal and practical links to the story of education in Somerset. The scene is the fashionable city of Bath in the last quarter of the C18th. The group became known as **The Blue Stocking Circle.** It is relevant to our story because of one family, the More family consisting of five sisters**.** The More family are important not only for the school run by the five sisters in Bristol, which attracted much contemporary praise and interest from eminent people, but for one particular sister, Hannah, who brought ideas and connections from this wide-ranging group of prominent women and turned them into practical reality through her extensive philanthropic work which included establishing local village clubs and schools. It is this latter aspect with which we will be particularly concerned. But first some background.

Born in Bristol in 1745, Hannah's mother was from a farming family and her father was an educated gentleman from a Presbyterian family who, having lost an inheritance in legal battles, was lucky enough to find a patron who set him up with the Headship of a school in Fishponds (Stapleton) then at the edge of Bristol. This was an endowed school, which not only taught the 4 Rs (reading, writing, 'rithmetic and religion) but also provided clothes, taught crafts and offered apprenticeships to some pupils. Hannah was the fourth of five sisters who were all well-educated in languages and literature at home (but not in mathematics as her father believed this was too difficult for girls). All the sisters were intelligent and could be very charming – which proved useful in raising money for later projects. The More sisters worked as a team, though Hannah was the most gifted and also lively, attractive and a good conversationalist. Several of the sisters continued their education in languages at the Baptist Academy in Bristol – noted for its broader and more liberal curriculum – where the sisters made further useful contacts among its visiting speakers. Wanting to be financially independent, the More sisters, set up a girls' boarding school first in Trinity Street, then in Park Street, which was large enough to house 60 scholars and their teachers. This establishment quickly became highly successful – in part, thanks to the many influential contacts the young women continued to develop.

From its beginnings in 1758, the school attracted the attention of many eminent people: leading preachers of the day, Charles and John Wesley, the anti-slavery campaigner William Wilberforce and social hostess **Mrs Elizabeth Montagu**. Hannah began to be noticed, partly as a result of a well-received play, *In Search After Happiness*, written for her pupils, but which attracted much attention - including that of a leading actor at the Bristol Theatre Royal, William Powell, whose daughters attended the Mores' school. The play was written *'to promote a regard for religion and virtue in the minds of young persons'.* Although said to be pious and platitudinous, given that it was written by a sixteen-year- old-teacher for her charges only a little younger than herself, it was greeted warmly. Thus Hannah first became notable as 'the poetess of Bristol': the initial success led to Hannah writing several more plays which were then taken up by London performers including the famous David Garrick, of whose family she became a close friend.

These literary successes, together with the independence won from a settlement of £200 a year (as a result of being jilted after six years of engagement to the indecisive Edward Turner, a landed gentleman with an estate at Belmont, near Wraxall), allowed her the freedom to move to London and mix in the social, political and literary circles of the day. This heady life-style led to many further influential contacts which later provided invaluable support for several of her social and educational projects. These were set up to help bring basic literacy and employable skills to village children around the Mendip area.

Hannah's links with these eminent people was helped by her friendship with the pre-eminent hostess of Georgian London, Mrs Elizabeth Montagu, who was active from the 1750s till her death in 1800. Mrs Montagu (a cousin through marriage to Lady Mary Wortly Montagu) is regarded as the founder of the Blue Stocking Circle. This was a very informal group of articulate, well-educated and well-connected women who were frustrated by the submissive role which society allotted to them and who wanted to engage *'in conversation rather than cards'*, to listen and learn from intelligent dialogue and not only to participate in the social and intellectual currents around them but actively to effect some change. The group wanted to establish greater gender equality and opportunities for women, the key to which was believed to be through education. It was a diverse group and held conflicting ideas as to how they might achieve their goals and even what their goals should be. In the words of the founder, the ultimate purpose was *to 'think for ourselves, & act for ourselves'*, rather than being *'so perfectly of ye Rib of Man as Woman ought to be'*.

The only requirement for membership of the Blue Stocking Circle was a strong desire to discuss, analyse and examine the problems of the day. Despite the fact that most members advocated only mild changes to society, they (gently) broke the cage and set the stage for the more revolutionary groups and movements that would follow. By participating in regular meetings and focusing on philanthropic goals the Blue Stocking Circle members worked to help those less fortunate – whether by creating Sunday School classes or directly assisting poor families – without seriously challenging the society in which they lived.

How the group acquired the name, Blue Stocking, is not clear. One notion is that it stems from a certain Benjamin Silliton who was invited to attend a meeting and arrived in every-day, coarse blue woollen stockings instead of the usual white silk ones for social occasions. This amused his hostess, who liked the idea that it could underline the informality of the meetings and the group's intention to do good for those less fortunate. Another possible origin could be a deliberate echo of a similar group which had been meeting in France, wearing the blue stockings of the artisans they intended to support. The name soon became firmly fixed in the group's imagination after the publication of Hannah More's poem entitled *Bas Bleus* where she explains the importance of communication and its positive effect on those who participate:

Range—study—think—do all we can
Colloquial pleasures are for man.
Yet not from low desire to shine
Does Genius toil in learning's mine;
Not to indulge in idle vision,
But strike new light by strong collision.
Of CONVERSATION, wisdom's friend,
This is the object and the end,
Of moral truth, man's proper science,
With sense and learning in alliance,
To search the depths, and thence produce
What tends to practice and to use.
And next in value we shall find
What mends the taste and forms the mind.
If high those truths in estimation,
Whose search is crown'd with demonstration;
To these assign no scanty praise,
Our taste which clear, our views which raise.
For grant that mathematic truth
Best balances the mind of Youth;
Yet scarce the truth of Taste is found
To grow from principles less sound.
O'er books the Mind inactive lies,
Books, the Mind's food, not exercise!
[ln. 318-342]

Precocious and vivacious young Hannah was easily accepted into this group. Among her admirers were the politician Horace Walpole, the constitutionalist and MP for Bristol, Edmund Burke, man of letters Dr Samuel Johnson, diarist Samuel Pepys, the artist Sir Joshua Reynolds (whose daughter Frances painted her portrait), and many others – indeed, anyone who was anybody in London society! Having decided she was not for marrying (none of the More sisters married though they took the title 'Mrs') she developed a series of close friendships with many older intellectual men whose conversation and patronage she valued and, also, several churchmen who later held important and influential posts such as the Dean of Gloucester and Bishops of Bristol, Bath and Wells, Salisbury. Some of these men were able to offer support to Hannah in her later 'hour of need'.

The members of the group were often involved in setting up such Sunday Schools, following Raike's model, as noted earlier, which chimed well with their own desires to *do* something in and for society. While they did not view themselves as revolutionary, the group was important as, by being a recognised Circle, its adherents set themselves apart as serious, educated, interested and participatory female members of society who actively wanted to effect something useful.

Several of the group made important contributions to the practical development of such education. Among such women was **Anna Barbauld,** well-known for her many critical and literary writings but also for *Lessons for a Child* and *Hymns in Prose for Children (1788-9).* These were a revolution in children's literature. For the first time, the needs of the child reader were taken seriously. Barbauld demanded that her books be printed in large type with wide margins so that children could read them easily and, even more importantly, she developed an informal conversational style as though between parent and child. This 'catechetical' approach dominated in books for children for several decades. *Lessons for Children* was a four-volume, age-appropriate reading primer. Many of the stories were based on ones she had told her own son. In keeping with the high moral tone of the times the stories included basic concepts about society and behaviour, simple ethics and, unusually, it included principles of 'botany, zoology, numbers, change of state in chemistry... the money system, the calendar, geography, meteorology, agriculture, political economy, geology, [and] astronomy'. *Lessons for Children* and *Hymns in Prose* had, for children's books, an unprecedented impact; they even influenced the poetry of William Blake and Wordsworth and was remembered by adults years later – Elizabeth Barrett Browning claimed she could still quote from them when aged thirty-nine!

Another Blue Stocking member, whose work included items for children, was **Sarah Trimmer**, who wrote many classroom books including *The Spelling Books*. She received so many requests for advice on starting Sunday schools – including from Queen Charlotte – that she wrote *The Economy of Charity*, a guide to setting up such schools which was highly recommended by many important figures. *The Spelling Books* were a very popular collection of stories with embedded key words (similar to a modern 'contextualised approach') from which children could learn meaning as well as the spelling. It was published by the SPCK and therefore had an immediate and widespread impact. The stories themselves were considered innovative: they emphasized the ordinary lives of ordinary children *'who climbed trees, played with fire, threw cricket bats at sheep and begged in the streets'* - with appropriate moral lessons about the consequences! The books were even adopted by the renowned **Dr Andrew Bell**, around 1800, and were used in his schools – as we shall see in the next chapter. Sarah Trimmer wrote many other books for classroom use and also a guide for teachers – *The Teacher's Assistant* – which showed how to organise and instruct a class of children using the new, more dynamic 'catechetical method' (questions and answers instead of the deadening method of rote learning) a method which had already been promoted by Anna Barbauld.

iii. The character of the Mendip Schools

To return to **Hannah More**: after a series of deaths – David Garrick in 1779, her father in 1783 and then Dr Johnson in 1784, Hannah abandoned the frivolities of city life and, inspired by the evangelical Clapham sect, she turned increasingly to religion. She left London to return to the west country, setting up home in Blagdon, Wrington, Cowslip Green and finally Barley Wood. She was now older and wiser, confident in herself as a writer and inspired to tackle some of the dreadful poverty she saw around her. On a trip to Cheddar, while showing her friend, **William Wilberforce**, the beauties of the area, they were shocked by the poverty. Wilberforce wrote to her urging action, *'The cliffs are very fine but the poverty is dreadful. If you will be at the trouble end, I will be at the expense'.* This prompted her efforts to establish a number of village Sunday Schools, Female Clubs and Schools of Industry. Villages which had such clubs or schools included Cheddar, Axbridge, Congesbury, Wrington, Wedmore, Yatton, Sandford, Rowberrow, Shipham and, also, in Blagdon and Nailsea (both controversially). It is to this part of Hannah's life that we now need to turn in more detail.

Debate was raging about education by the end of the eighteenth century. Hannah could draw on plenty of existing expertise and resources. Cheddar was the first of many of the More sisters' Sunday Schools. It became the model for subsequent ones. The village, 'of about 200 hovels', was occupied by people considered lawless and wild, who earned a living from cheese-making, spinning and knitting. Several families lived in the surrounding caves and sold bits of stalactites to tourists already coming to experience the 'romance of the caves'. The vicarage was in the gift of the Dean of Wells, but had had no resident curate for years. Rather, a 'galloping curate' rode over from Wells each Sunday. It was a common abuse at a time when many clergy were considered fox-hunting, hard-drinking men with little concern for their flock. There were, of course, others: dedicated scholars (who might also neglect their parishes) or, committed men who worked hard to improve their parishoners' spiritual life even if not empowered to affect their physical lives.

We must remember that the benefits of education were not considered self-evident at this time. Many opposed even Sunday schooling for the labouring classes for a variety of reasons: local farmers believed that schooling would ruin their workers by educating them above the rank in society for which they were destined; religious groups jealously guarded their right to instruct their members in their beliefs; politicians were afraid that if such people learned to read the Bible they could also read seditious pamphlets; parents needed their children to earn for the family so some of them wanted the children to be paid to attend and, the children, themselves, found the additional discipline burdensome on the only day without long working hours. Hannah and her younger sister Patty set out to persuade them otherwise. They rode across the countryside visiting farms and homes along the way. To the farmers, they claimed that education would keep the poor from robbing their orchards, poaching, and might reduce their own contribution to the poor rates! To the religious and political conservatives they suggested that the teaching of religion could serve as a means to reinforce divine duty and be a means of instituting social control. To the parents, they reassured them that their children would not be sold overseas (as had been rumoured) and that the children would learn skills to help them get jobs to earn more for their families.

Cheddar itself, as we have already noted, was the beneficiary of Sarah Comer's bequest of 1751 which provided an endowment for a School of Industry. Such schools aimed to teach children to read from the Prayer Book and Bible but, also, to acquire skills which could enable them to gain local employment, such as spinning and knitting together with sewing, cooking and household skills to fit them for domestic service. It appears that the Comer Trust was slow to be put into effect. Land for a school was only purchased in 1787. But, between 1787 and 1837 there was sufficient money in the Comer bequest to apprentice 106 young people.

Eventually the Mores found a suitable-sized building, in need of repair, which could house the children. It was adjacent to land belonging to the Comer Trust. The school opened on 25th October 1789. Building on Raike's foundations, the Mores introduced innovation in the pedagogy they developed within the classes. In the classroom they tried to make learning entertaining and varied: teachers were advised to use singing when the young scholars tired and when energy and attention waned. Unusually for the times, the Mores argued that to get the best out of children their affections needed to be 'engaged by kindness', echoing Locke's advice that '*Nothing that children are to learn should be made a Burden*'. While outside the classroom they extended the range of activities provided and, in particular, courted publicity concerning the schools, which they hoped would then encourage others to develop further initiatives.

Even the original Mores' School for Girls in Bristol had been noted for its happy atmosphere (not always the case in schools of this period) and Hannah tried to make her new Sunday Schools for the poor enjoyable too. When the children were tired or restless, they stood up and moved to another part of the room – to sing hymns. However, the Mores – focusing on the education of poor children – still believed it was a fundamental error to consider children as innocent beings rather than as beings of a corrupt nature and evil disposition. This contrasted strongly with the then current ideas of Rousseau concerning the natural innocence of children compared to the corrupting influence of society, echoed in Blake's *Songs of Innocence*.

The end of the C18th was still an early stage in the promotion of education beyond the middle-classes. To encourage poorer children to enrol and then to stay, the Mores offered 'incentives'. A penny was given to each child who arrived in time for Morning Prayer on four consecutive Sundays. Every other month a gingerbread treat was handed out. Once a year good scholars received gifts of a Bible, Prayer Book or Tract. Clothing was also distributed annually: boys received a pair of shoes, hat or shirt, while girls were given a calico apron or a cap. These were tangible benefits which were a real incentive to families living in the depths of poverty.

The Sunday Schools were charitable ventures, funded by private contributions from sponsors. Money had to be raised by constant campaigning and appeals to circles of wealthy contacts. In this respect, the Mores were well placed, but it was still a constant battle to keep funds flowing in. The yearly cost of the More's Cheddar Sunday School is reflected in a surviving invoice, reproduced in *Hannah More and her Circle*,1867 by Mary Hopkins:

House rent	*£ 7*
Repairs, whitewashing benches	*£ 2*
Salary for Headmistress	*£ 30*
Under-teachers	*£ 10*
Bibles, Prayer and other books	*£ 8*
Caps, tippets - 100 girls	*£ 15*
Shirts - 20 young men	*£ 5*
Club subscriptions and expenses	*£ 6*
Incidental charities	*£ 6*
Total	***£ 89***

We can see that the invoice shows a predictable expenditure on books for reading and also materials for the sewing of caps, tippets and shirts in which the girls were to be trained.

The prime purpose of the Sunday Schools was to teach children to read. Methods and materials to this end were developed.

a. Learning to read. This was expected to be achieved quickly, in a matter of months. The old fashioned 'horn book' with its alphabet was still in use. This listed the letters, in upper and lower case, in alphabetical order. This was often followed by consonant-plus-vowel listings such as *ba be bi bo bu* and vowel-plus-consonant *ab eb ib ob ub* etc. (similar to the 'synthetic phonics' approach currently favoured).

To follow on from learning their letters, children could move to using Sarah Trimmer's *The Spelling Book*. We have no direct evidence that this was used by the Mores but, given the popularity of the books and also the Mores' links with the Blue Stocking Group, they must have been aware of them and it seems highly likely that the books were used at the Cheddar School. These were normally lists of words in order of 'difficulty'. Sarah Trimmer was unusual in that she put the words into a story context to help give meaning – and greater motivation.

Below, are brief extracts from Trimmer's *Ladder to Learning* – a series of carefully graded stories to support children learning to read. These are arranged according to syllabification, so that Step One had stories with only one syllable words, Step Two with two syllable words, and so on. From the extracts from two levels, below, we can see the moral content offered and also the demands made on a young reader.

Step the First *[one syllable]* ***The Wolf and the Lamb***

One hot day a Wolf and a Lamb came at the same time to quench their thirst in the waters of a clear brook. The Wolf had a will to taste the flesh of the Lamb, so, he would straight way fall out with the Lamb ... [and cause a fight...which he then regretted...] etc...

Moral: The worst of men know so well that they ought to be good
that when they do wrong they try to make it seem right.

Also, *Fox and the Crow, Horse and the Man* and many more.

Step the Second *[two syllable]* ***A Foolish Stag***

A Stag, who chanced to come to a clear fountain to quench his thirst, saw his own image in the water. He noticed a pair of branching horns, and thought,
"How sweetly these antlers become me. What a noble effect they produce."
While the fool was giving himself these airs, he was startled by a pack of yelling hounds. He fled swiftly into a thicket where his horns became wedged among the branches. The hounds soon came upon him and tore him to the ground.

Moral: Those things most pleasing to the fancy are often hurtful
to our real welfare

Whilst nowadays we would question the phonetic complexity of one syllable words such as *quench, cause, fight* and *straight*, this idea still forms the basis for the reading formulae used extensively from the 1970s to grade readers. These early teaching aids give fascinating insights into beliefs about learning and the methods used at that time. Further, it has also been suggested that while the children learnt these texts by heart and recited them using this formal language, it did nothing to help them express their own ideas and feelings for everyday purposes. This resulted in a wide mis-match between 'display' oracy, and 'everyday' oracy.

This discrepancy applied less to the favoured question-and-answer teaching method. As an illustration of this catechetical method of teaching, suggested by Anna Barbauld and used by Sarah Trimmer, the following is a brief extract from Trimmer's *The Teacher's Assistant* - a system of questions and answers carefully sequenced to lead to the 'right' conclusions. Socrates himself might have approved!

A catechetical form of Q and A
Lecture: God the Creator
Questions: Who alone can create?
Can mankind make things?
What are your gown and flannel made from?
Where does the wool come from?
Who made the sheep?
Is it not good that God supplies us with the means to
fashion clothing?

Here was religion and logical thinking linked to daily life: working from the experiences of children to lead them to wider considerations. Good, modern 'child-centred' practice!

Hannah, too, produced many further items for reading and instruction in the form of the popular *Cheap Repository Tracts* intended for 'society's unfortunates'. The most famous of these stories is probably *The Shepherd of Salisbury Plain*, describing a family of phenomenal frugality and contentment. This was translated into several languages. Two million copies of her similar short, simple and didactic stories were circulated, in one year - some even reaching communities in America. They were intended to teach the poor to rely upon the virtues of sobriety, humility, industry, reverence for the Constitution, distrust of the French, and to trust in God and in the kindness of the gentry - hardly revolutionary.

Reading materials were increasing rapidly in this period of 'chap' books (a corruption of 'cheap'). In particular, children's books were becoming recognised as an independent market. Important additions to the available reading materials for children resulted from the work of one particular man, **John Newberry**. By 1740 he had started publishing books, first in Reading and then London. He is credited with being the first to make children's books central to his publishing enterprise. There were recognisable characteristics of Newbery's books. He borrowed techniques from other publishers, such as binding his books in Dutch floral paper and adding woodcuts (some by the celebrated artists John Bewick and Stothard) to make the books attractive. The books were strongly made, with good print, wide margins and quality paper (some gilt edged): it all added up to a 'Newberry brand'. The content was wide-ranging and the style lively. He also used his stories to promote other books and even products – such as Dr Fever's Powders! Newbery's firm published around one hundred titles for children, which included stories, ABC books, novels and magazines – many of which were specially marketed as Toy Books. He is believed to have commissioned authors, written some books himself, as well as published manuscripts sent to him.

In common with the 'mood of the moment' he appears to have adopted Locke's views that '*children may be cozened into a knowledge of the letters; be taught to read, without perceiving it to be anything but a sport, and play themselves into that which others are whipped for*'. He also argued that children should be considered 'reasoning beings' and suggested that picture books be created *for* children. Newberry seems to have put these notions into practice. He also made his books relatively cheap. Even cheaper, were the wood-block editions (which disappeared around 1790, except in chapbooks) and coloured plates (where colouring was done by an 'assembly line' of children who added one colour in one place). The first to be successful was *A Little Pretty Pocket-Book* which cost only 6d – or 8d when sold with a ball or pincushion! This book was a collection of information and games, riddles and even advice on a proper diet. The main message was always that hard work will be rewarded so, '*learn your lessons ... and one day you will ride in a coach and six*'.

One of Newbery's best-selling stories, *The History of Little Goody Two-Shoes*, went through 29 editions between 1765 and 1800 (editions were commonly 2000 copies). It was possibly co-authored by the dramatist Oliver Goldsmith, while Dr Samuel Johnson is thought to have edited another popular title – a compilation of English rhymes, *Mother Goose's Melody, or, Sonnets for the Cradle* (London, undated, c.1765). Newbery also published a series of books written by "*Tom Telescope*" that were wildly popular, going through seven editions between 1761 and 1787 alone. These were based on the emerging science of the day and consisted of a series of lectures given by a boy, Tom Telescope. The most famous is entitled *The Newtonian System of Philosophy Adapted to the Capacities of Young Gentlemen and Ladies.*

At least three Blue Stocking authors were published by Newberry: *The Governess or Little Female Academy* by Sarah Fielding (sister of novelist Tom Fielding) was a best-selling title, as was *Fabulous Histories* or *Robins* by Sarah Trimmer, which sold two editions every three years for a whole generation at least. The *History of John Cheap, the Chapman*, *Parley the Porter*, and *Stephen of Salisbury Plain* and other favourite tracts, were written by 'the Quaker lady', Hannah More, about 1777.

By the time John Newberry died, he had established a unique reputation for his children's books as well as a distinct branch of literature. Although the books seem very pious and didactic to modern readers, they must have revealed untold treasures for young readers who otherwise only had religious books to read. The last legatees of this ancient firm, Messrs Griffith & Farran, survived into the twentieth century, still publishing children's books. A final tribute to his role came in 1922, when the Newberry medal was created in his honour, which is awarded each year to the best children's book published in the United States.

b. Additional benefits. While reading was considered essential - to be able to read the Good Book – Hannah seems to have regarded the teaching of writing with suspicion. It was only taught to exceptional scholars and then it was taught by a separate master often in a separate location. Primers and tracts remained the basic diet. But the new materials, teaching methods and content alone were not sufficient inducement for some pupils to attend the new schools and develop the reading habit. Other incentives were offered. A penny was paid for correct recitation of the ninth chapter of Isaiah, the Beatitudes, and some of the Psalms. Children then progressed to the Catechism, which was framed and hung on the classroom walls. Further reading progress led to the New Testament and the Book of Common Prayer. Not easy reading material, but it suited the civilizing goals of the school. Then there was the lure of the Great Feast in the form of a summer picnic, when the children were taken in decorated carts to a local beauty spot with baskets of food, processional flags, ending with a recitation competition and prizes to be won!

The Mores knew that the success of the school would depend on the teachers they appointed. At Cheddar they were fortunate to find Mrs Barber and her daughter Betsy. They were paid £30 p.a. plus free rent of a house and garden (worth 7 guineas), and an allowance of coal and candles. Additional under-teachers received £10 p.a. This was the accepted rate at the time. The Mores always tried to find intelligent, religious, industrious people - preferably a couple, so the wife could teach the girls and the husband the boys.

Not content with teaching children, the Mores moved on to working with adults. On Sunday nights, meetings were held for parents. Programmes were developed to suit the needs of different ages and levels of those who attended. A printed sermon might be read, a prayer read and a hymn sung. Sometimes an instructor would explain the difficult words. However, no 'extemporaneous' prayers or instruction took place, for this would raise angry protests of being 'Methody' and could lead to trouble and even broken windows. Further classes were added during the week, too.

In addition, in several Mendip villages, the More sisters encouraged Clubs which were set up along the lines of the men's Friendly Societies. These were mutual benefit societies where each member paid in one penny a week in order to receive support at a future date. According to the Rules of the Society, in Cheddar, a woman could draw 3s 6d for her family while too sick to work herself, receive 7s during the 'lying-in' period after a birth, while a guinea might be made available for a funeral. Sometimes a successful Club might attract a legacy from a lady of the manor so the fund could become quite considerable. Another feature of such Clubs was the intention to teach village women how to cook cheaply and healthily, according to recipes supplied by the Mores and collected in a book *The Cottage Cook*. Agricultural labourers at this time only earned between 6 and 8 shillings a week – Somerset labourers were some of the worst paid. A skilled woman could add nearly 3s by spinning wool, and children could earn 1s a week for scaring crows or stone-picking, while a dilapidated two roomed cottage would be rented at 50s a year. Every care had to be taken to eek out the wage so the family could be fed. This could have been rich soil for the revolutionary ideas from across the Channel, during the period leading to the French Revolution – hence another cause of fears about the appropriateness of educating the poor.

The Mores' efforts to improve conditions led them into many detailed areas of housewifery. Bread-making and beer-brewing were promoted (in preference to gin or foul water). Community fuel schemes were initiated: a village baking oven was built and fired three times a week for all the households to use. This cut down on fuel which was becoming scarce as heaths were enclosed and turfs and faggots increasingly difficult to find. Care and attention given to a small garden plot could be critical in keeping a family going through the 'hungry months' before the new season's vegetables could be harvested. Hence, they offered 'education' in a broad format.

At Cheddar, Shipham and Rowberrow such Clubs throve well. The annual Club Day was celebrated with gusto, in a similar way to the children's Sunday School outings. Cakes and tea were served, fine speeches from a representative of the local gentry were delivered, a homily which both exhorted and warned and, finally, presentations of white woollen stockings (knitted by the Mores themselves): 5s and a Bible were handed to any girls soon to be married.

In all, the More sisters set up schools at Axbridge, Barnwell, Barley Wood, Belmont, Blagdon, Cheddar, Congresbury, Cowslip Green, Flax Bourton, Nailsea, Rowberrow and Shipham, Wedmore, Weston, Winscombe and Yatton. Out of these 16, not all flourished: some were short-lived and soon quietly melted away, others became embroiled in controversy and ended in heated and protracted public exchanges. Nailsea and Blagdon stand out for very different reasons.

Nailsea was a mining area, where the glass-makers were the dominant economic group. It was considered a wild, rough environment and the people savages. The sisters found the conditions in which these people lived 'greatly transcending all we had imagined'. One cannot but admire the courage of these two middle-aged, middle-class women riding into such areas, unchaperoned, with the intention of trying to convince such fierce families of the gentle virtues of education. Nevertheless on their first visit they won the promise of 27 children for a new school.

The community of Nailsea ruled itself in time-honoured ways. The 'Headsmen' ran the affairs of the parish with the welfare of the people at heart. They took to the idea of a school immediately and willingly undertook the running of the enterprise. They agreed that among themselves, they too would attend, in pairs, forfeiting a shilling for absence from work. When they had accumulated 14s they spent the money on a gooseberry tart for the little scholars!

But this intense interest and participation spelt trouble for the More sisters who were used to doing things their own way. The Headsmen soon fell out with the young couple from Bath who came to teach at the school. Mr and Mrs Younge had been recommended for their zeal and industry – but not necessarily for tact. After many angry meetings the Mores were forced to withdraw the Younges and place them elsewhere. Meanwhile the Headsmen elected their own teacher from among themselves – a young collier, too injured to continue in the mine. His training was paid for by the Headsmen and he soon made an excellent teacher, till his own death. It was a lesson in community democracy which the Mores needed to learn.

Blagdon was another turning-point. The controversy which broke out between 1800 and 1804 is an interesting reflection of the unease of that time. The Napoleonic Wars were raging across the Channel and fear of social or political unrest was very real. The controversy also represents the fierce battle between different religious sects which was to dominate and bedevil education developments throughout the nineteenth century. A series of problems arose because of clashes between disgruntled curates (who perhaps saw their leading role in caring for the spiritual well-being of their flock being undermined by the intrusive Mores), defiant teachers recruited on a mission, an unyielding stance from the Mores, and no senior clergyman to serve as referee.

The problem started in Axbridge where a teacher had had to be removed because of 'rashness and indiscretion'. Having been moved to Wedmore to work alongside an unwilling existing teacher, local opposition to the school and suspicion of the evening meetings for adults (thought to be dangerously nonconformist) became more vociferous. The Conventicle Act of 1664, which banned nonconformist meetings was still (theoretically) in force and punishable by transportation. Similarly, the Test Acts (restricting Roman Catholics) were also still law. To disregard the Anglican Church was to disregard its Head – the Monarch – and, in earlier times, that would have been construed as treason. Though such measures were no longer enforced, they could still be used as a threat and emotions whipped up to a hysterical pitch. The curate at Wedmore, Mr William Eyre, was a friend of the curate at Blagdon, Mr Thomas Bere. Forewarned, Mr Bere began to watch the Blagdon school more carefully.

Mrs Bere started to attend the Monday evening meetings for adults. She reported that the meetings were Methodistic, characterised by extemporaneous prayer (rather than prayers from the authorised Book of Common Prayer) and that members were encouraged to give 'personal testimony' concerning their own spiritual state (such testifying was considered a threat to the established scriptures and authority of the Church and its clergy). Everyone was up in arms. Letters flew back and forth between local clergy, local gentry, magistrates and anyone else with grudges. It became a very personal attack on Hannah More herself who was accused of being Methodistic. After all, her father was from a Presbyterian family, she had attended a Baptist Academy, she was known to the Clapham Evangelical sect etc. etc. etc. Hannah mustered all her well-connected Bishops, Lords and Ladies to counter the scurrilous posters and insidious pamphlets in circulation. The very level of her activity in setting up schools, clubs and other charitable efforts was tainted as 'enthusiams' which were dangerously 'evangelical'. The school was closed, the teachers dismissed and Hannah relapsed into ill-health and possible breakdown for the next two years. Being an educational philanthropist was not for the faint-hearted.

As she gradually recovered, Hannah turned again to her writing and less to the active supervision of her schools. She had first been asked by Beilby Porteus, the Bishop of London, to write something in simple words so the uneducated would not be dazzled by words like equality or liberty. The first venture had been *Village Politics by Will Chop, the country carpenter*. An extract will illustrate the nature of the story:

Jack: *What's the matter?*
Tom: *Matter? Why I want liberty!*
Jack: *Liberty? That's bad indeed! What, has anyone fetched a warrant for thee? Come, man. Cheer up. I'll be bound for thee. Thou art an honest fellow though thou dost tipple and prate a little too much at the Rose and Crown.*
Tom: *No, no. I want a new constitution!*
Jack: *Indeed! Why I thought thou wast a desperately healthy fellow. Call for a doctor directly!*
Tom: *I'm not sick. I want liberty and equality, and the rights of man.*
Jack: *Oh now I understand thee. A Leveller and a Republican!*
Tom: *Nay I am a friend to the people. I want a reform.*
Jack: *Then the shortest way is to mend thyself.*
Tom: *But I want a general reform.*
Jack: *Then let everyone mend one.*

So, that's the French Revolution dismissed – Britain can sleep safely!

The first of these Cheap Repository Tracts was produced in March 1795 and Hannah produced them monthly for three years. Over two million were sold! Since the early success of the moral (rather than political) *Shepherd of Salisbury Plain* she was encouraged to produce many more stories in a similar vein: *The Two Shoemakers, Black Giles the Poacher, Betty Brown the St Giles Orange Girl, The History of Mary Wood the House Maid* and *The Lancashire Collier Girl.* All these stories followed the same moral tone and drew upon incidents Hannah had witnessed in her own life, tales from the recollections of her mother's farming family, or ones she had been told by others. They were down to earth and surprisingly different in style compared to her earlier literary efforts.

In different vein she published *The Manners of the Great* in 1788 which urged the importance of reforms in high society so that they might seep downward. This was followed in 1799 by a further book, *The Strictures on the Modern System of Education of the Female*, which focused on the frivolous nature of the upbringing of young society ladies. The latter sold 19,000 copies! but was more in the nature of a rambling homily on how young girls should be brought up to acquire virtuous habits. As she grew older, Hannah became more conservative and less tolerant of views which were different from her own. The Romantic poets, Coleridge and Southey, called upon her out of respect for the *grande dame*, but left feeling disillusioned.

The death of her elder sister, Mary, in 1813 was soon followed by that of Elizabeth in 1816, Sarah in 1817 and her dearest Patty in 1819 – the last loss broke her heart. Eventually Hannah was persuaded to move to a small house in Clifton, nearer to her remaining friends and away from her servants who, she believed, had been pilfering the household stores. At her death she left £ 30,000 to be distributed between 70 charities, yet she left almost nothing for the continuation of her schools. She seems to have shifted her attention to the causes of the emancipation of slaves and the protection of indigenous peoples of America, and lost interest in the Mendip schools which she and Patty had worked so hard to establish.

Nevertheless, her contribution throughout her long life to the development of basic literacy and employment skills and to women's mutual benefit clubs had made a major difference to the lives of many hundreds of women and girls. It had also changed the attitudes of many who lived in the area around the Mendips, including those who were in positions where they could also *do* something, just as the *Bas Bleus* had intended.

We can now turn to a very practical pioneer, Rev John Poole, who focused his experiments beyond the Sunday Schools to the village day school he helped to create and where he, himself, taught alongside the teachers for nearly 50 years. He also trained teachers to work in other nearby schools to which he gave continued support. Visitors from far and wide came to what developed as a model for other villages, not just within his own neighbourhood but far beyond.

Chapter 3

Rev John Poole: Model School at Enmore, the work of Lancaster and Bell, and the emerging national organisations for education

The focus now turns away from exclusive attention on individual philanthropists who, in Somerset, have so far proved to be predominantly women. Instead, we find the beginnings of national organisations which become institutionalised and assume a dominant position in channelling educational changes. The focus of attention also introduces the enduring battle of the C19th – between the Churches and the State, in their efforts to take control of the development of education for the masses.

In Somerset, attention moves from the Mendip Hills south of Bath, where the More sisters operated, to the south-west and the quiet Quantock Hills, where **Rev John Poole (1770-1867)** was born in the village of Over Stowey, became minister in the neighbouring parish of Enmore and, later, set up an important model school. What little we know about John Poole comes indirectly through references to him in books relating to his better known cousin, **Thomas Poole**, whose claim to fame lies in his friendship with the Romantic poets – Coleridge, Southey and Wordsworth. These friendships are noted in *Thomas Poole and his Friends* by Elizabeth Sandford (updated 1996, originally *Mrs Sandford and her friends* by the said Mrs Henry Sandford,1888, sister-in-law to John Poole).

The Poole family was from a very different social class to the Mores, but it was also a long-standing family in the area. We hear of a Prudence Poole 1630, James Poole, teacher in Cannington in 1662 and Nicholas Poole, priest at West Quantoxhead in 1761. They continue to figure in the local landscape – when Rev Poole in Fitzwilliam (Taunton) in the 1880s supports a school with Lady Slade. The branch of the Poole family at the centre of this story derived its prosperity and standing from its local business, which drew its strength from the dominant wealth of the region – sheep. They were tannery owners. Both cousins had been educated locally but, while Thomas was destined to take over the family business and for whom, therefore, further education was not considered necessary, cousin John was sent to Oriel College Oxford and later took Holy Orders, becoming a priest in the village of Enmore close to where he had been born.

Both cousins are known to have supported Sunday schools in their respective villages of Nether Stowey and Over Stowey, from 1789. Thomas himself, despite his formal education being curtailed by his father in favour of going into the family tannery business, was a great reader and continued his own education through avidly devouring books to keep abreast of current ideas. Thomas always seems to have admired his cousin and there was no apparent jealousy. He asked John to teach him Latin and he taught himself French so he could read documents coming from revolutionary France.

Apart from revolutionary politics, Thomas was also a friend to the Romantic poets Coleridge, Southey and **Wordsworth**. Having met Coleridge and Southey on their famous walking holiday from Oxford in 1794, which took them through Somerset to the Quantocks, he became a pivotal figure for the newly married but impoverished Coleridge by finding him local accommodation and giving him further practical support as well. Wordsworth soon followed his friend Coleridge and also came to live close by. Thomas Poole's illustrious friends were frequently in trouble and even accused of treasonable activities when their habit of long night-time walks on the hills overlooking the Bristol Channel was referred to the local authorities as being suspicious. One story has it that a government agent, tracking them on a nocturnal walk, reported that their discussions were about Spy-Nosey – in fact the philosopher Spinoza! Whether apocryphal or not, it reflects the tensions of the times. It seems that Coleridge, in particular, delighted in shocking the more serious-minded cousin John, by coming out with outrageous ideas just to watch his reactions. Southey was later to write an autobiography of the influential educationalist, Dr Andrew Bell, whose work was also admired by John Poole: whether John's work was also admired by Southey we do not know, but we do know that Wordsworth was very interested and Tom often passed on information through their letters.

In keeping with several enlightened individual philanthropists, Thomas built up a considerable private library of his own. He then opened up a Book Reading Room in his own house to which anyone could come to read and discuss current topics of interest. Like his cousin John, he was a passionate supporter of education and, after the successful development of the nearby school by his cousin, Thomas funded the building of a school in 1813, in his own village, to be run along the same lines and staffed with teachers trained by cousin John. Thomas also encouraged the setting up of Friendly Societies which typically collected membership dues to create a fund to support members in difficult times. His efforts at local support extended to women too. A Women's Walk – thought to have started around 1806 – still takes place on the Saturday nearest to Whitsun. The associated Women's Benefit Society lasted till 1975.

Meanwhile, cousin John had been appointed Rector of neighbouring Enmore village, in 1796, although it was not till October 1801 that he and his growing family moved to that village. Rev Poole remained Rector of Enmore for 60 years and was also Chaplain to the local Earl of Egremont who supported him in his educational goals. John was '*a reformer at heart but of sober and temperate fashion*'. He always declared that he wished his life to be useful. He took his ministry seriously, aiming to preach his sermon 'in Saxon', crossing out words of Latin origin, so that his parishioners could better understand him.

However, John Poole was also radical in certain respects but, as a man of the cloth, he went about changing his world in a quieter manner. He set up a new school in his village of Enmore in 1810, which came to be considered exemplary. The school became a model and was referred to by many as a blueprint for the subsequent movement of the Anglican society mentioned below, though the school came into existence shortly before the establishment of the National School Society.

To understand Rev Poole's contribution, we must go back a few years and, also, travel many thousands of miles. For, his efforts are preceded by two influential men: Joseph Lancaster and Dr Andrew Bell.

i. The origins of the Monitorial System

Joseph Lancaster, 1778-1838, was a Quaker, born in Sheldon, Birmingham. Growing up in this rapidly industrialising region and aware of the dreadful social and (im)moral conditions children lived in, he became determined to take action to improve access to education for the children of the poor. In 1798 he opened his first school in **Borough Road, London** followed soon after by a teacher-training establishment. He was able to inspire others to contribute to his projects, even members of the Royal Family. Recognising that the cost of education consisted mainly in the salaries of teachers, he devised a method of teaching whereby one schoolmaster was responsible for 300 or more boys, all accommodated in one large schoolroom. The basic teaching of the younger children was undertaken by older ones, called monitors, who taught in small groups on either side of the schoolroom, while the Schoolmaster could watch all the groups simultaneously. It was repetitious and dull, based on recitation of texts as a means of 'learning to read'. The poet Southey reputedly noted that despite his opposition to corporal punishment, he would rather be beaten than subjected to Lancastrian discipline.

Nevertheless, children were taught to read, instilled with discipline, given moral instruction and effectively prepared for the kinds of jobs many of them would have to take in the new industries. Mindful of the need to adapt and meet the expectations of the growing numbers of admirers, Joseph Lancaster wrote *Improvements in Education* in 1803 as a guide for other entrepreneurs who might similarly wish to educate their future workforce. He even toured America to talk about his educational ideas and was well received.

In 1808, following some financial problems, his efforts were transformed into the Society for Promoting the Royal British, or Lancastrian, System for the Education of the Poor. This was formed to help Lancaster organise and stabilise his financial affairs. The name was later changed to the **British and Foreign School Society**, in 1814, as it is known today.

At the same time, **Rev Dr Andrew Bell, 1753 - 1832**, was deploying a similar system in far off Madras, where that part of the Empire shared a similar educational goal for similar economic and moral reasons. Who started their system first, who should therefore win the 'credit' as founder of the monitorial system has long been debated. Perhaps they both had similar ideas independently of each other: after all they were trying to solve a common problem – how to educate more for less.

Fife-born Bell came from a humble, though enterprising family. Yet he was destined for fame and eventually buried in Westminster Abbey. His father was a barber and wig-maker, but had earlier been a clockmaker, made apparatus for the University physics labs and helped in experiments. Andrew was educated at Grammar School and then University. As a young man he travelled as a tutor to Virginia, then as a science lecturer to Madras (India), where he found himself working at the Male Military Asylum – a boarding school for orphans and the illegitimate sons of native women and British soldiers.

He found the teaching methods abysmal and was at a loss to know what to put in their place, until one day he came across an open-air native school where younger pupils were being taught their letters by older ones, by inscribing them in the dry sand. The other teachers in the Asylum school were reluctant to try anything new, so he co-opted an intelligent older pupil and showed him how to teach the younger students. In this way, the monitorial system was born.

Within a year of his return from India in 1797, he had published a report on the Male Asylum. The full title is interesting – "*An Experiment in Education made at the Male Asylum in Madras, suggesting a system by which a school or family may teach itself under the Superintendence of the Master or Parent*". By the next year, **St Botolph's School in Aldgate, London** and the **Industrial School in Kendal** had adopted the system.

Interestingly, the list of early experimental locations includes the Lake District, where Wordsworth was then living. An account by a colleague of Bell's, teaching in Grasmere Parish School – the very village in which Wordsworth lived – describes how he was in the classroom when an elderly gentleman entered and questioned him about his methods. Subsequently, **Dorothy Wordsworth**, the poet's sister, who had met Bell when he visited the school at Grasmere, remodelled and largely rewrote Bell's manuscript on the Madras School in order to make it easier for the reader to follow: (unfortunately) Bell discarded it. In addition, as mentioned, one of Bell's biographers was the poet Robert Southey who was part of the web of friendship begun in the Quantocks. Thus, Bell's work, the interested Wordsworths and John Poole's innovations in Somerset were all linked through this network of personal contacts.

This might have been further substantiated after 1801, when Bell was appointed Rector of the parish of Swanage in Dorset. Soon he had 13 Day Schools and 3 Sunday Schools running on the Madras system in the county and, within his own parish, he set up benefit societies, social clubs and a cottage industry in straw-plaiting. By now, the Madras system was being adopted by many schools all over the country, and Bell was being sought after for advice on its implementation. Being so (relatively) close by, it is hard to imagine that Rev John Poole would not have heard of him, maybe visited and had discussions with him.

Professor Meiklejohn, another of Bell's biographers, explains the characteristics of Bell's system (quoted in the website of Madras College, Fife):

> *Before Dr Bell's plan, the master 'heard' all the lessons; and forty-nine children were always more or less idle while the fiftieth was occupied in 'saying' his lessons. But now the children were to teach each other; each child was to rise or fall in his place in class according to his accuracy; or even to fall or rise from class to class as the little boys were arranged in divisions.*
> *One of the boys taught and, when one child was reading, all the others listened; and the next boy corrected when an error was made. The lessons were always very short; and each child prepared what he had to without a single mistake. Literacy began with learning one's letters by tracing them on a board strewn with sand, leading to reading where letters were joined up into syllables and the syllables into words. The steps in learning were kept short, the idea being to encourage pupils by the immediate reward of seeing the results of their efforts. As Bell put it, the aim was to 'get everything perfect'.*

Many of his practices lasted for decades: even a hundred years later, in the primary school, the practice of pupils moving places according to performance continued, and many were taught to read according to the syllabic method. Other ideas of Bell's show him to have been years ahead of his time e.g.

> *Each pupil to find his own level and be encouraged to teach / share with peers;*
> *Small learning steps and each learned perfectly before moving on (mastery learning);*
> *A system of monitoring individual progress (paidometer);*
> *No corporal punishment, and a strong emphasis on Moral Education.*

Bell was an energetic organiser and, based on the success and spread of his new system, he lobbied to set up a national organisation. Alarmed by the success of Mr Lancaster's (non-conformist) schools, the Church of England swung into action. A certain Joshua Watson, having made a fortune in the City as a wine merchant and Government contractor during the Napoleonic Wars, had retired from business in 1814 at the age of forty-three in order to devote his time and energies, for the remainder of his life, to the service of the Church of England. In 1814 Joshua Watson had became Treasurer of the SPCK, (Society for the Promotion of Christian Knowledge) which had branches all over the Empire. He had increased the annual income of the SPCK to an unprecedented figure which raised his standing in the Society. At the same time, he became interested in missionary work in India where he must have become aware of the educational work of Dr Bell.

After lengthy discussions with key Church members, including the Archbishop of Canterbury, the **National Society for the Promotion of Education Amongst the Poor** was established on 16th October 1811. At the founding meeting, a statement about educational goals was recorded: *'That the National Religion should be made the foundation of National Education, and should be the first and chief thing taught to the poor, according to the excellent Liturgy and Catechism provided by our Church".* The primary stated objective was *"to teach [children] the doctrine of Religion according to the principles of the Established Church, and to train them to the performance of their religious duties by an early discipline":* the secondary objective was *"to communicate such knowledge and habits as are sufficient to guide them through life in their proper station'.* This was interpreted as imparting a limited amount of secular instruction – reading, writing, arithmetic - based upon the monitorial system, already devised by Rev Dr Andrew Bell, in Madras.

The National Society became highly active in many aspects of education, from the publishing of books and provision of equipment, to the training of teachers. The mission of the Society was to found a Church school in every parish in England and Wales by offering grants to potential founders, on condition that development was fostered on the Society's principles.

The new organisation was partly in response to issues raised by controversies such as that relating to Mrs Hannah More and the Curate of Blagdon. The Society, therefore, set out to clarify what should be taught, how and by whom. There was, however, great variety in the types of school within the country. We find that there were 596 elementary schools of which 111 were private Dame Schools. Others were charity schools, sometimes dependent on individuals such as the Mores' school in Cheddar, or small village enterprises often run by the parish priest (Lawson and Silver 1973). By 1833, 154 schools were already called National Schools, but many were not in fact members of the National Society, though they probably agreed to many of its aims – and thereby won access to grants.

Nevertheless, the founding of these two national organisations marked a major change. For the first time the idea was recognised that there was a need for a coordinated national approach. Education, as we have seen, had been the province of individual philanthropists. Yet, with the nonconformists successfully organising schools nationwide in response to the growing need and now increasing demand – from the poor – for education, inevitably, the Church of England also felt the need to react. It was not yet considered the business of the State to intervene or provide education, as this was seen as a threat to the autonomy and independence of the religious organisations. It was the beginning of a long battle between the religious organisations, each trying to protect its own influence.

Meanwhile, the Madras System expanded rapidly, leading to the personal founding of several establishments including the Madras College in Bell's home of Fife. In 1812, the Society had 52 schools with 8,620 pupils; in 1813 the number had risen to 230 schools with 40,484 pupils. By 1816 around 756 schools were attached to the National Society. Yet, as with Lancaster, the personalities of both men did not make them good at committee work or financial organisation. Bell was reportedly hurt to find the leadership of the Society given to Joshua Watson.

Instead, Bell turned his attention to his next concern which was to see his system introduced in his home town in the two principal schools - the Grammar School and the English School – as a preliminary to getting the system adopted in these sectors nationwide. It is against this background that we can now consider the work of Rev John Poole, in Somerset.

ii. The School at Enmore

As already stated, **Rev John Poole** had become involved with an existing Sunday School and was aided by the Earl of Egremont (a keen local supporter of education).There, he introduced the teaching of 'reading, writing and reckoning' and not just Bible reading. He believed, *'It is not natural to confine a child's attention through the whole day to the subject of religion'.* The Sunday School attracted 60 children from amongst the small village population, but this soon dropped once the Day School opened which offered wider opportunities.

We can conveniently access information about the origins of schooling in the village, as summarised by a recent Headmistress, Sybil Laver, in a booklet written for the 175th anniversary in 1985. It seems there were already at least two dame schools in the village. In 1810 Rev Poole persuaded Mrs Bailey (who held her school in one of the Park Cottages) to reorganise her school according to a new system under his direction. The children were later moved to a larger cottage nearer the church (possibly in the old Poor House buildings, linked to the Earl of Egremont). In this new location, there was one schoolmistress who taught reading and needlework, while 5 or 6 older pupils acted at 'monitors' and taught the younger ones. Rev Poole provided sand, slates, books and soon enlarged the space available by creating a separate space for the Infants. He added desks for writing – quite rare at the time as little writing was usual offered in such elementary schools and, if it was, it would be done on the children's knees, on their slates. Underneath these desks were long lathes which formed a cradle where bonnets and hats could be kept. Rev Poole, himself, taught daily in the school to set the example he expected others to follow. Incentives were offered to the staff: the schoolmistress earned 2d a week extra for each child able to write on slate, and 3d for those who could write well enough to be allowed to use the more expensive paper.

We know a considerable amount about the organization of the school through the then widely read book *The Village School Improved*, published by Rev John Poole, in 1812, with further editions needed in 1813 and 1815. (The title echoes that of Mr Joseph Lancaster's, published a few years earlier. In the preface John Poole pays tribute to both Lancaster and Bell). In this book he describes a new form of the 'monitorial' method – adapted to the small village context rather than the city or grammar school. A relative, Mrs Joseph Anstice (quoted in *The Friends of Thomas Poole*) later wrote, *'You have no idea as to the celebrity of the school.'*

Its organization, style of teaching and pedagogical principles were soon to attract considerable attention from local notables as well as national figures. It was of particular interest to Wordsworth, now living in the Lake District, to whom cousin Thomas Poole often sent up-dates. It is believed to have been reflected in some of the sentiments expressed in a lengthy philosophical poem, *Excursions, (published in 1815).*
In *Book Ninth: Discourse of the Wanderer* the Sage declares

> *"O for the coming of that glorious time*
> *When, prizing knowledge as her noblest wealth*
> *And best protection, this Imperial Realm*
> *While she extracts allegiance, shall admit*
> *An obligation, on her part, to teach*
> *Them who are born to serve her and obey;*
> *Binding herself by statute to secure*
> *For all the children whom her soil maintains*
> *The rudiments of letters and inform*
> *The mind with moral and religious truth."* [*l* 293-302]

"...Prudent caution needful to avert
Impending evil, equally require
That the whole people should be
taught and trained... [*l* 356-359]
From culture, unexclusively bestowed
On Albion's race in freedom born
Expect these mighty issues: from the pains
And faithful care of unambitious schools
Instructing simple childhood's ready ear
Thence look for these magnificent results." [*l* 392-397]

Wordsworth was unusual in calling for the *State* to take the duty of providing education, as was his call for education for *all*. He certainly believed that great results could come from the pains and care of modest, 'unambitious' schools – such as in the village of Enmore. Although Wordsworth always promoted the idea that much could be learned from nature around us which was sometimes the best 'school', nevertheless, he also recognised the need for more formal education of children, as

"...On themselves
They cannot learn, nor to their own hearts
To know what they must do: their wisdom is
To look into the eyes of others, thence
To be instructed what they must avoid:" [*l* 143-147]

iii. Establishing a sustainable form of village education.

In the *Village School Improved*, Rev Poole set forth arguments for educating the poor – not yet universally accepted as a legitimate goal. It was feared that once educated, the poor would have higher aspirations and be unwilling to perform the lowly tasks currently assigned to them. He believed that, *'The humblest individual now has continual occasion for some acquaintance with writing and arithmetic. Of this the poor are now sensible. Parents are universally desirous of this instruction and their cordial concurrence is essential to prosperity'*.

He also recommended village education on two further grounds. He believed it would help to sustain the local community by educating the children within the village from 8-13 years old – and prevent the children of more prosperous farmers being *'sent to an inferior boarding school in a neighbouring town where, if they escape moral corruption, often acquire a distaste for country employments. Whereas, by receiving their education within their own parish their connection with the parish remains unbroken'*. Further, he then liked to train and employ the more promising scholars as teachers in his own, or neighbouring schools. In fact the motto of the school is *'Those who are taught here must go out and teach others'*.

He included arguments that such education would help to integrate the community, for *'There is also beauty in a system which brings under one roof the rising generation of the labouring poor and those who will be their future masters or mistresses, and which places the former under the guidance of those very individuals .. who will be their employers, advisors and protectors'*. Hence, he tried to reassure those who thought that educating the poor would lead to an exodus from village to town in search of new jobs resulting in an assumed increase in overcrowding, unhealthy and immoral living.

To John Poole the practice of the 'monitor system' was not for the sake of economies (by which, instead of paid teachers, older children taught the youngsters). Instead he believed that the evidence of learning needed to be demonstrated in both oral and written form and, that the best evidence of learning was by showing the ability to communicate your own learning to others and thus to teach them. It was for this educational reason that an adapted system of monitoring appealed to him.

Further, he wished to encourage more students to gain an education and also to retain those children of the wealthier farmers by offering a wider curriculum. Thus, while he frankly admitted, '*There may be people who question the propriety and necessity of introducing subjects such as English Grammar and Higher Rules of Arithmetic in the elementary school*', he nevertheless felt it was proper so to do. This, too, would support his aim to nurture the sense of community which he believed suffered if many children left to go to city schools. He also believed that living in the countryside was healthier and beneficial to all children.

Within a year of opening what he called a 'new improved village school', Rev Poole was already receiving visitors to observe the workings of the new method. In 1812 visitors included the MP Francis Horner and the local diarist Rev William Holland of Over Stowey who became a regular visitor. In fact the school became such a wonder that Mrs Sandsford wrote, in 1888, '*The institution rapidly attained great celebrity and was visited from far and near by people of all ranks and even foreigners. Indeed it was commonly believed that hardly anyone could teach arithmetic like the teachers trained by Mr John Poole*'. Cousin Thomas Poole had such confidence that he sent his beloved and fatherless niece, Elizabeth, to the school at Enmore before sending her to Wells to learn Latin and Greek. She later became a great campaigner for education, through her own book *Female Education*. Other family members also left children with aunts and uncles to be educated at Enmore, like his sister Mrs. Penelope Anstice, who left her son Joe. Rev Poole later adopted him and sent him to Oxford to continue his studies.

Other schools opened in imitation: Nether Stowey School opened on 22nd March 1813, for 85 children with Miss Price as mistress. The school was supported and funded by cousin Thomas Poole, while John Poole advised, approved and regularly visited. By April 27th it already had 118 new recruits! Jane Turner was later the assistant at Stowey, after being educated and trained at Enmore. She later moved on and set up her own school in nearby Cannington. A similar, though smaller school opened at the same time in Over Stowey, Rev Poole's home village. Rev William Holland notes in his diary (published under the title *Paupers and Pig-killers*) that John Poole visited the schools often and that his plan for combining the Bell and Lancaster systems had been developed to 'great perfection'. It seems that Rev Poole was soon overwhelmed by letters from all parts and that he was '*indefatigable in the pains he takes*'. Rev Holland even records a trip, in Nov 1815, in a gig to Zoylandsee (probably Weston Zoyland) to visit another school set up on Mr Poole's Plan '*where the management has been assigned to John Poole*'. We also know that in the nearby village of St Decuman, two further Pooles are listed as Rectors: first, Henry 1798-1834, then Robert 1834-1884. Robert, also set up a school – no doubt with help from his relative, John Poole. We also find the Poole family as active supporters in the school in Eastover Bridgwater, also, North Curry. Later, and further afield, there is also a Rev John Poole in Batcombe supporting his village school in 1847.

When John Poole opened the elementary school for village children it was originally for just 25 children, but it expanded quickly. Most 'scholars' were fee-paying (showing the strong desire for children's education amongst the often poor local parents). At first Rev Poole undertook most of the teaching, but he soon found he needed increased support to give him more time for training visiting teachers as well as, presumably, for his pastoral work. The rapid expansion in the early years shows the growing desire for education and also the success of his methods:

in 1812	70 pupils (including many older scholars, with no previous schooling)
by 1815	100 pupils (including Sunday School pupils)
by 1833	60 pupils (day pupils only) but,
by 1872	32 pupils

The village population fell by a third from the 1820s (due to urbanization) and never recovered. This did not greatly affect enrolments till the Agricultural Depression in the 1870s and 80s, when large-scale emigrations were common in the poorer rural areas – by which time John Poole had been dead for more than two decades.

Rev Poole, through his publication *The Village School Improved*, provided very practical suggestions for others when setting up their own schools. He gave guidelines for the optimum size and space for schooling: the Enmore classroom was 27' x 16' (over 400 square feet). At first Poole suggested 6 square feet per child, but by 1848 his planned new building would have allowed 12 square feet per child – more room for 'active learning'. He even gave details on the size and spacing of desks: suggesting a size of 10' 6" long and between 26" and 31" high, depending on the age of the children. He recommended that these long desks should be placed parallel to the shorter side of the room, just 1' 6" from a long wall, thus leaving space for passage along either side and plenty of space at the front for groups to come out for 'recitation'. He also recommended that all desks should face forwards (as in the Lancastrian system), rather than along the outer walls (as was common in the Bell system).

What is particularly fascinating about *The Village School Improved*, is not just the precise organisational and physical details, but the exact pedagogical details of what and how children should be taught. To begin with, we are given the Daily Routine of the school:

Each day begins with Prayers
9-10.00 Write copies from copper-plate copy-sheet, pasted on wood to save from injury.
9.30-12.00 upper class to be divided into reading and arithmetic groups (second class too young for arithmetic)
2.00- 4.00 girls are engaged in needlework, knitting, straw-plaiting (with regular breaks), while boys continue as in the morning...
End of the Day: Q/A from Catechism

All tuition is to be supplied by the scholars from the 7th and 8th classes who become the teachers for an hour at a time. From 10-14 minutes is allowed for preparation of the 'lesson words' for dictation.

This is very similar to the plans set out for the school in North Curry in 1820, which describes itself as an Improved School, set up on the lines of Enmore's Improved Village School. Like Enmore it aimed to teach boys reading, writing and the common rules of arithmetic, and the girls to be taught the same (even arithmetic!) with the addition of useful needlework and knitting.
The guidelines were as follows:

I 9.00 and 2.00 school opens, scholars to be assembled.
II Boys, who learn to read, write on slates etc, and girls shall pay 2d a week and ½ d for the use of books and slates.
III Payment to be made on Monday morning.
IV All to attend Sunday School.
V The parent to bring any new scholar.
VI Any child found guilty of lying, swearing, stealing, Sabbath-breaking etc and persisting after due admonition shall be expelled.

Rev Poole acknowledged the work of both Lancaster and Bell, but made it clear that his approach differed in important ways. Other schools which adopted the Lancastrian and/or 'Madras' system included Timberscombe (1803), Winscombe (1813) and, more briefly, Williton (1811) and Watchet (1820). His prime motivation appears to have been to contextualise learning wherever possible, in order to give it meaning and reduce the reliance on mere rote learning. To this end, he preferred to use small books, rather than rely on word cards, to reinforce reading skills, and to expect good comprehension which also motivated the scholars. He emphasised, *'Nothing should be repeated from memory until accompanied with questions to clarify its meaning'*. Thus, reading and ciphering lessons should be held *with* questions, written dictations should be *linked* to the content of reading lessons, the interrogative mode should be used in religious instruction, and even numerals and punctuation should be taught *through the context* of a meaningful written dictation. However, he appears to have recognised that some things, like spelling, needed a hefty dose of rote learning. In this case, he advised reading words syllabically and alphabetically, both forwards and also backwards – as a real test!

Having established such a successful system, which was clearly much admired by many leading figures of his day, he was understandably concerned to provide a sure foundation for the continuance of the school after his lifetime: it needed a system that worked independently of any particular person.

First, he set about planning a purpose-built school and successfully applied for a government grant in 1837 (only available since 1833, but requiring to be equalled by local subscriptions). Yet it was not till 1848, with land bequeathed by Mrs Sophia Gould and Mr Nicholas Broadmead that building could begin. (Interestingly, a Sarah Gould and her sister Mrs Mary Scott gave land for a school nearby in North Curry at a similar time.)

Rev Poole then gave 2.63 acres of land and 2 cottages known as Dix's cottages (sometimes given as 'Pixes') into a Trust, to ensure financial support for Enmore School. By 1875, the Trust provided £38, while government grants amounted to £18.6s.0d. and by 1883, the Trust still provided £38 while the grants had increased to £51.17s.0d. The cottages, near the pub, were eventually sold in 1959 and the land in 1972.

The early model school later became a Voluntary Controlled School and latterly a Foundation School. It continues to be a model of high achievement and 'caring pastoring' - just as the Rev John Poole might have hoped. The extracts below from his manual outline many practices which are again current. Of particular interest is the teaching of writing: the division of letter shapes into straight and curved, and into those formed by anti- and clockwise movement, the use of sand trays to *feel* the letter shapes – only serving to demonstrate the revolving fashions in education.

Details of the syllabus used in the model school of Rev John Poole, Enmore, W. Somerset.

First Class

Equipment: Flat-topped desks with a shallow trough for dry sand
Aim: The Alphabet
Method: In pairs, children must trace the letter or numeral on the given card.
The teachers watch and listen to children sound or name the figure.

Capitals are taught as follows:
I H T L E F A V W M N Z K Y *[straight before curved]*
O U C G J D P B R Q S *[anti-clockwise before clockwise]*

Small letters taught in alphabetical order.
Groups of 3 are called out to read from the alphabet chart.
The board is made with rows of [hook] pins. Letter cards with holes can be rearranged so the order can be altered. Only those which are already known, plus the one to be learnt are shown: the rest are turned blank side outermost, so as not to distract.

Procedure: If a mistake is made the next child is asked.
The teacher himself in no case corrects an error.

Second Class

WRITING: attention to correct formation, capital letters taught first.
Each child traces over the card, then makes the shape - in sand first with a finger, then by holding an implement, such as a skewer.

Small letters taught in the following order:
l t b i n m h p u v w j y c e o a d q g x r s k z f
Individual letters taught first, then in pairs, then three or more...

When all letters can be correctly **produced in sand**, the children are then provided with Warren's patent **engraved slates**, and they progress to writing short words.

READING: from Mrs Trimmer's *Charity School Spelling Book, Pt I*
Elementary syllables, or easy monosyllabic words, on large print cards.

SPELLING: from Lindley Murray's *English Spelling Book.*
Teacher **demonstrates** the spelling and sounding of the syllables
then requires **each child to repeat**,
then the next card in the set line, repeated three times.

Procedure: Children are tested by pointing randomly to any of the day's cards.
When a child can both read and write these syllables they move to the next stage.

Third Class. ***(Age 5 or 6 years)*** approx. 10 pupils in each class

The day's words are dictated and children write them on slates.

These **writing words** must be **related to** the children's **reading** ***tasks*** *[which gives focus on meaning rather than rote repetition so prevalent in much of Victorian education]*
Every word which may present difficulty is **presented to them** and **forced to their attention** 7 or 8 times during the half hour lesson.
[this in accordance with current research on memory]

READING: To read with accuracy and pronounce with propriety
Lesson Words: So, (pre-teach) "give" "g-i-v-e", "give"... Children write and then present their slates frontwards so the teacher can check. When 12 words have been thus completed,
Teacher says "Shew (sic) slates"
Teacher and monitor check any errors and the results are marked on the monitor's slate. This method saves time and prevents noise: then the command is given "Clean slates"

Note: The words to be presented should appear in the reading book written so that *syllables are separated*, and should be placed in a separate section, not at the top of the reading exercise, so that when the child is required to read the (key) words, they are not in view.

Materials: The English Spelling Book is purchased in sheets, each sheet can be divided into smaller parts covered with thicker paper: each part costs 3¼ d

Monitoring: ***Particulars of each lesson are copied into a register book at the end of each day***

READING: After 10 minutes for this presentation, a further 20 minutes is allowed for reading. Each class "Lead out" to a vacant part of the class (either at the front, or between vacated rows of desks), so that the **school mistress can inspect** all classes.

Reading books are given out. *First*, a **single word** of the text is **read out**, in turn, by each child in quick succession. The task is **equally divided** between all, and the **attention of all is secured** so as not to lose the sequence of the words. *Then*, each **child reads whole text**, in turn.

If any error is made the next random child starts. No correction is offered until whole class has tried. *[This requires children to listen to and monitor each other]*
If a class finishes before the others, teacher asks children to spell words from earlier lessons. When all have finished, teacher says "Lead in". All return to benches.

SPELLING WORDS: those which pose problems and need constant repetition are noted on slates and dictated, written and inspected on return to desks. Then covered and spelled again. *[visual, aural and kinaesthetic reinforcement]* This takes 5 minutes.

Note: On the **second reading** of a monosyllabic text, emphasis given to **intelligent reading**, with proper tone, emphasis, pauses. Children taught to count 1 at a comma, 2 for semicolon, 3 for colon, 4 for period. This continues for about a week.

When reading ***word by word*** is successful, child then reads each word, in turn, ***backwards*** (in reverse order) to prevent reading from memory.

Reading and understanding: When reading completed, Questions are asked from the *Teacher's Assistant* ('TB') and also extemporary questions to encourage the habit of scrutiny and reflection.

Fourth Class
READING: Two-syllable word readings: Instructive fables. Catechism. Mrs Trimmer's *Charity School Book Part II*
Questions after the reading will also include questions about the spelling rules, accented syllables

e.g. de- scrībe, de- clāre, but dīs- tance, dīs- crete

ARITHMETIC: Arabic numerals written... 12 Twelve etc

Dictation: "1 - 2 - twelve", and "X - V – fifteen"

Fifth Class
READING: Parables, Miracles, Discourses and Prophecies

Sixth Class
READING: As above plus *The Sunday School, History of Hester Wilmot* and other productions *from Mrs More's pen.*
Watt's *Divine Songs*

Seventh Class
The Shepherd of Salisbury Plain; History of Tom White, and The Postilion [by Mrs Hannah More]
Historical Questions and Answers for the Mendip Schools
Mrs Trimmer's *Abridgement of Scripture History*
All the above from *Messrs Rivington, Hatchard, and SPCK*

Eighth Class
READING: *A Concise English Grammar, Common Prayer Book, Fox's Duty; Lessons for Young Persons in Humble Life and Two Shoemakers [Mrs Hannah More]*

Question and Answers for the 7th and 8th classes are varied.
Attention to Words: explain words, previously dictated, and their meanings.
Questions to elicit ancient opinion, custom, circumstance.
Attention to Meaning: despite trials, it is found that a concluding lecture on explanation or instruction of a text is not helpful. It is important to break text into short Q and A sections to retain the attention of such young children.

CIPHER: Children begin to cipher at 7 or even 6 years.

ARITHMETIC: begun at 8 or 10 years
By means of progressive sums, knowledge is easily attained, *without* dictating keys to the procedures for each sum *(as suggested by Bell)*
Occupying just one hour a day in the summer and ¾ in the winter, within 2 years children are able to operate

4 Rules and Reduction
Rule of Three - direct, inverse and double
Practice
Tare and Tret
Interest and Percentages
Cross Multiplication or Duodecimals
Extraction of the square and cube root
Vulgar and Decimal Fractions

iv. The spread of schooling in rural Somerset in the early C19th.

As we can see from the Rev Poole's involvement, interest in schooling was developing fast. From the story of Enmore we can also learn that a new school did not always mean new, purpose-built premises: Rev Poole's first school, in 1810, was in Mrs Bailey's Park Cottage, then in rooms in the Poor House and only three decades later was a new building constructed.

As the decades passed, there was one further factor which continued to be the focus of fierce debate throughout the century: what, if any, was the role of the State in the provision of education? Any involvement by the Sate was fiercely resisted by those who feared it would undermine the authority and autonomy of the Church – or Chapel.

Opposition was strongest from the Anglican Church which defended its right to continue being the main provider. New 'Dissenter' groups sometimes also resisted State intervention, believing it would promote the 'Established' Church orthodoxy at the expense of the various sects which were now legally tolerated and growing rapidly.

However, the voluntary sector could not cope with the demand for education and the necessary funds were simply not always available. So, gradually and carefully the State began to become involved. In 1833 the Privy Council set up a Committee to investigate the condition of elementary schooling. (Being in the Privy Council not Parliament, it was hoped that it would take politics out of the discussion). The Council offered grants to help with building work. But with money came the desire to check its use, so an Inspectorate was set up in 1839 – initially only to 'inspect' those schools which accepted a grant, which itself often had to be met by equal contributions from the parish by donations or subscriptions. Soon the Council was offering blue-prints for school designs to guide parishes in economical and efficient use of their grants, as well as exercising increasing control over what and how the curriculum was taught.

Training Schemes, for teachers, were key to the viability of the schooling ventures. Further, to ensure the success of the schools, the quality of the teachers was a vital ingredient. Rev Poole, himself, as we have noted, trained his own teachers in the methods he wished them to use. But the celebrity status of Enmore Village school often meant that he constantly found himself robbed of his own teachers who were lured away to start other ventures elsewhere. So, he started a programme of training for other schools which could send their teachers to observe, to learn and then take ideas back to their original schools.

The need for training was recognised early and from 1805 the Lancastrian organisations (later, British and Foreign Schools Society / BFSS) opened a training institute in **Borough Road**, London to train monitors in their system of teaching. Plans were made for further schools based on uniting 'Works of Industry' with 'Useful Knowledge'. One such school was planned for Maiden Bradley, then in Somerset (now Wiltshire). Other training establishments were opened in Southwark and also Dublin. Soon afterwards the rival Anglican (Bell) organisation (National Society / NS) opened a training establishment in **Baldwin Gardens**, London, (which soon moved to Westminster) and then at Bishop Auckland near the cathedral city of Durham, also at Norwich and Winchester (Rich 1972). At this stage Oxbridge was still uninterested in promoting popular education. These early establishments recruited older students (19-24 years and 21 years respectively) who had already received some secondary education. The average length of the course was at first only 4-6 weeks, but soon lasted between 3-6 months. In the case of Baldwin Gardens, however, completing students were expected to be future

Heads of Schools rather than mere classroom teachers and were, thus, given instruction in management rather than practical pedagogy such as that taught at Borough Road.

The descriptions of the early Colleges give some indication of the courses which students had to follow. The first Bell school at Baldwin Gardens, describes the methods as 'learning by doing'.

a. *To work through the manuals of method, then implement them by 'taking a class' starting at the youngest 'in the sand', and working to the top [class] over a period of 8 weeks.*
b. *To work through the actual textbooks to be used in class (e.g. the mono-syllabic spelling book, and the syllabic reading method – reading each syllable and then the whole word)*
c. *Experience a criticism lesson – a lesson prepared by a trainee, watched by peers and staff and then criticism given to improve the trainee's technique. (Rich, 1972).*

The criticism focused on *Matter, Method, Illustration, Language* or, in 1871, *Theme, Evolution, Illustration, Recapitulation* – not dissimilar from current trends in training establishments.

Yet, in these early days, the moral imperative was paramount – both as regards the purpose of the schools as well as the model behaviour of those who would be teachers. Propriety was everything. Rich notes that the Minutes of the Ladies' Committee (1814) at the institution in King's Road, London declared that, regarding the female trainees,

1. *They should be habited in cotton or queen stuffs – plain muslin handkerchiefs, caps with no lace, and plain straw bonnets.*
2. *The cloathes (sic) should be neat and suitable for the schoolroom, with no white petticoats.*

The Rules for Life at the National Society training establishment in the Barrington School, Durham also indicate a strict regime, both in terms of behaviour and also scholarship.

1. *Cleanliness, propriety and regularity of attendance are pre-requisites for admission.*
2. *The scholars shall be educated as masters and ushers in public schools.*
3. *The scholars are to keep a register of their lessons and studies, their writing and ciphering, of what they have taught others, and show it to the Master every Sunday.*
4. *If a scholar does not appear to have made adequate progress at the quarterly exam they shall be dismissed.*

In addition, teachers who married were usually required to leave. This was frequently the custom till after the Second World War when, with a shortage of men (particularly after the First World War) and with gradually changing social attitudes, expectations began to alter. We find, however, that in rural areas expediency often took precedence over distantly designed regulations. Widows were accepted as were wives of known villagers who 'stepped in' when other applicants were not suitable. Wives of the Headmaster were often employed as sewing mistresses or mistresses of the infant class.

This approach would probably have met with approval from Rev Poole who strongly believed in the importance of education and service to the Poor through the Moral and Christian example of the teachers he trained and supported in his neighbourhood. He was indefatigable in his promotion of education till his death in 1867, two decades after the new, purpose-built school was completed in his own village of Enmore.

It was not until the 1840s – still within Rev Poole's life time – that a network of Teacher Training Colleges emerged on the national scene and, only later still, that the burden of meeting this need from local initiatives alone was lifted. At first this was achieved through the Diocesan Colleges, thus keeping close control of the religious training of future teachers. A few 'Dissenter' Colleges also provided a flow of students which, together, could enter the schools with at least some training.

Issues surrounding the status and training of teachers will be elaborated in Part III.

Part III

Changing Patterns of C19th Schooling: Inside the Schools –

Funding
Building
Staffing

The changes reflect the altering balance between both
the previously dominant individual school sponsors
and denominational schools,
and the newly expanding role of the State.
The growth of the Privy Council Committee for Education
and the part played by the newly formed Inspectorate became
the keys to educational development during the early C19th.

Fig. iii

Key National Dates

1785 **Sunday School Society**

1790s ***Literary and Philosophical Societies, Useful Knowledge Movement***
also Robert Owen's ***Mechanics' Institutes,***

1796 **Society for the Bettering and Increasing of Comfort of the Poor Pauper Children -** Schools of Industry for learning to spin, sew, plait, cobble etc

1797 **Dr Andrew Bell** *An Experiment in Education* (Madras)
1798 **Joseph Lancaster** school for public education of every poor child
1803 *Improvements in Education* Lancaster's US Lecture tour
1808 **Society for Promotion of Royal Lancaster System for the Ed of the Poor**
Became, in1814, **British and Foreign School Society** (*BFSS or BrS*)
1811 **National Society for the Promotion of Ed for the Poor** (*NS*)

1820 Parish Schools *can be* supported from rates + fees from parents (2-4d per week). Teachers to be appointed by Vestry.

1833 **Committee of the Privy Council on Education** set up.
Money distributed *indirectly* though the NS or BFSS
1839 **Grants** for Teacher Training and advice for Teachers' Houses
Inspectorate established.

1833 **Factory Act**} children to have two hours of schooling
1842 **Mines Act** } every day
1844 **Ragged School Union** started by *Lord Shaftesbury (176 schools by 1861)*

1840 **Teacher Training Colleges** e.g. Whitelands and Borough Rd
1846 **Launch of Pupil -Teacher apprenticeship scheme**

1846 First *direct* **Treasury Grants** for school buildings
1853 New capitation grants in rural areas, 1856 in towns

Somerset Examples

Examples appear, later, in Somerset: *1860s Wrington, Cheddar, 1852 Frome, 1861 Rode*

Schools of Industry, Female Clubs, Sunday Schools
e.g. *Cheddar, Winscombe, Shipham, Carhampton*
Several Mendip Sunday Schools aided by **Hannah More**

Schools using the *Madras system*: 1802 Timberscombe, 1813 Winscombe

1810 **Improved Village School** at Enmore, under **Rev John Poole**
Also, book of same title – guide to setting up village schools on an adapted model of the Lancaster-Bell system

Examples of early Somerset schools built by subscriptions, parents or levied rates
1827 *Othery, Lamyatt, Rode; Wembdon, Woolavington, W Camel*
1840s *Weston-Middlezoy, Moorlynch, Chilton Polden, Fiddington, Meare, Brent E,* also *Long Sutton*

1833 **Impassioned speech** by AJ Roebuck, MP for Bath, for state education added pressure for government involvement, initially through grants
1834 *Limington, Coleford Infants* built by subscriptions, **Diocesan and National Society monies** distributed from 1833 Privy Co grants;

Later, Factory Schools e.g. Evercreech 1860s

Later, Ragged School e.g. Bridgwater 1860s

Further **Treasury Grants** increased school building opportunities e.g.
1846 *Ash, Montacute, Monksilver, Pilton, Walton* schools built.
1847 *Martock School (opposite Church, now Youth Centre), Mudford Enmore, North Curry, Coleford, Milborne Port, Barrington* also built

Chapter 4
How the Schools Were Funded: Charities, Benefactors and Government Grants

From the first tentative steps towards developing village schooling in every part of England, the venture had invariably relied on the interest, capability and willingness of individuals. From the C17th these may have been from significant local families or from the clergy who taught boys in their own house or a religious meeting place. These contributors might include local landowners (Lords Portman, Poulett), priests (Rev Poole, Woodeforde), businessmen (Thomas Poole, Clark and Pinney families), philanthropists (Hannah More, Richard Ellsworth) and many others who all made major contributions to funding rural schooling. Occasionally, as at Nailsea, a group of villagers might gather together – one of whom agreed to teach the others to read, reckon and write.

As we have seen, during the C17th and C18th education was left to private individuals. These individuals typically left charitable donations, gifts or bequests, in their wills, in order to support a wide range of different educational functions. Their charity gives a fascinating window into local current concerns and the hopes for future generations in their village. It is interesting to note that, as long ago as 1670, schools had also been given some State financial help, by means of special exemption from the Hearth Tax which was applied to other buildings.

i. The education charities

a. Range and variety. These were initially the main source of funds and, over the centuries, a wide range of charities was set up. They fall into certain patterns in terms of their income and their purposes, as can be seen from the following table:

Sources	Purposes
Rents/interest from land/property	To fund fees for scholars
	To pay salary of School Teacher
	To bind and place apprentices
	To purchase clothing for 'scholars'
	To buy equipment: books, paper, spinning-wheels…
Gift of Land or Property	To build/use as School Room or School House
To give 'support'	To show interest: listen to Singing class, look at Needlework … 'help' when needed
	Give one-off monies for specific items

From Collinson's *History of Somerset* (1789) we find that most charities appear to have been set up in the C18th, though there are some in the C17th, and from the Directories we find a few in the C19th. The latter tend to be donations of land to erect a purpose-built school room, which would imply that many of the earlier schools were housed in a variety of non-specific buildings.

The charities set up across the county are not evenly distributed: it seems to depend on the generosity of a particular local person – more often a local resident, successful businessman or a priest. However, the pattern appears to reflect the rise and spread of schooling itself in different locations at particular periods. Thus, in the C18th several schools are found around the port area of Bridgwater and in a swathe of land across the Levels and the Polden Hills, then east towards Milborne Port. Another concentration occurs around the Mendips – almost a 'backyard' to philanthropic worthies from Bristol and Bath. Other focal points are around the manufacturing (textile) centres of Chard, Crewkerne, Bruton and Evercreech.

An early charity was in High Ham where, in 1598, Rev Adrian Schaell gave 120*L* to be invested and the interest used for *the encouragement and maintenance of a School Master to instruct the poor of the parish in reading, writing and arithmetic.* This was to be accomplished in a House near the Church, held by the Parish from the Lord of the Manor. The School Room was to be on the ground floor for 60 pupils, while the master had the use of four rooms upstairs and the garden.

Another early arrangement was in Trull, in 1609, where two schools were maintained by charities which, in 1820 had 18 children each with Bibles, Testaments and copies of Dr Watt's *Hymns for Children*. Rydon North Petherton also had an early charity set up in 1687 to educate poor children, while another charity existed in Wedmore from the same period. Ten other C18th schools are recorded in the hundreds of Whitely, Polden and North Petherton. A similar charity is recorded in Wiveliscombe in the south-west, also in Winsham, Chard, Crewkerne and Hinton St George in the south, and in Cucklington, Marston Magna, Abbas Combe in the south-east.

Several Charities included opportunities for children to be placed and bound over as apprentices: 1604 Sir Francis Popham in Wellington instructed that children should be placed in apprenticeships in husbandry and, on completion *'to be given 3L 6s 8d for stock to begin to live with.'* Other examples can be found from Anne Harris of Midsomer-Norton in 1731, Henry Werriot of Shepton Beauchamp in 1733, also Elizabeth Morgan of the same village and Sarah Comer in Cheddar, both in 1751.

As far back as 1656, the Church Warden's accounts in Wrington note sums of money for the repair of a School House – usually signifying the teacher's residence – in which the school might also have been held. These charities were often even-handed in their approach to boys and girls, or became so through subsequent additions, which is itself remarkable. For example in Wrington, Mendips – before it became associated with Hannah More – the Charities Commission, reporting between 1819 and 1837, noted that:

> *In 1704 George Legg* (gent, dissenter) *gave 9 acres of land named Poor Ground, the rents from which are distributed amongst six boys and six girls in keeping each and everyone of them at school in Wrington to be taught and educated to read perfectly the Holy Bible, and after they were so taught to keep another twelve poor children at school;* Also, *a boys' school for twenty to thirty children are taught reading, writing and rudiments of arithmetic, the master to be paid 8L pa being part of income from the 9 acres; what remains is to be applied to a school of industry where particular attention is to be paid to the Holy Scriptures.*

In 1798 Mr Smith's Charity adds 50*L* invested *so that the dividends thereof might be applied in the support of a* ***Sunday School*** *and in purchasing religious tracts. The boys and girls at the* ***School of Industry*** *are to be taught to read, and the girls also to sew and knit.*
1840 Bragg's Directory notes 50*L* in stocks from Mrs Webb, also for the same School.

b. Setting up a Charity was not without hazards. The Charities Commission noted that the 1782 Trust willed by Ann Castlemain in Wedmore was refused by her representatives. In 1761 Symons Cardinbrook in Winscombe willed certain monies but required the parish to raise a further 200*L* to build a school, which they failed to do, so the building was seriously delayed. This 'matching' of monies has a familiar modern ring and came to be included on many occasions from the mid C19th, particularly with regard to receiving grants from the National (CoE) or the Foreign and Home ('Dissident') Bible Societies or, later, the government.

Shepton Mallet illustrates a different issue: not this time with the Trustees but with the beneficiaries. The Strode Charity set up in 1627 established Almshouses, a Chapel, a School for 12 poor children, and School House for a teacher. In the C18th Mr Dunkerton took the post and all went well. However, on his death in 1766, his son John usurped the post, kept the house and used the income for his own purposes, suffering the house to go into decay. This 'imposter' was eventually sent to jail. The Trust was thrown into disarray until 1803, when Rev Thomas Smith was appointed to restore the reputation of the school. He was given a free hand. It seems he first repaired the house, then reopened the school as a private boarding school where he instructed pupils in classical and general literature: 12 boarders were lodged on the premises (the charity children?) and the others in some of the apartments in the old almshouses which were converted to accommodate 20 more boarders.

Two further charities were also established: 1730 by John Curtis who left monies for up to 4 children to be taught to read, write, cast accounts and the principles of religion before being apprenticed; and Gapper's Gift for 4 orphan girls to be educated, clothed (one blue gown a year till aged 16) and then also apprenticed. Where these children were educated is not clear.

In the case of Wrington, further difficulties arose, again not common but not unique. The Trust lands and monies seem to have been 'in the hands of Mr Walley' who appears to have done little except to credit himself, in 1785, with 30*L* 8s 2d 'for the instruction of children'. Perhaps he was the Parish clerk or sexton who sometimes acted as village schoolmaster if there was no willing curate or paid teacher. Eventually the Vestry assumed responsibility and undertook *'to apply the interest to pay a master or mistress to teach spelling, reading, sewing, knitting or netting as to them that should appear proper, to provide spinning-wheels or other instruments for the children, and in the hiring of a room for these purposes'*. It was only by 1813 that we discover that the committee had erected a dwelling house and two school rooms: *'the boys were taught by a master and the girls by a mistress, at different ends of the room'*. Interestingly, the Commissioners' Report states that the school was *'carried on first on Lancaster's and afterwards on Bell's system'*. However, on learning that the school was to teach the Church catechism, the Dissenters discontinued their subscription and established their own school in 1808. This rare level of detail shows us not only how children were taught, but also reveals the religious battleground that education long proved to be.

c. The administration of charities was another contentious issue regarding the terms for the Trustees themselves. They were usually *appointed* and *named*, with specified action to be taken on the death of any member. **Milverton,** however, gives us a fascinating insight regarding *elections* to Trusteeship. In 1721 Mary Lamb set aside *'£300 for purchasing land, the rents thereof to be forever employed in educating in the principles of the Christian religion of the Church of England, 40 poor children viz.20 boys and 20 girls'*. Monies were also set aside for renting a school house, for books, paper, ink and quills. Mary Lamb was clearly distrustful (presumably with reason) and stipulated that the books should always remain in the school house! But it is the procedures for elections which leave little doubt that she considered skulduggery to be rife. She determined that all elections [to Trusteeships] *'be made openly and publically in the school room between the hours of 10 in the morning and 3 in the afternoon with at least four days' notice being publically given, and that there should be a book of account kept and fastened by a chain and locked to some convenient place in the school house'*. So, no shadowy dealings possible in such daylight elections, no chance of mis-appropriation of funds either! One wonders what elections were often like – remember, this is at a time of rotten boroughs and the open buying of votes for the still very limited seats in Parliamentary elections. Or perhaps she was just a control freak!

d. Rewards: Referring to the C18th, education was still often not an attractive proposition as it took children out of the labour market, so a carrot and stick approach was sometimes used to encourage attendance. For this reason clothing was sometimes provided by the charities. In Crowcombe, Bishops Lydeard, South Petherton, Shepton Beauchamp clothing was offered. In West Coker, girls were given a white gown and petticoat for constant attendance. In North Petherton and in Evercreech each child was given a blue coat, either at Easter or Christmas as 'an inducement'. In Kilmersdon clothes were offered as a reward for 'constant attendance'. These clothes were frequently specified to be blue as this was the cheapest and most readily available dye. This led to several of the charity schools becoming known as Blue Coat Schools.

A particularly interesting reward was offered in Frome, in the shape of a silver pen. This was to be awarded alternately to the child with the best handwriting and to the child who was best at casting accounts. While in Nunney, a 'fair crown piece' was given to each child who could recite their catechism.

ii. The operation of the schools

a. Curriculum: One feature of C18th charities was the frequent inclusion of instructions such as 'education in the principles of the Christian religion', or, 'to teach the children to read the scriptures' or, 'to teach the children of the poor to recite their catechism'. Thus, Religion was often the objective and Reading a means to that end.

A further feature was the inclusion of training or instruction, particularly for girls, in sewing, knitting, spinning and also – often for the boys – netting [similar to coarse tatting]. This occurred in a geographically wide range of villages – from Carhampton, Cannington, Winscombe, Wrington, Chewton Mendip (where girls were to be taught scripture and knitting only), Shepton Beauchamp, Chard and Kingsbury Episcopi. Specific 'Schools of Industry' were established in Wrington and Cheddar in the mid C18th. This was where girls – and, in the evenings women – could learn spinning and knitting. Sarah Comer and Hannah More, as we have seen, continued and developed these schools.

The subjects to be taught were specified by certain charities: some restricted themselves to Reading and Religion (Carhampton, Blagdon, West Coker, South Petherton), others included Reading, Writing and Arithmetic or Casting Accounts (Cheddar, Wrington, Churchill, Shepton Beauchamp, Stratton on Fosse). Rarely, as at Winstaunton, further subjects such as Grammar and Geography might be added *'for those children for whom it was apparent that they might turn knowledge to advantage'*.

Occasionally, as at Wanstrow, a charity provided the means, for those who could benefit, to attend a neighbouring 'better' school, such as in Bruton, or, an exhibition *'to attend a college or house of learning in the University of Oxford'*, such as willed by William Owsley, 1779, in Crewkerne. Somerset had close links to Wadham and Exeter Colleges at Oxford.

A vocational slant, in the C19th, was often included as we can see in Bruton, where the Sexey foundation (started in 1619) later opened a Training School for Girls in 1877 to prepare them for service or for spinning. The crafted products which were made could be sold to raise cash for the school, the girls keeping a little for themselves as an incentive. In 1892 a Boys' Trade School opened in the same town for 11-18 year-olds and also took boarders from surrounding villages. Such additional schooling continued the vocational tradition found in earlier 'continuing/night schools' which were sometimes attached to elementary parish schools and were open to pupils over the leaving age and to adults who had never had schooling.

b. Materials to be used in schools.
A few charities specified other purposes for which their monies were to be used, for example to purchase necessities for the school as at Kilmersdon, Middlezoy, Timberscombe, Shepton Beauchamp. Items such as books, paper, ink, pens or quills are mentioned. Frequently the main use of the charity money was to pay the teacher's salary.

An interesting example of a very detailed Charity is the one set up in 1714 by Richard Ellsworth of Bickham, near Timberscombe. This gives very specific details about equipment to be purchased and also includes many other features which recur elsewhere – and some unique ones!

10*L* towards teaching the poor children of the Parish to read, write and say their catechism
10*L* towards buying Spelling Books, Bibles, Prayer Books
an *Answer to All Excuses for not coming to Sacrament*
the Church of England's *Man's Companion*
200*L* towards building a charity Schoolhouse and Library at the cross of Triscombe
200*L* to buy books for the Library, to be chosen by the Bishop and lent to clergy and others
10*L* yearly for books chosen by the Archdeacon
30*L* for a gallery to be built in the church for poor people and their children
40*L* yearly for 2 scholars of the parish who are to enjoy 20*L* each for 7 years

Despite, or maybe because of the detail, the requirements became cumbersome: only one hundred years later, was a school house or even a master established. Possibly the Parish had been expected to raise the rest and had failed to do so. This entry also states that the school, in 1804, was conducted on the lines of Bell's *Madras System* – the one adapted and promoted by Rev John Poole. Ellsworth's was a wide-ranging charity which also offered exhibitions of £5 pa to promising scholars at nearby Cutcombe and even as far away as Stogumber.

Another charity is worth quoting in detail as it is unusually specific and gives a valuable picture of schooling. In Chard, the Corporation had acted as Trustees for William Symes' monies gifted in 1671. It notes that

The school room is 40' long, sufficient to accommodate 50 boys, and with apartments that may accommodate 20 boarders. The master educates about 30 boys, so long as they come decently clothed. The day boys receive their education for the sum of 2 guineas a year each, where they find their own

implements. All are taught arithmetic, writing, English grammar and reading. If they are sufficiently advanced they are taught geography and the elements of mathematics for additional remuneration. He also instructs the youth in the Catechism and to read the Bible. He receives members of the established Church and of dissenting congregations.

It seems a remarkably open-minded and liberal establishment.

iii. Changes in funding

a. The Role of Local Gentry. By the C19th when school-building became more popular and more necessary as numbers grew, several Lords of the Manor and main landowners contributed to building a new School Room and often a School House for the teacher as well (App. 4). This was the case with Lord (later Viscount) Portman who was responsible for building North, and South Barrow schools and, later, the combined Barrows' School. He was also prominent as a contributor and supporter in many other villages, across a wide geographical area including Brompton Ralph, Broadway, Bicknell, Misterton, East Coker with Chinnock, and Sutton Montis. Other prominent landowners, who supported several local schools in their various holdings included Sirs Thomas Acland and Alexander Hood, Lords Poulett, Egremont, Carnarvon, and the Luttrell family of Dunster. Each of these was actively involved with education, particularly in the far west of the county and also its eastern borderlands, where villages were scattered, sparsely populated, predominantly agricultural and frequently in dire poverty.

Ladies of the Manor also gave financial support for specific projects in the late C19th such as for funding a Sunday School in Montacute (Mrs Phelips), or to build and stock a public Library, or Workingmen's Clubs, Reading Rooms or Lecture Halls (Lady Slade in North Petherton, Lady Waldegrave in Radstock and Lady Augusta, daughter of Lord Poulett). These Ladies, and often the vicar's wife and daughters, also gave general support by showing an interest and 'dropping in' to hear the progress in Singing or to see improvements in Needlework. This kept both teachers and pupils on their toes: their efforts were sometimes rewarded by a day's holiday, or an invitation to tea and buns at the Manor! These visitors might hear the children read, or even undertake to 'teach' on a regular basis. This probably meant working on reading or needlework or even music with a small group, as this was thought to be in keeping with using their feminine 'accomplishments' and 'doing good'. There were few other working opportunities for such women which were deemed socially acceptable.

What is perhaps of greater interest are the *untitled* non-aristocratic donors and sponsors of education. Who were they and what motivated them to give considerable sums to this new enterprise? Local individuals had often come to the fore to set up endowments and trusts as we have already seem. By the C19th they were likely to help in more visible ways, as in building a school or donating land. C19th land donations are evident in Long Sutton, Charlton Mackrell, Cadbury North. There were also C18th examples when land was donated for a school, as in Kilmington by the banker Mr RC Hoare in 1830, and by James Bennet JP in North Cadbury in 1875, while James Clarke gave a House to be used by a teacher and as a School in Lovington in 1715, where adjacent land was added later to build a separate school building. Other examples of different sources include:

the Vestry at Winscombe, 1813
Voluntary contributions at Wemdon, 1825
Churchwardens at Westonzoyland, 1842,
five farmers in Othery 1877 (£555 for the school and £320 for the School House)
friends of the Rector at Withycombe, 1866.

In examining some of the early new-builds we can see the results of enlisting private help from the school account books e.g. Limington 1834, which lists the subscribers. We find:

Educational organizations:	an individual, through the National Society gave £35, while the Society itself gave £5.
Ecclesiastical sources:	the Rector gave £10, the Archdeacon £5 and the Rural Dean £5. a further Rector, from Herefordshire, gave £2. 10s.
Educational institutions:	Wadham College which had just acquired the living, gave £5 while an individual Fellow from the College gave £1.

Other individuals' names follow, including 'A Friend to the Poor' who gave 10s. Eventually £135 was raised which went a long way towards meeting the costs of £205, including the conveyancing. Perhaps the builders were patient and accepted the rest later (Plate 3).

A mixture of sources is still evident fifty years later, in 1895, at the time of a rebuild at East Harptree, but the ingredients are different:

Educational organizations:	£45 (National Society £20, Diocesan Education Fund £25);
Local companies:	Bristol Waterworks gave £21, the local Brewery 3gns;
Amateur events:	School Concerts raised £15 17s 10d, while local Theatricals raised £18;
Finally, local individuals:	a significant contribution of £138 – Kettlewells £86 13s 4d, Hopes £46 6s 8d, Lady Waldegrave gave £5.

The total raised was £241 17s 10d, while the costs amounted to £272 6s 10d. Again, this small discrepancy was perhaps deferred.

However, the second example took place in a very different context: one in which government funding had been available since 1833 (indirectly) and from 1846 (directly) to those schools which would accept inspection in return. Yet where schools chose not to accept government grants and the strings attached, they had to resort to measures as at East Harptree.

Other mechanisms existed to raise money such as by subscription from the local gentry. This was often done at the time of the building of new school and also to maintain it. During the wave of expansion in the last quarter of the C19th following the setting up of School Boards, we find specific local rates for education being introduced: Fiddington, 1874, had a 'voluntary rate' of 6d in the £, but some householders 'declined', while Kingston Seymour, 1888, resolved to have a rate of 6d in the £, but 'many refused' (luckily local benefactor, Mr Kettlewell, paid the deficit), but in other areas, an officer was appointed to persuade and collect from the 'volunteers'!

This gap between income and expenditure led to frequent fund-raising activities to avoid real hardships in the school. In 1871, Brewham school charged for evening Readings held in the School Room to which, presumably, many came; by the 1880s Chaffcombe (and others) held concerts to raise money. The girls often seem to have been a source of earning for the school through their needlework: sometimes to order, sometimes through Sales of Work – which might be held at specific times like Shrovetide and Christmastide as at Westhay. All such outcomes were recorded in separate account books which schools had to keep (Plate 4). By the 1930s Whist Drives and Dances were held. Horsington Caretaker complained bitterly as a Ballroom Polish was applied which was treacherous for the children!

b. Changes in state involvement. At the beginning of the C19th the two main organisations began to offer opportunities for schooling: the Dissident-leaning (Lancastrian) British and Foreign Schools Society and the (Anglican) National Society. These organisations, through their contacts amongst the wealthy members of their respective memberships, were in a position to raise considerable sums of money. However, the debate concerning whether education should be funded at all and by whom was still inconclusive: a correspondent from Huntspill voiced the opinion in the Monthly Magazine (1815) that *'dependant charity debases the human mind – I am against giving money to the poor who accept it and then abuse it'*; some believed it undermined parental responsibility.

Campaigners had for some time been demanding state involvement in funding. This was fiercely contested by the rival religious groups who feared loss of control over their curriculum, in particular, that over the teaching of religion. After an impassioned speech by **AJ Roebuck**, Radical MP for Bath, calling for *'the urgent necessity for a state system for the universal and national Education of the Whole People"* (Dent 1977), a significant event occurred in 1833. Government at last became involved in the provision of education in England. (Schools for the army had received state grants since 1812.) Initially this was through a Committee for Education in the Privy Council, which thereby made it less 'political' and hopefully avoided the 'party politics' of the House of Commons. However, being dependent on the counsels of His Lordships also meant that Bishops, too, could voice their strong and often negative opinions on the merits – or otherwise – of state 'interference'. The Council had powers to offer 50% of the proposed cost of building a school for children of the Poorer Classes and, from 1835, recommended building a School House to accommodate the teacher, but no additional funds were offered. The purposes, amounts and mechanisms for distributing the money varied.

At first, monies were distributed through the two main national organizations – The British and Foreign Schools Society and The National Society. Thus funding was *indirect* and the problems of distribution handed to the organisations themselves. Many schools preferred to keep their independence and rely on private subscriptions, voluntary rates, 'sacrament money' and the (variable) parents' pence – the fee for each child. Within five years, the National Society built 700 schools and the BFSS 200 (Bagley, 1969). It was estimated that the two Societies, between their foundation in 1811 and 1837, set up 3,500 schools - not necessarily in new buildings. A further significant move came in 1846 when schools could apply *direct* to the Treasury for grants.

The matching of grants by local subscriptions appears to be the case in Martock – where a plaque in the original school building opposite the Church (now a Youth Centre) states that:

These schools,
erected with liberal subscriptions
from the inhabitants of Martock
and its neighbourhood,
aided by grants from Her Majesty's Treasury,
from the incorporated National Society,
and from the Diocese of Bath and Wells
was opened in January 1847.

Possibly a similar situation arose in nearby Ash, which opened a year earlier and in Enmore and North Curry where land was donated and dormant plans implemented in 1847. These schools were quick to grasp the changed grant opportunities. Between 1839 and 1859 (when such grants stopped) £1 million had been granted for building, enlarging, repairing or furnishing Elementary Schools (Seaborne 1971). Kingston Seymour made an application for grant in 1857 – just before the grants stopped - where the educational provision "*was next to nothing*." In fact a situation is described where "*An old man, unfit for office, taught reading and writing in a small unhealthy room*" (Pudner and Thomas, 2008). With the advantage of a grant, a school for 60 pupils was proposed with dimensions of 37' x 16' x 15' which would cost £700. The application was successful and land was donated by the Lord of the Manor, Mr Pigott.

From 1839 further monies were offered for the provision of (mostly Diocesan) Colleges in which to train teachers. By this time, the desire for accountability, led the government to assume the right to inspect any school which accepted a grant, so a nation-wide **Inspectorate** was established – initially of only two men, increased to six just four years later. This was also perceived by some as interference that might affect the denominational character of schools linked to the two religious societies.

c. Budgeting: To turn first to income, most schools required a parental contribution. This was partly in the belief that it was the parents' responsibility to care for their own children: in Chillington children paid ½d in 1835, though by mid-century it was more typically 1d a week per child. Other schools varied the rate according to what it was believed the family could afford. In Charlton Mackrell the school charged just 1d *per family*. This must have been a real help and an encouragement to send all the children of the family to school. While, in nearby Monteclefe, graded fees were suggested by HMI, in 1851:

> *'Labourers 1d, and children of those earning more than 12s a week 2d, and all tradesmen and others should pay 4d a week.'*

According to the East Lydford Parish records of 1875 a school was erected and endowed by the Vicar J J Moss. It expected to charge in the following way:

> *'The children of the labouring classes were charged 2d a week for the first child from each family and 1d a week for each subsequent one, but 2d a week when over 9 years of age. All other children paid 3d a week.'*

In 1879 East Harptree School Board adopted a similar policy, where 'class' referred to the social class of the parents, not the class in which the pupil was placed. Unfortunately fees for Class I are not mentioned, but,

> ... *'Class two paid 2d per child,*
> *Class three paid 2d for the first child, and 1d for any subsequent child'.*

Social class is the clear criterion at Horsington too. In the same year the Managers decided that artisans should pay 2d for their first child and 1½d thereafter. They then helpfully define 'artisan' as *all who rent above an acre of land* – blacksmiths, masons, carpenters, painters, plasterers, shopkeepers – and that *'endowment money should be used for the remission of fees for those who are regular attenders'.*

Linking fees to attendance was another device used to encourage better attendance. At Fiddington, in 1886, all children in Standard IV and above *'to be charged an extra 1d, to be returned when the child passed all items in the Higher Standards exam'!*

We not only find a long and strong tradition of the local gentry paying subscriptions or giving donations to fund the maintenance of the school, payment of the teachers or as a general contribution to school fees. We also find that certain children were sponsored by a specific local resident to whom they were expected to demonstrate progress. Some children appear to have gained sponsors to help defray the costs, not only for attending but for the items need at school. We find a record at Monteclefe School for Girls and Infants, that some girls had only slates and not copybooks '*as they had no-one to buy them*'. Children in some Levels schools seemed to have been less fortunate in obtaining sponsors: some did not attend '*for want of clothes*' (IsB 1887), '*they are sent home for not paying their pence*' (IsB 1888), '*some came in indecent clothes*' (IsB 1883). '*In November there are many absences as children don't have boots*' (Chf 1895), and '*the children can not put on their boots for their chilblains*' (IsB 1899). Sadly, no sponsors were able to come forward to help. It seemed that little could be done without individual acts of charity which were so prevalent in the C17th, as at Oakhill 1762, when 5s was given to the school '*for such as their friends are unable to pay for them*' and, a century later, when specific children were '*supported by Lady Strachey and numerous residents of a superior class*'. Again, we find similar charity in the following note: '*Through the liberality of Sir W Trevelyan one child in each family received a pair of winter boots*' (Ntc 1898). [1]

Similar poverty is evident in the mining area of Coleford**.** In an era of widely held distinctions between the 'deserving' and 'undeserving poor', an understanding of local conditions was a necessary prelude for any gesture of charity which could only be recommended on proof of virtue. For example, Rev Sandys in 1879, commented on the poor condition of some children's boots. The Head satisfied him that '*the parents were in great poverty, the family being out of work by the closing of the coal-mines. Rev Sandys then requested me to obtain a new pair of boots at his expense.*' Later in the same year he was asked to pay the fees for a child lately orphaned. The following year the Revs Yevens and Sandys paid the school fees of two children who had achieved full attendances for 13 and 15 weeks respectively – which was repeated the next year, too. In May, the School Attendance Officer requested fees from the Board of Guardians for those families who could not afford to pay and, in December, handed over to the school 2s 6d for fees. In 1883, the Guardians paid for those families removed to the Union (Poor House) on account of their poverty. The next year, a member of the school committee paid for a child. In this school, therefore, several different sources of help were successfully approached in order to tide over families in real need.

Yet despite these difficulties, many parents tried desperately to find their own school penny – whether for entirely educational motives is unclear. The significance of the ubiquitous 'school penny' was described, by the poet George Crabbe (1812), in quite un-educational terms

> ' ..... *busy wives who pay*
> *Some trifling price for freedom through the day…*'

Perhaps this was the feeling of many hard-pressed mums!

Costings: We have detailed accounts for some establishments which give a fascinating insight into the running of the schools. As the charities relating to larger schools, often in market towns, they do not give insights into typical village schools. We can turn, instead, to a more characteristic village example at Blagdon. The end of year accounts for March 1883 are given as:

[1] Abbreviations for school references given in fig i. Map of Regions of Somerset, p.11

Income from	
Committee of Education	*£ 61 03 04d*
Grant from local rates	*£ 65 00 04d*
Fees paid by parents	*£ 42 14 00d*
...by Guardians	*£ 3 04 00d*
Total	***£173 2 07d***

Expenditure	
Salaries of Mr James, Miss Cook	*£ 140 07 09d*
Salary of Articled Teacher Wood	*£ 7 17 06d*
Temporary Monitor	*£ 12 00d*
Books and Stationery	*£ 10 13 04d*
Fuel, lighting, cleaning	*£ 2 06 00d*
Furniture and repairs	*£ 8 10 10d*
Rent, taxes, insurance	*£ 2 15 02d*
Total	***£173 02 07d***

Balanced to the last penny!

In November, an additional entry shows that the School Fees of Pauper Children, £1 15 08d were paid by the Guardians of the Poor, from the local Poor Rates presumably.

Another, much later, example is from Monteclefe Managers' Minutes Book for 1906 (this is after the newly formed County Council's Committee of Education had taken over responsibility for local schools). Further, as school pence had been abolished since 1891, the difference between income and expenditure had to be met by the County.

Income from	
Grant	*£ 155 07s 06d*
Sales of Work	*£ 1 17s 09d*
Total	***£ 157 05 03d***

Expenses	
School House rent	*£ 20*
Commercial Union	
Fire Insurance	*£ 2000*
Salaries: Head Ada Taylor	*£ 90*
Miss Peacock	*£ 36 18s 10d*
Miss Gross (Inf)	*£ 40*
Monitor	*£ 6 10s 00d*
Total	***£ 2193 08s 10d***

As we can see, Insurance was now the substantial new cost, following policies introduced by the great reforming Liberal government of 1906.

d. Evolving criteria for award of grants.

Having once got involved in funding schools, periodic changes were made to the grant system with the aim of always trying to get *'better value for money'*. One way of achieving this was through better accountability and inspection. Two new incentives for this drive came from the fact that after 1856 the Department of Education was made accountable to Parliament rather than the Privy Council, closely followed by an urgent need for economy following the Crimean War. Another way of improving costs was believed to be through decentralising the management of the budget and was intended *'to cut the appalling waste'* believed to be inherent in the previous system. Any shortfall would have to be met locally – through church funds, a parish levy or donations. Money to be spent was now given directly to the School Managers who had the task of negotiating individual staff salaries, deciding what monies should be spent on the care of the buildings and on equipping the staff with appropriate teaching materials. The policy seems to have worked for, in 1861, government costs for educating 855,000 children amounted to £813,450 while in 1865 1,016,500 children cost only £636,800 i.e. the cost had been halved from roughly £1 per pupil to less than 10 shillings per pupil (Bagley 1969).

There were detailed mechanisms for how the monies given to School Management would be 'earned' by the school. The new payment system was implemented through the **Revised Code of 1862.** Its impact was far-reaching. First, it was linked to the level of educational achievements reached by the pupils. Teachers now taught with the sole aim of getting the maximum number of children to perform adequately at the annual inspection, during which the pupils were questioned on what they could remember of the lessons taught. It was learning by rote and payment by results. However, it is important to note that 'results' were not the sole criterion. Secondly, the new criteria required a judgement relating to the parents' cooperation, as part of the grant was dependent on attendance records and, thirdly, grants were dependent on an evaluation of the specific responsibilities of managers to provide adequate accommodation and materials. Thus funding was intended to promote a three-way partnership between teachers, parents and management. Other criteria were added later as we shall see below. However, any form of government funding was still strongly resisted by some denominational groups who continued to fear that accepting such money and the concomitant inspection would limit their freedom to give religious instruction on their own terms.

Curriculum Content to be tested: From now on great attention was paid to the *Programmes of Work* which had to be submitted to the Inspectors for approval, then taught, finally tested. Approved schemes of work were copied into the Head's Log Book which, together with the teacher's note-books (none of which have survived for examination) had to be available for inspection. This intensified after the 1870 Act, which supported the setting up of Board Schools run by locally elected Managers. This meant that schools run by or linked to the two trusted national organisations – the British and Foreign Schools Society and National Schools Society – no longer exercised a position verging on monopoly: hence the perceived need for even greater accountability to ensure standards.

The criteria for a 'pass' in the Inspectors' examinations for each class (I-VI) can be judged from the table below:

Requirements for Annual Examination Code of 1862

Pass Standard Reading: intelligible, dictation legible and common words spelt right,
Pass Standard Arithmetic: correct in method and at least one sum accurate.

Reading
I Narrative monosyllables
II One of the narratives next in order after monosyllables, in a reading book used at school
III Short paragraph from a reading book in school
IV Short paragraph from a more advanced reading book in school
V A few lines of poetry used in the First Class of the school
VI Short ordinary paragraph in a newspaper or other modern narrative.

Writing
I Form on blackboard or slate from dictation, capital, small and manuscript letters
II Copy, in manuscript characters, a line of print
III A sentence from the same paragraph read slowly once, then dictated in single words
IV A sentence slowly dictated once, a few words at a time, from a book of the First Class
V Another short ordinary paragraph in a newspaper or other modern narrative, slowly dictated once, a few words at a time.

Arithmetic
I Form on the blackboard or slate, from dictation, figures up to 20; name at sight figures up to 20; add or subtract figures up to 10, orally
II A sum in simple addition or subtraction, and the multiplication tables
III A sum in any simple rule as far as short division inclusive
IV A sum in compound rules (£ s d)
V A sum in compound rules (weights and measures)
VI A sum in practice or bills of parcels.

It was the start of teaching by objectives and teaching to the test

Selman (1967), noting the changing criteria, states that between 1862 and 1871 the 3Rs were compulsory, as was girls' needlework. At first the 3Rs were tested with regard to Reading (emphasis on accuracy, re-tell and, only later, on reading expressively and responding); Recitation; Writing, (emphasis on handwriting, spelling, dictation); Arithmetic (mental and paperwork). Religious Knowledge was tested separately by the Diocesan Inspectors.

The **Blagdon** Logs show that the possible Grant was 12s per pupils (8s for passing the 3Rs and 4s for regular attendance), with extra for Needlework. From 1867 one or two Special Subjects could be added. These earned extra grants and were thus attractive, but more subjects meant more work for both teachers and pupils. The most popular were Grammar and Geography, although History could also be considered. The maximum number of class subjects was soon limited to two. Schools did not always make the grade, so HMI might comment, *'Grammar and Geography only just qualify'* (Ctc 1880) which served as a warning to the teacher before the next Inspection. Worse still was the comment, *'I am sorry I cannot recommend payment of a grant under Article 19c as the examinations of Grammar and Geography were a failure'* (Kgd 1878).

By the 1880s a significant shift came when Special Subjects were referred to as Class Subjects: the emphasis was now on general proficiency of the whole class, rather than on individual performances. English or Science were added as options and Singing, which was divided between 'singing by ear' (which could earn 6d), or 'singing by note' which required the ability to read music (usually by the newly-promoted Sol-fa notation method) which could earn a further 1s. Blagdon managed to earn a full 1s. For the Girls, Cookery could win a grant from 1882 and Laundry from 1890: these subjects were intended to *'fit girls for household duties'* and intended *'to set a high value on the housewife's position'* (Horn 1989).

More changes came with the developing curriculum during the 1890s, after elementary schooling at last became free as well as compulsory. English was no longer compulsory as an exam, neither the 3Rs. But, in the curriculum, Object Lessons for the Standards (not just Infants) were compulsory though not examined. Also by the 1890s, Drawing (of a technical nature, for Boys) joined Needlework (for Girls) as a compulsory and examined subject and these too could earn grants which were especially necessary as the materials were consumed and needed regular replacement. The dreaded HMI report might be given, *'Needlework was not good enough for grant this year'* (Bgd 1888).

By the turn of the century, although Cookery, Gardening or Woodwork were being offered, finding the facilities for these in remote village schools was not always easy. This was important as the grant system had changed yet again. A single unified grant of between 22s or 23s was given based on average attendance. The system of awarding Grants based on examining Class Subjects was abolished, but, Grants were awarded for Practical Subjects only – again to help cover costs, and as a stimulus to include them.

Attendance and Tone assessed. Apart from achievement results, throughout the C19th other criteria were included. These gradually shifted in importance so the balance altered. Among these additional criteria was Attendance. Registers had to be marked twice daily. Absences and irregularity became significant. They were no longer merely the pupil's loss, but also the school's loss. Attendance officers were appointed whose job it was to round up the truants and to warn parents who did not send their children to school. Eventually, they could be reported, summoned and fined by magistrates. But with the stick came the carrot: children were given attendance tickets to 'win', prizes were awarded to good attenders, prestige could be gained – and financial benefit too.

To the desirability of attendance was added good Organisation and Discipline. So, the 'behaviour and tone' of the school was also assessed. 'O and D' became gradually more highly rated but, being so subjective to assess, it was difficult to know how to prepare in order to impress the inspectors.

From 1875 to 1881 the previous 5s grant for good average attendance was reduced to 4s, but instead a further 1s could be earned for good Organisation and Discipline. 'Organisation' applied to the planning of schemes of work as well as to the ordering of the children. Thus the size and composition of the class began to matter and affect the way children worked and how the teacher worked. Not being well organised meant that children might not be using time effectively, as having to wait a long time before being attended to, or because the teacher was not using their time effectively. 'Discipline' meant compliance and 'time spent on task'.

Premises: Whilst the curriculum was a key factor in determining grant, criteria measuring the 'Effect of the Premises on the Quality of Learning' were also considered. This was the area in which the managers took responsibility. However, an important change in the management of schools had taken place: new School Boards. We need to backtrack a little.

The growing costs of running a school had increased beyond the capacity of many small parishes. For some years individuals had spoken up for a new method of management.

Since its first conference in 1869 the **National Education League** (which counted amongst its supporters the campaigner for children's right to education rather than to work, Charles Kingsley author of *Water Babies*) had pressed for compulsory, free, non-sectarian schools, inspected by government and maintained from rates. Kingsley claimed that *'from 27 years' experience as a parish person I know that voluntary action is a failure in country parishes'* (Lawson and Silver, 1973). But, the government had to win over the religious groups as well. As so often, a battle for souls took precedence over the betterment of minds.

Such campaigning led to **Forster's 1870 Education Act** which established schools run by School Boards *'where provision for education is not otherwise made'* (this was to avoid competing with established denominational schools which remained partly outside the new government grant-funded school system). It is estimated that, at the time of the Newcastle Commission 1858, 40% of children aged 5-10 did not attend school, often owing to no accessible provision, also to the income lost by attending and the cost incurred by doing do.

It was *'to fill the gaps at the least cost of public money, with least loss of voluntary cooperation and most aid from parents'* and *'to preserve freedom of conscience and integrity of religious instruction'*, for *'no catechism which is distinctive of any particular denomination shall be taught in school.'* This was the famous so-called **Cowper-Temple Conscience Clause**. This Clause, over which battles had raged in Parliament in order to pacify the religious lobbies, allowed children *not* to attend religious instruction classes if the faith of the individual was different from that of the school. Few Logs mention it. In a rare example of a religious stand, the Head of Horsington School received a letter, in 1904, saying:

> *'Dear Sir, Please do not teach my children the catechism, Mr P'.*

In addition Blagdon Log noted, in 1926:

> *'Admitted one boy who wishes to be excluded from Scripture Lessons'.*

Both Williton and nearby Watchet mention operating this clause (1872,1873 Directories) and, in 1892, HMI requested that a copy of the Conscience Clause should be made available in schools. No other mentions have been found. This seems to reflect the mood 'on the ground' which a subsequent Commission noted:

> *'The poor, when selecting a school, look entirely to whether the school supplied good reading, writing and arithmetic. I have heard of no instance in which religious teaching formed the grounds for withdrawing a child from a school'.*

Between 1870 and 1896, particularly after compulsory education came into force from 1880, over 2,500 new School Boards were set up, nearly half of these in communities of less than 1000 people and thus in small rural settlements where voluntary funding was in short supply (Lawson and Silver, 1973). Many other existing schools also became Boards Schools, so by 1896 there were 2 million children in 5,700 Board schools. However, 2.5 million children continued in 14,500 Voluntary schools run by denominational groups. The new Boards increased local responsibility, as the representatives – including women – were directly elected from among all parish ratepayers for limited terms and, therefore, were directly accountable. The representatives, however, were drawn from much the same social groups as before – even the same families – and, being local rate payers, they were keen to keep down the rates and thus to manage the school with greater 'efficiencies'. The basic grant per pupil was now 10s, with the possibility of more by passing in the 'special subjects'.

Attention turned to the buildings themselves and to the Managers' contribution to the success of the school. Often the first area of concern was with the need to separate the Infants into a different room, outside the traditional large main Hall. From the late 1870s, extra grants could be won by having a separate classroom properly equipped and furnished for these younger children. Thus Blagdon earned 8s per Infant pupil in 1882. Further, these Infants did not have to be examined – a source of easy money? No wonder very young children were admitted. Later, the same principle applied to separate rooms for older children who might be applying for scholarships for secondary places. Additionally, from the 1890s, HMI reports regularly comment on the heating, ventilation, lighting in rooms and, of course, the state of the 'offices' [toilets]. Only from the 1890s, when drill became an added curriculum activity, did the condition of the playgrounds come under scrutiny.

Yet another management change came with **Morant's 1902 Act**. He was no lover of School Boards, regarding them as *'the mistake of getting together a lot of people whose sole hobby is education and letting them have the run of the public purse'* (Bagley 1969). School Managers elected from among the parents, together with appointees from the new Local Education Authorities, now put the government back in the driving seat. Funding again came *indirectly* through the LEA. Throughout the C20th education has become one of the 'big spending' departments of government and this, in turn, leads to cries of 'economise' at every economic downturn. We can see this increase in the following costs:while, in 1902, the cost per child was £3 0s 9½d, it rose after the new 1906 Liberal government reforms (including costs for the new school insurance, medical services, free meals, juvenile employment bureau, continued provision for the deaf and blind and, for the first time, for the 'mentally deficient') to £4 15s 2d in 1913, which thereby increased the education bill from £8.5m to £33m. [It was not until the 1988 Baker Act and, later still, the setting up of Academies outside LEA control, that funds were again *devolved* to individual schools to manage and money became more *directly* accessible.]

However, denominational schools could still 'opt out' in terms of some aspects of government control and therefore from certain areas of funding. Another key moment in the funding of schools came with the **Abolition of School Fees Act** 1891, according to which School Boards could agree not to charge fees. Instead grants could be obtained, but with grants came inspection so, once again, special provision had to be made for 'denominational' schools.

Once this greater State involvement began there was further continuous evolution, a shifting of goalposts, a constant flux. We can see how the criteria spread from results, to learning, to an even greater interest in the suitability and appeal of the school buildings, to quality of teaching provision and, finally, to the welfare of the child.

From the mid-C19th the building of new schools, then of training colleges contributed to the enormous and dramatic expansion of the schooling system in general. It is to the buildings that we turn next.

Chapter 5
What the Schools Looked Like: Distribution, Styles and Furnishing

In trying to trace the school buildings, investigate their distribution, style, layout and the changes which occurred, it is appropriate to remember where the data are to be found and their nature. Again, we have to accept the fact that the data are not consistent or complete and often ambiguous. It remains a challenge to interpret and check. Hence the following is not exhaustive and the conclusions tentative.

We also need to remember that a school is often mentioned, particularly in the early period, but with no indication of where, or in what kind of accommodation. From documents such as Vestry accounts, it is clear that many villages had little opportunity for new build. However, they might hold community facilities in the form of a Church House, a Poor House, even Almshouses in which spare accommodation may have become available. It is in these buildings that schools were often housed. Thus a 'school' cannot be assumed to be synonymous with a dedicated 'school building'. For example, even the important and much visited school of Enmore, began in a cottage in 1810, moved into rooms in the Poor House, and did not achieve a purpose-built school till 1847. We can also find details of accommodation, albeit incomplete and ambiguous, in the Trade Directories. From these we read that schools are held in a wide range of places, for example

a. in a Church/Chapel – often a side aisle or Vestry as at Chilton Trinity 1868
b. in the 'parvis' room over the porch, as possibly in Porlock, Ilton, Corfe and Wedmore
c. in buildings associated with religious organisations such as a priest's house
   Chantry House Wedmore 1707, or *Rectory* – Marston Magna 1736, N Cheriton (girls)
   Church House: Aisholt 1662, Croscombe 1668
   Poor House: the upper floor used as a school, while residents kept to the lower floor e.g. Over Stowey 1840, Charlton Musgrove 1818, Spaxton 1825, Wrington 1840, Ashcott 1852, Crowcombe, and perhaps Enmore 1830s, while Chilton Polden 1840 and Penselwood 1847 were on the *site of* the Poor House;
d. glebe cottages: Marston Magna 1840, Creech St Michael 1846
e. private properties/cottages: Enmore 1810, Aisholt 1846, Cossington 1849
f. conversion: malt-mill Henstridge 1813, or barn Somerton West End 1875
g. part of the Town Hall was made available by the Corporation in Ilchester 1814
h. several schools were accommodated 'in the churchyard' (within the graveyard) such as Merriot 1808, Yarlington 1836, Shepton Montague 1846, Coombe St Nicholas, and two 'grammar' schools Shepton Mallet and East Coker or, 'adjacent to the churchyard' (just the other side of the churchyard wall) Curland 1866 and Buckland 1866, Curry Rivel, Dowlish Wake.

We can also find examples of how existing buildings were used in the details of some charity documents. In 1668 Elizabeth Carew funded a school in Crowcombe: *There is an old house* [Church House]. *On the ground floor the poor of the parish are lodged. On the upper floor is the school room.* This appears to be a not unusual configuration. Further, in 1868 William Chapman in Westonzoyland gave monies to furnish the interior of the school *to provide two classrooms and an infant gallery and accommodate a total of 148 children.* This division of the main Hall – often with a curtain or a wooden partition – as well as the provision of a gallery, became standard practice until the turn of the century, after which the policy changed to allow infants space to move and HMI recommended the immediate removal of such Infant Galleries.

The lasting legacy of school buildings allows us to plot the where and when of their distribution, note in which styles they were built and what features exist. Finally, we can surmise the relationship between changes in buildings and in pedagogy. These considerations will serve as the main focus in the following sections.

i. Type of School: denominational variety and alternative educational provision.

In the mid-C19th most Somerset schools, referred to as Parish or Parochial schools, were dependent on local funds and grants from the two main educational societies. The Church of England (CoE) schools could also call upon the Bath and Wells Diocesan Fund and, later, all could look to the government. Many schools described themselves as **National**, which indicated that they at least had a 'relationship' with the (Anglican) *National Society.*

However, there were other types of schools, the **British Schools.** These were associated with the 'non-denominational' *British and Foreign Schools Society*. Such potential rivalry could serve the community well by providing plenty of opportunities, or, it could divide and undermine efforts and delay the implementation of educational provision. Several villages, also had chapels belonging to Wesleyans/Methodists /Independents; in addition there were Baptist, Congregationalist, Bible Christian and Moravian groups. These appear to occur more densely in particular areas: Baptist Chapels in Bridgwater, Curry North and along the Poldens, also in the adjacent hundred of Abdick in the central Levels and to the south in textile manufacturing areas around the hundreds of Kingsbury Episcopi and Crewkerne; while many Wesleyan, Baptist and Congregational Chapels were to be found to the east from around Milborne Port in the hundred of Horethorne and north to the mining areas of Kilmersdon. In these districts, in the larger settlements, there are often two schools - National and British, often of similar size. Not many villages had only a British School: examples include Blagdon Hill an adjunct to Pitminster, West Pennard, Lullington and Rode near Frome, several of which became Board Schools after 1870.

A few village records show that Quakers supported the local CoE school: at Greinton (1819) there was 'Quaker support' for the local CoE school, and at Long Sutton - for a while. Further, Quakers set up a separate school in Winscombe (1808) which merged into Sidcott Quaker school in (1848), and in Pawlett (1860). Quakers may have been influential in setting up a Commercial school in Chilton Polden (1838) and Shapwick (1847), and in the east at Beckington (1861). A group of local farmers, after a religious controversy in Northmoor Green near Bridgwater, set up its own school and similarly at North Petherton (1860s). Congregationalists had a school in Othery (1867) which became the Board School ten years later, and also in Bridgwater in (1830) which became the Board School in (1878).

British Schools (sometimes also referred to as Wesleyan) existed in North Petherton (1861-78), Wincanton (1859–71) and Chard (1861-83), where they all became Board schools; Cheddar (1866-94), then again during the reorganisation in 1902, and Milborne Port (1850-1909); in Bridgwater (between 1824 and 60) when it became the Arts and Science Institute, and Midsumer Norton (1875-98), then as a Higher

Elementary School, before adding a Teacher Centre in 1912; Frome 1843-63, Rode/Road 1860, West Pennard 1878. Baltonsborough (1861-1902) was an interesting case as it seems to have had several schools – the National, Moravian, as well as St Anne's School for the daughters' of clergymen.

The tables overleaf show the development of school building across the county, with the same uneven distribution profile we have seen amongst the early teachers and the Sunday Schools, the reasons for which were suggested in Ch. 1. Again, in Table 5.1 we can see the dominance of regions 2, 7 and also 9 in terms of areas which moved early to set up schools – these being the areas with a higher number of non-conformist chapels and possible rival schools (either Sunday or Day School). We can also note that regions 5 and 8 (and 1) were also ready to provide schooling, being areas with higher levels of manufacturing / mining which may well have created a greater demand for skills in reading and casting of accounts that local inhabitants were willing to supply. These are also areas with higher levels of non-conformist congregations.

The 'Dissidents', believed to be particularly keen to encourage individuals to read their own Bible, were often found to be some of the earliest to promote popular education (which was thought, by the traditionalists who held sway in many villages, to be potentially subversive). Many of the pre-1833 village schools were often started by such groups with Dissident leanings or by those linked to the more evangelical ('Methody') wings of the Anglican Church. However, other schools were built (often later) by the local squire, firmly in the Anglican mould but with a desire to educate 'his villagers'. Details relating to school size and village size can be found in App. 5.

Key to Hundred groupings

1 Winterstoke, Brent+Bempstone Huntspill+Puriton
NW (Mendips)

2 Cannington and Andersfield Petherton N, and Whitely
W(Quantocks+ Poldons)

3 Carhampton and Williton
W (Exmoor)

4 Kingsbury W, Taunton Deane, Curry N, and Abdick
SW+Levels

5 Kingsbury Episc, Petherton S, Crewkerne, Houdsbo'+Stone
S Central borderlands

6. Martock, Tintinhull, Pitney, and Somerton
Central

7. Horethorne, Norton-Ferris, and Catash
SE

8. Glaston, Wells, Whitestone, and Bruton
East

9. Kilmersdon, Frome, Chewton,
NE + Mining

Table 5.1 Distribution of schools:
% built in each period x region

	1 Mend	*2* Qntk*	*3 Exm*	*4 Lvl*	*5 Sth*	*6 Cnt*	*7* SE*	*8 East*	*9* NE*	**100%**
1901 1870	6	15	12	***22***	***15***	***13***	1	10	4	***98***
1869 1846	***10***	10	***15***	9	11	8	12	11	10	***96***
1845 1833	8	***27***	3	3	5	5	***19***	10	***19***	***100***
Pre 1833	18	9*	13	4	18	4	9	9	13	***97***

* many schools existed in other buildings, which only became purpose-built after 1870s.

Table 5.2 Distribution of schools:
% built within each region x period

	1 Mend	*2* Qntk*	*3 Exm*	*4 Lvl*	*5 Sth*	*6 Cnt*	*7* SE*	*8 East*	*9* NE*	
No of Parishes	26	37	33	31	35	26	28	33	26	* 275
1902 1870	20	32	30	***56***	37	***47***	3	27	11	
1869 1846	***52***	***35***	***57***	37	***43***	*43*	***61***	***55***	***50***	
1845 1833	12	***27***	3	3	6	8	***26***	12	***27***	
pre – 1833	16	5	9	3	12	0	6	6	12	
100%	*100*	*99*	*99*	*99*	*98*	*98*	*96*	*96*	*99*	

* excluding settlements over 2,000 in population, or less than 200 and with no school.

ii. Styles of build.

While we can plot the distribution of schools in time and place on a map, in this section, the issue of style and layout will be addressed. We often believe that there is a recognizable and typical style of 'village school'. They can be spotted in many villages, often helpfully called *The Old School.* However, names can be deceptive, for sometimes the current owners do not distinguish between the School House (the accommodation for the Teacher) and the School (where the scholars went). This confusion is further muddied by the fact that a Master's wife might have had a class of 'little ones' in a room within the nearby School House. In only a few cases is the architect's name or main sponsor's name available (see App. 5). This was because, as in the case of medieval cathedrals, the master builder built using his experience without the need for architect's plans.

This use of 'master builders' may also account for the fact that schools were often built in a domestic style, or even as a barn, as these were the kinds of buildings in which builders had experience and confidence. Money must also have been a key factor in most situations: thus designing in a familiar style, in which the builder was confident such as a barn-style or common vernacular would be an obvious choice. Hence, the 'Tudor style' with square top windows and mouldings would probably be cheaper and more familiar to the village builders than the 'Gothic style' with pointed windows. Similarly, gable-ends rather than the rare hip-style roof-lines would also be an obvious choice.

In fact, schools come in all shapes and sizes, though there are common elements. The real give-away is the presence of an external bell (about 20%) though this might be a gable-end bell, in a stone-housing atop a gable or porch, or a wooden bell-cott on the roof. A few, such as Merriot and Hinton St George, have a tower-housing for their bell, whilst Eddington has a clock-tower and bell-cott. The other identifiable feature is the double entrance separating Boys, from Girls and Infants (only 7%). These occur in schools which differ widely in size and style, for example modest West Camel (Tudor 1837), yet elaborate Queen Camel (Gothic 1872), and also Montacute (1847), W Pennard (1856) and Rode (1860) – one of the very few remaining Methodist schools. Interestingly, on looking closely, there are also a few examples of a single-entry porch containing twin doors which can serve the same segregation purpose (e.g. in the south Limington (1834), West Hatch (1858), Isle Brewer's (1869), and towards the east in Baltonsborough (Moravian 1859). Even without these details the school usually has an obvious lofty Hall with a large dominating window at one end and side windows set high so children cannot see out and be distracted.

If we look systematically we may be able to trace other patterns relating to school building. The difficulty lies in the fact that there are so many possible variables which may influence the design of the build: shape of the plot, local materials or cost. There is also the likelihood that local individuals may have influenced the design: members of management or Vestry, a lord of the manor or key sponsor or the architect he might have employed. If these were an influence it was certainly not consistent: each build seems to have been an opportunity to try out a new idea.

Finally, there is the possibility that beliefs about 'seemliness' may have played a part and it is here that religion may enter the frame. The buildings themselves reflect these different traditions: Dissidents, building Academies in the larger towns opted for a 'Palladian' style, or even adopted an austere Classical style. Most preferred the plain 'Tudor style' with square top windows, stone mullions and moulded hoods. This was also offered as one model by the 1840 Committee of Council on Education which tried to take a neutral stance. In contrast the Anglicans often preferred the 'pointed' style with 'ecclesiastical', or 'Gothic' windows. This was intended to emphasise austerity, discipline, simplicity and 'seemliness' (Seaborne, 1971). It did not become very common in Somerset till later in the century, particularly after the Board schools were built, with substantial government grants. Somerset, however, had a reputation for being a rather rebellious, 'dissident' county and many of the school buildings appear to be in that style: in fact around 80% of the village schools are 'Tudor' and 20% 'Gothic' – though several contain features of both.

Once State monies began to flow guidelines were also offered so as to standardise and economise by having a particular style to help architects, who of course had rarely had to build schools before. The Church of England Buildings Committee advised a barn-like structure with a single-cell space (as at Barrington 1848). The Privy Council offered a series of sixteen alternative plans based on current expertise, as best adapted to various systems of instruction (Seaborne, 1971). Later, in 1841 the major architect, A.W.N. Pugin – designer of the Houses of Parliament - published *The True Principles of Pointed or Christian architecture*. This, it was suggested, should be used in school building, to reinforce religious aspirations.

To guide the new interest in school building, The Royal Institute for Architecture (founded in 1834) held relevant books such as *Designs for schools and school houses* by HE Kendall (1847), and *Schools and School Houses* by L Clarke (1852), and the weekly periodical, *The Builder*, which started in 1843, also regularly gave advice and suggestions. Seaborne (1971) estimates that the architect's fee was generally about 5% of the build cost.

a. External characteristics: Thus both the period of build and religious persuasion are often reflected in the external appearance of the building. Several are in the 'Tudor style', for example Lamyatt (1829), Limington (1834), Hazlebury Plunknett (1858) and Odcombe which has both Gothic windows in the larger Hall and Tudor ones in the smaller classroom. Wrington is described as 'in the pointed style' costing £1,500 for a new build sponsored by Lord Poulett in 1857. Only one school is described as in 'perpendicular style', at Cossington (1870). Several noted as 'in the Gothic style' include Stogursey (1860) and High Ham (1867) both by *John Norton* (the latter since demolished), Minehead (1867) and Upton Noble / Batcombe (1842) designed by *RJ Wither*.

There were indeed some spectacular designs amongst the wide ranging schools. Amongst the most impressive must surely be Nettlecombe towards Exmoor: a huge building in a tiny village intended for 150 scholars in 1819, designed by *R Carver* at the expense of the Lord of the Manor (who had just cleared all the village houses from the area around his estate, as 'they spoiled the view'). It is characterized by Dutch-gable ends on a two storey building – perhaps intended for boarders upstairs and for the teacher's accommodation. Dutch-gables can also be seen on Thomas Poole's school in Nether Stowey, now the Public Library, on which *Carver* was believed to have been consulted. These gables also appear on the ends of the Poor House which was, in part, used by Rev John Poole's school in Enmore.

Another beautiful building is Charlton Mackrell decorated with encaustic Minton tiles in the main Hall (now the gym) including 'worthy quotes' picked out in coloured tiles around the arches and in texts around the wall, all of which cost £2,500 in 1853. This was paid from the Brymer Fund as a memorial to Archdeacon James Brymer. Originally a single room (approx 15m x 6m) abutting the Teacher's House, the design was by *C Giles*, erected by Snaith builders. Milborne Port is another elaborate design 'in the Tudor style' built for 250 scholars in 1864 and costing £2,000, supported by the Medlycott family, designed by *Henry Hall*. This magnificent school used a local '*native stone, Forest marble plinths, with Bath stone windows and dressings*'. It also had an arcaded entrance, and a small clock tower at the rear. A tiny, very humble, but delightful surprise is Chillington (1861) built by Earl Poulett: from the outside, a wreck due for demolition, yet inside it has a decorative moulded plaster-work ceiling!

Materials and Roofs: Apart from the availability of money, other influences will be the local availability of materials. In the case of Somerset, stone is plentiful in most areas – red sandstone in the west, golden Ham stone in the centre, blue lias towards the east. The majority of schools were built with stone walls (20" thick according to specifications at Brewham 1861) and have gable ends. Exceptions do exist. A hip-roof can be found at E Coker (1851), N Cheriton (1863), Bower Hinton (1870) and half-hip at Cutcombe (1875). The interior roof-space was usually a 'high open space'. This was intended to allow the noise to disperse, but resulted in rooms impossible to heat adequately. Down on the Levels and at the edges of the Quantocks bricks made in Bridgwater were easily accessible and therefore used – Chedzoy (1878), Middlezoy (1843), Westonzoy (1842), Othery (1877), later additions at Meare (1874) and Westhay (1891) and, earlier, in East Brent (1841), North Curry (1847); Nether Stowey (1813), Crowcombe (1872), and also Nettlecombe (1819).

So, Middlezoy school, dating from 1843 but altered in the 1860s and 1903, is of *'orange-red brick, with a low schoolroom attached to a two-storey teacher's house.* Westonzoy had a distinctive design: in 1868, *'a 4-bay, 2-story, hipped roof design with simple Gothic windows was constructed, in brick'*. Nearby, the Othery build of 1877 is described as a *'red-brick 3-bay villa style'*.

In some designs a combination which mixed stone and brick was used, as with the decorative yellow quoins at Goathurst (1876), while at Luccombe (1881) decorative brick quoins were used in a stone-build. Other techniques were tried: in 1870, Muchelney the Vestry agreed to build a school using *'local lias rubble'*, while in North and South Barrow (1860) the identical schools were built of brick using a *'rat-trap bond'* (alternating stretchers and headers but turning the bricks on their sides so they presented a higher side outwards and thus built upwards more quickly, using less brick, and creating a space (rat-trap) between front and back facings which was 'tied' by the headers).

Whilst roof shape may be distinctive, roofing materials also varied. Only Allerford School, built around 1820, retains its thatched roof (now a Museum). Elsewhere either slates or tiles are used, sometimes in patterns using shapes, such as scallop, or colour-contrast to form bands or diamond-shapes.

In terms of siting, as early as 1509, Dr Colet (Dean of St Paul's London) advised: *'As Elementary scholars must of force be near unto their parents, schools should be placed in the skirts of towns, near fields for exercise'* (Seaborne 1971). However this advice seems to have been largely ignored. We find that the majority of village schools are within a stone's throw of the church or chapel to which they were linked, often close to the rectory/vicarage. They are thus likely to be central to the village and more conveniently accessible.

b. Alternative layouts. Despite the diversity it is still possible to discern a pattern of building layout and the alternative ways in which buildings developed and grew.

Stage 1: 1800-1840s
Single-cell buildings consisting of a small rectangular room which can be found in small villages. These smaller schools had Halls of modest (approximate) proportions[1]:

e.g.	10 x 6m (Fivehead 1874)	9 x 7m (Misterton 1874)
	8 x 6m (Puckington 1862)	7 x 4m (Sutton Montis 1841).

[1] Where the author has ''paced out' dimensions, they are given in (approximate) metres; where dimensions are noted in a Log, they are given - as recorded - in feet and inches.

These were intended for 30-60 pupils. Guidelines were given as to how many square feet should be allowed per child, which was re-calculated more generously in the 1890s. We must remember that absenteeism was high. Rarely was the whole school present, though children do seem to have made an effort to attend when the inspectors came: if the school performed well there might be free buns or a ½ day holiday!

Some much larger single Halls were built in the 1900s, which were used for several classes within the same space. HMI was soon urging them to put in partitions to form two, or even three separate classrooms, as at Keinton Mandeville 21 x 5m (1902), Writhlington 20 x 7m (1901), also earlier at Chilcompton 18 x 9m (1875) and Queen Camel 24 x 6m (1872).

Stage 2: 1840-1870s
Accommodation extended either *in-line*, or more commonly added at the back to form a *T-shape* or *L-shape*. This often depended on the siting of the original chimney so that it could be shared by the extra room. Thus in a smaller room with a single central chimney, an extra room could be added to form a *T*; while in a larger hall with two chimneys along the rear wall, the addition could be at one end to form an *L*. If the chimneys were on the end walls, then an *in-line* extension would be logical. Of course, all this depended on the shape of the site itself.

Another alternative was to place two Halls back to back, in *parallel* alignment (Bawdrip, Batcombe). In some larger schools a mix of approaches evolved, thus at Merriot the new Board School had an *L*-classroom, with a *parallel* block, one of which was *in-line* extension.

Stage 3: 1870-1902
Where a (two-storey) **Teacher's House** was provided, it could be placed in a number of alternative positions relative to the School Hall. Examples can be found *in-line*, in *L*-, or *T*-formation, with the Teacher's House at one end and the School Hall at right-angles. An alternative pattern was to place the Teacher's House at one end of the site with a parallel high-ceilinged school hall at a few yards' distance and link the two adjacent buildings by a corridor (which often became an administration block or further classroom), thus forming an **H-shape**.

Stage 1 Single-cell School Hall: rear chimney and front porch

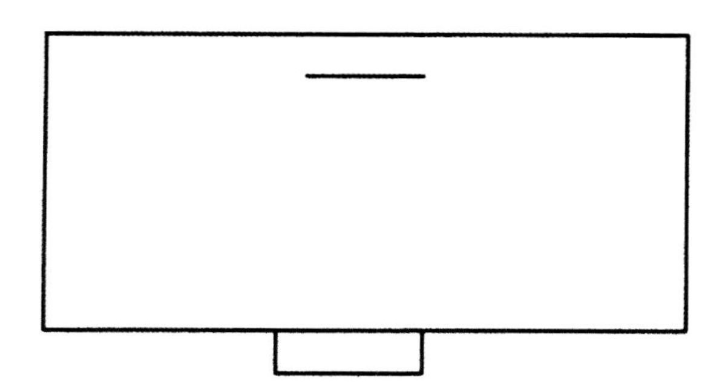

Examples across time and geographical spread

Lamyatt 1829
Limington 1834
Long Load 1860
Luccombe 1881

Stage 2. L- , T-shape School Hall, or in-line classroom *(right)* **- often depending on original site of chimney**

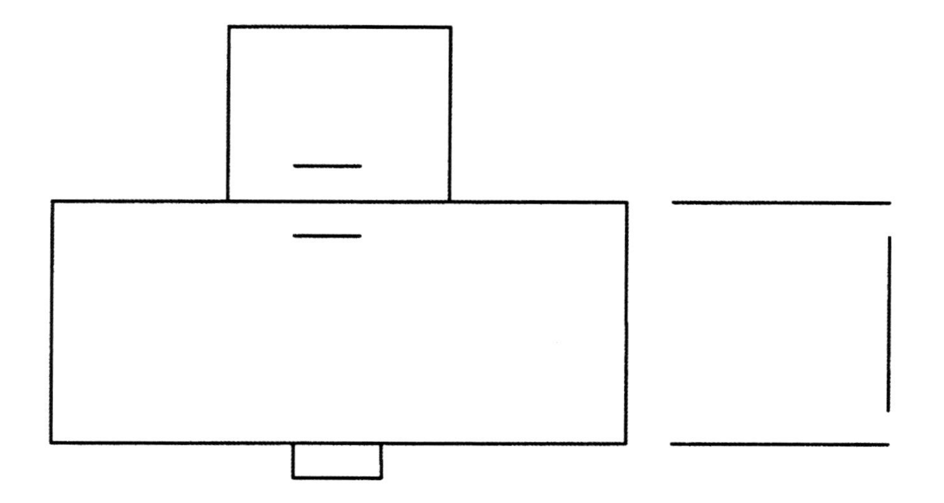

L – Ash 1846
Kingsdon 1872
Ilton 1875

T- Withycombe 1866
Wedmore 1861
West Bampfylde 1857

In-line extension
Dowlish Wake 1840
Odcombe 1831, '87
Pitney 1875, '94
Barwick 1830,
Pylle 1875, '99

Stage 3. H-shape with (linked) School House for Teacher

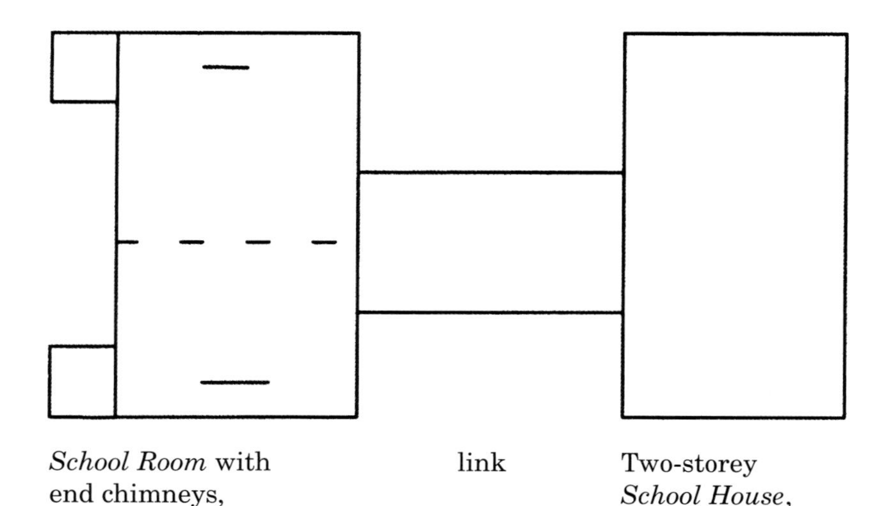

School Room with end chimneys, possible to share with in-line extensions

link

Two-storey *School House*, for Head's use.

Teacher's Houses:
In-line: Meare 1840
Withypool 1886
L-shape: N Curry 1847
Misterton 1874
T- Skilgate 1861
Enmore 1847
Sutton Montis 1841
S Brewham 1861
T- Broomfield 1849 with later transverse classroom to balance Teacher's house

H- Rowberrow 1863
Sandford 1872
Brompton Ralph 1877
Chilton Cantillo 1852

Plate 5

Cottage School, Cheddar 1790s

Poor Ho, poss school (top floor), Enmore 1800s

Othery Churchyard School, 1827

Limington 1834 + ***twin entry, single porch***

Blagdon 1842 + ***bell-cott***

Cutcombe 1875 + ***½ hip-roof***

Enmore 1847 + ***Teacher's House on right, H-shape adds***

N Curry 1847 + ***Teacher's House on right, L-shape***

Plate 6

Nettlecombe / Yard 1819 + *Teacher's House on left*

Skilgate 1861 + *Teacher's House on left, T-shape*

Chillington 1882

Stove + ceiling

Triple blackboards

Chaffcombe 1878

Isle Brewer's 1869

Meare 1840 + bell-housing + *Teacher's House on left, inline*

Westhay 1891

Plate 7

Blagdon interior 1842

Allerford (Museum) interior + long desks

Enmore interior 1847

Milverton (decorative) 1835

W Huntspill (decorative)1897

Meare (decorative)1874

Charlton Mackrell 1853 + *Teacher's House on right*

Minton encaustic tiles interior

Monteclefe Girls + Infants 1851

West End Somerton barn conversion 1875

Plate 8

Horsington 1855 gothic + ***Teachers House off right***

Writhlington 1901

Kingsdon 1872 + ***bell-cott***

Keinton Mandeville 1902 + ***gable bell***

West Pennard 1856 + ***double entry***

South Brewham 1858 + ***Teacher's House on left***

Coleford Infants 1834 + ***hip-roof***

Teacher's House **Coleford National +** ***gable-roof*** **1847**

Post-1902 the newly appointed County Councils often integrated accommodation from neighbouring schools to create larger, more 'efficient' units and thus much larger and better equipped schools. This may be in an extended, in-line arrangement, with several classrooms either side of a main entrance with the now expected administration, school kitchens and service rooms, a sports hall and larger assembly space.

Stage 4. Classroom block with central Assembly Hall

Administration and services block

Examples: often used for larger, secondary schools rather than elementary/primary.

Post-1944 some schools experimented with square 'activity-based' buildings comprising a central hall for marching, drill, indoor sports and areas for music, art, cookery and carpentry. Separate classrooms led off this central shared area (development at Keinton Mandeville and Somerton). By the heady late-1960s and 70s, open-plan classrooms and team-teaching were tried with emphasis given to creativity and self-expression. But this was mostly abandoned when new demands of the 1990s saw the 'back-to-basics' movement and increasing pressure for exam results and league tables which seemingly put an end to many of these ideas.

Stage 5. Activity 'square' layout

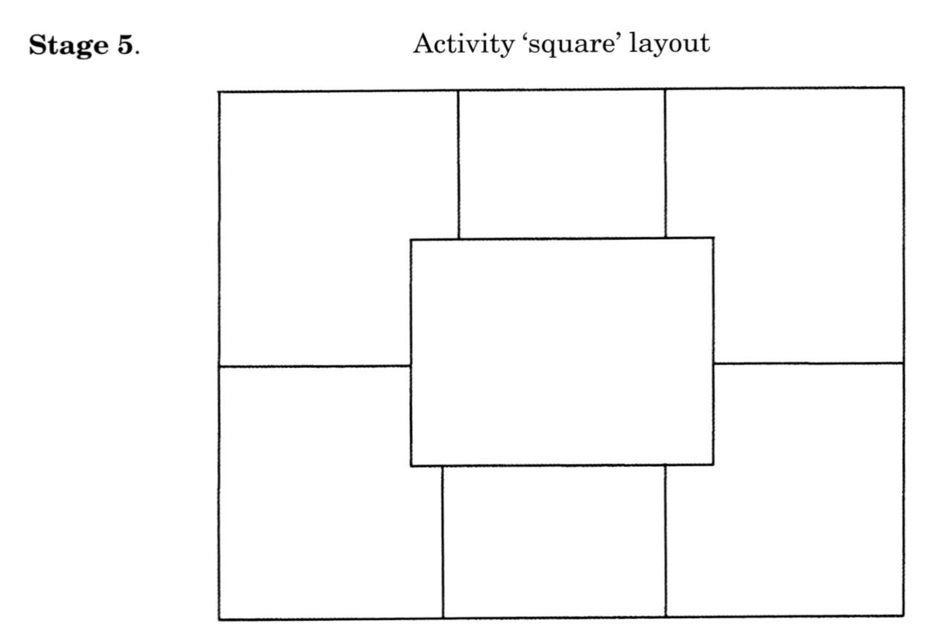

Classrooms surrounding central Hall

Examples: Keinton Mandeville and Wood Street Somerton.

c. Internal Plan and Layout of the Buildings

The 'barn style' was pervasive till well into the mid-C19th. Originally, this was considered suitable for the 'monitorial' method of teaching which had been so dominant from the beginning of the century. We have very specific instructions to suit this teaching technique, which were published and disseminated by both the main societies. The costs were initially estimated as £1 per child, rising to £2 10s by 1842.

1805 Lancaster's *Hints and Directions for building, fitting up and arranging school rooms*	1816 National Society *Sub-committee proposals for Schools using the Madras system*
Size: 7' per child Desks: facing front, Bench: 16 children per 22' bench Aisles: 5' wide to allow easy flow Walls: lime-washed to disinfect (renewed annually) Walls: hung with baize to reduce reverberation of sound Floors: hard brick/rammed clay as wood too noisy Flues: at floor level for heat to avoid open fires Offices: closets and urinal stalls with sloping floor	6' per child, at cost of £1 per child 2 rooms (1 for boys,1 for girls) Desks in military square Seats for ½ the children as other ½ will be standing to read or recite in monitorial groups, in the centre Sand trays for the younger ones to practise making letters Tables for the girls' sewing Brick floors Flues for heating

Drawn from Seabourne,1971.

A scale of sizes was offered by the BFSS in 1831 in the *Manual of the system of primary instruction founded 1814, from the Royal Lancastrian Association 1810.* viz. for 304 children, 62 x 34'; for 72 children 30 x 18'; 40 children 16 x 16'.

However, all this was about to alter with the change from the monitorial system and the adoption of the new pedagogic approach of the 'simultaneous' method from the 1840s. This involved having a 'class' led by an adult who taught the 'class' all together, simultaneously. It was considered to be more effective than the small groups led by young monitors and the whole 'supervised' by a single master. This new method had been successfully pioneered by David Stow in the Glasgow Normal Seminary. For the first time, the intention was to create 'classes', consisting of scholars at approximately the same level of learning (though not necessarily the same age), each class requiring its own adult teacher. In effect, village schools continued as before but, after the introduction of pupil-teachers from 1846, it was they who took the separate 'classes' rather than a trained adult. Nevertheless, the changes eventually led to a need for separate 'classrooms' which clearly effected the plan and layout of the school building.

Further waves of school building stemmed from four significant government policy changes: **1870 Forster's Act** which supported the provision of new Board Schools, where a sufficient one did not already exist, and 1876 making education *compulsory* for those of 5-13 years, or who had passed Std IV.
1880 Mundella's Act which made education *compulsory* from 5–13 years or, with exemptions from 10+, *if* the child had passed Std V (and later VI)
1891 Act which at last gave *free* and compulsory education for all children from 5-14 years but, with a minimum exemption age: this rose to 11 in 1893, 12 in 1899, until the ...

1902 Morant's Act which made education compulsory for all from 5-14 years, with no exemptions. Figures relating to these can be found in App. 6.

This entailed the considerable and continual need for the outlay of yet more money to try to keep up with new regulations and policies. Thus we find that hard pressed, strapped-for-cash School Managers or Boards cannot or will not find the funds for 'necessary improvements', despite constant pressure from Inspectors' Reports. These details emerge in the Managers' Minute Book or in the Head Teacher's Daily Log and demands for improvements sometimes drag on for years.

In general, the classrooms must have been cramped and crowded: the guideline allowance from 1862 was 6' sq. ft per older, 8' per younger child but, by 1910, it had altered to a more generous 10-12' per older child and 9' for infants.

We can get an idea of the building size and pupil density (sq ft per pupil, and cost per pupil) from the (approximated) details below:

1847 Enmore	27' x 16'	for **70** @ **£ 277**	***6** sq ft pp*	***£ 4 pp***
1847 Batcombe	33' x 20'	for **103** @ **£ 550**	***6** sq ft pp*	***£ 5 pp***
1861 Brewham	51' x 18'	for **138** @ **£711**	***6** sq ft pp*	***£ 5 pp***
1877 Cutcombe	37' x 24'	for **152** @ **£ 930**	***6** sq ft pp*	***£ 6 pp***
1857 K Seymour	37' x 16'	for **60** @ **£ 740**	***10** sq ft pp*	***£12 pp***
1886 Withypool	33' x 20'	for **70** @ **£ 970**	***10** sq ft pp*	***£14 pp***

Partitions: By the end of the C19th HMI were no longer content to comment on the external suitability of the buildings, but also made additional, increasingly detailed recommendations about the internal furnishings of a school. Recommendations were made on the organisation of parallel benches or long desks in separate classrooms, and to partition the hall with curtains (Seaborne 1971) so as to reduce the noise from other classes sharing the same Hall space. This was indeed the case at Allerford (now a Museum) and East Harptree (1880). Of course, a curtain did little to dampen the distraction of noise from other classes while the children chanted their lessons so, later, sliding wooden partitions were added (still visible at West Hatch, now the Village Hall) or folding ones at Chaffcombe (1893) with a glass panel added in 1896. In nearby Chillington, all children were still in a single room in 1910, though not long afterwards a store room became used for the 'babies': a specific classroom was never built.

At Somerton Monteclefe, in the report at the beginning of 1870, HMI identified the organisation of the school as faulty. They suggested that the Managers should arrange for the girls and the infants to be taught separately – until this time all children were in one Hall, with Infants and their gallery at one end. Clearly any separation had both staffing and accommodation implications – for which money would be needed. It was six months before the temporary solution of a dividing partition was installed, under Lady Smith's supervision! Sixteen years later, overcrowding had again worsened and odd spaces were pressed into classroom use. By 1908 we find two recesses are also being used for teaching purposes.

A partition replaced a mere curtain at Writhlington 1910. At Blagdon, the large main room was only divided by a low screen until 1940, which was frequently commented upon by HMI and belatedly improved, while at Skilgate (1909) it only reached part way across the room. Partitions were eventually installed in North Curry (1911) and Somerton Boys (1912). Sometimes partitions had an inserted glass panel so the Master could still keep a watchful eye. After repeated recommendations by HMI at Monteclefe Girls, the screen erected in 1871 had glass inserted to decrease noise and increase light in 1914. Screens were similarly a bone of contention in Keinton Mandeville, though they did eventually achieve folding doors and, in 1915, an inserted glass panel and, similarly, at Coleford in 1925.

Gallery: Within the Infant classroom we often find the 'gallery', which figures in many Log Books and particularly in the Managers' Minutes. It was not a suspended, 'balcony-type' feature, but more like a mini football terrace – a tiered set of steps on which the little ones sat (Plate 9). This was considered ideal for 'object lessons', as even the ones at the back could see. The gallery was often placed along one wall of the classroom and thus accommodated many children without using too much floor space e.g. Somerton West End School building where the marks on the wall are still visible up to a height of about 5'. The gallery came to be used for many other lessons too, particularly ones where large numbers were brought together, as in Singing and for some 'simultaneous' lessons in 'class subjects' such as Geography.

Dates of installation vary, but we find HMI constantly urging Managers to install Galleries from the 1870s (OkBr 1871, Hsg 1873 – only achieved after 5 years (Clf 1878). By the turn of the century, however, all HMI were recommending the removal of the Gallery as being old fashioned,too restrictive (IsB 1895, OkBr 1910) and taking up too much space – in fact half the floor area of the 15 x 9' Infant classroom (KgS 1914). Thus by the outbreak of the Great War they had become a thing of the past – to conform to new notions about space for 'activities' and movement for the little ones. Only East Harptree seemed to retain theirs till 1930.

Following the removal of the Galleries, there was an effort to make the long desks and forms more comfortable by adding backs, but these were in turn soon replaced by dual-desks, with chairs. These were often fixed desk-and-chair combinations with elaborate wrought iron frames, available from specific companies making fixtures for schools. Under the new 1902 County Councils dual desks were gradually introduced (Ctc 1913, SmB 1913, Kgs 1914, KM 1920, Wrl 1924, SmM 1931). The desired type of desk could be selected from catalogues, after which the goods would arrive by train and carrier. It is evident from the Logs that these desks were fixed to the floor, for when there was an event held in the school – a fund-raising concert or whist drive, public lecture or meeting, an annual social event such as for the Ancient Order of Shepherds, or Brewery – the school had to be closed to allow time for the desks to be moved.

Separate Classrooms: Initially, the original, large, single Hall was shared: little ones one end, older ones at the other. In the last quarter of the C19th when the 'play-way' ideas and methods of Froebel were gradually becoming known in village England, pressure increased to create a separate space for the 'little ones'. This resulted in the development of an additional classroom which was often added when it came to be recognised that these infants needed more space for the sand, water, and craft 'occupations' which were becoming a part of their curriculum.

From the 1890s, as Elementary schooling became compulsory and the minimum number of years slowly increased, even more classrooms were needed. Further, secondary schooling was becoming available and the names of individual architects were given more frequently but styles remained diverse. Further building was required by way of alterations as, by the beginning of the C20th, there was fierce competition for Diocesan Scholarships and for the new Council Special Places and Junior County Scholarships. To help the older ones prepare for these ordeals, separate classrooms were added for the top end of the school. Gradually, every class had its own separate classroom.

Separate classrooms became standard for all new-builds once the County Councils took control from 1902. Another flurry of re-builds was undertaken as Councils sought to improve the standard of some of the older buildings and again after the introduction of free secondary schooling in Butler's 1944 Act. Each county produced a glossy booklet showing the new look for the 'schools of the future' and indicating how buildings could be expanded as needed. The new Secondaries, in particular, were spectacular in the 'acres of glass' to make the buildings light and modern-looking. This gave way to a new style of build created to meet new teaching policies with the coming of the experiments of 'open-plan' and 'activity-based' schools in the 1960s. Not many Somerset schools took these options, but Somerton Wood Street (1964) and Radstock Junior (1966) adopted these ideas, as did Keinton Mandeville in their extension plans of the 1970s.

When it came to building changes throughout the C19th, it is not always possible to discover whether this meant a new room – for overflow classes might also be held in other local buildings – or alterations and divisions of existing rooms. In addition, the names and status of a school may change – a school may change status from National, to Board (from 1870) to Council School (from 1902) – but it is often not clear whether this entailed moving to a new building which could either be an already-existing one newly acquired, or, a new-build. Without back-up from Logs or Managers' Minutes, or archived architects' plans (which are not always available) it is difficult to be sure of the architectural changes of individual schools.

As to size, in some cases the Directories give the capacity in terms of numbers of pupils which can be accommodated, but sometimes numbers of average attendees are given. Although square footage per pupil changed over the years, attendance often bore little relation to capacity, as in some cases (of over-generous benefactors) capacity and expectations far exceeded reality. The opposite could also occur and overcrowding was sometimes identified as a reason for poor performance.

Playground: The last element in the external built environment – the playgrounds – began to receive some attention in the late C19th. In some areas, mostly urban, attention widened to include this space from the 1850s and a limited amount of equipment was gradually introduced. In many rural schools, 'playground' was too grand a name for the patch of rough yard which gave access to the school. However, at Somerton Monteclefe school, in 1873, they already had swings installed in their play area, while at the other end of the spectrum, Charlton Mackrell only mentions apparatus in 1954. By the 1890s the curriculum included various kinds of Drill which needed a flat space on which the children could exercise. Frequent complaints were made about the poor state of playgrounds preventing children from doing their Drill, or being unusable if the weather was either too wet and muddy, or too dry and dusty. Somerton schools were lucky: the playground was improved in 1904, but at Kingston Seymour it took from 1914, when the playground condition was first highlighted, till 1922 before contractors came to level it. Flag-poles were erected at Blagdon in 1909, and Kingsdon in 1916 - when the first mention of the school celebrating Empire Day is recorded.

An example from Coleford School, in the mining area of Somerset, provides an interesting illustration of some of the difficulties faced by Heads with regard to playgrounds. It also shows the variety of funding which the Head needed to muster in order to achieve a positive result for the children. The playground proved a long-standing challenge to the Head, Mr Bassett, who commentated wryly about its condition, '*Black dust blows: a pond after rain, a mire after frost, a sandy desert in summer. It is perhaps a good illustration for Geography*' (1899). After repeated requests for repairs so that the playground could be used for those parts of the curriculum which required outdoor space – several different kinds of Drill and Marching activities – he managed to secure £20 allocated by the Managers and a further £20 donated by a private neighbour who shared his concerns. Various short-term measures were taken, but it again needed urgent attention in 1925. We only get part of the drama, as the evidence comes from the Managers' Minute Book, not from the Head's Logs (unfortunately missing). Three years later, increasingly desperate letters from the Head in support of the need for action were sent to the National Society (to which the school had been affiliated for nearly a century) and also to the Diocesan Fund. Clearly appeals had already been made, as the Managers note receiving a letter from the High Court and the comment that nothing further can be done. By 1937 the Council had been persuaded to give half the cost of asphalting 400 square yards of playground surface (not all the area). The Managers agreed to sell War Stock to raise £22 10s in order to get the job done. Eight years later there are more discussions (was this for additional repairs, or had the main task still not been done?). Again, the only documentation is in the Managers' Minute Book. This example shows us the slow response, the long-drawn out nature of the problem and the persistence involved before obtaining appropriate action.

Offices: Last but not least, the dreaded 'offices', the term used for school toilets. These were usually 'down the end' as far removed from the main building as possible, but gradually they were modernised, crept closer, till they were finally enclosed within the main structure. We find much about smokey stoves as well as smelly toilets in the Log Books. To remind us of the low level of sanitary conditions we need look no further than a relatively recent Langport District Sanitation Report, for 1956, to find what provision existed only sixty years ago.

We find only Charlton Mackrell and Compton Dundon relied solely on well-water: the rest had piped water. In terms of sewage disposal, Charlton Mackrell used a ditch, while Hambridge, Isle Abbots and Monteclefe had a cesspool, 6 others had a septic tank, just 5 were on mains, and 9 schools do not give details. In terms of the toilets themselves, 5 had a 'flushing device', 10 used pails, 6 had troughs (for boys), while 4 had 'other'. HMI repeatedly called for offices to be cleansed, emptied more frequently, the contents mixed with ash (one caretaker asks permission to use the product as manure), leaking roofs repaired, worm-eaten seats replaced, screens erected, cubicle doors positioned... the list is endless. Where any of the offices were located in relation to the school building is not always given. Many of us can remember ourselves, or from parents' tales, the horror of trekking out to a dark dank shed.

Repairs: The Logs and Minute Books document the reports, comments, complaints and recommendations which provide interesting insights as to what was expected by the educational authorities regarding improvements in *lighting, heating, ventilation, the 'offices'* , and simple *lack of space.* As we shall see in Part IV, HMI frequently appear to back the Head in their struggle with penny-pinching Boards and their efforts to get more money for repairs, fixtures, or fittings.

iii. Other educational uses of local buildings

There were two other forms of education which was sometimes available in the villages in the late C19th. These were the Night Schools (sometimes called Evening Classes or Continuation Schools) and the Reading Rooms (often part of a Working Men's Club or, later, one of the political clubs). Such amenities were very important for two different groups of people: at first particularly for those who had never had a chance to attend school and, later, for those who wanted to continue, but may have needed to leave day school early to earn but could still attend after work to better themselves. As so often in the story of education, it was in the more 'nonconformist areas' that the highest numbers of these two forms of schooling took place.

Night Schools: In terms of buildings, Night School (or evening classes) often took place in the village school itself. In several schools Night School only took place during the winter, when agricultural work was less pressing. Hence, we find Night

Schools were held in Winsham (1813), Charlton Adam, Marston Magna, W Camel (in the 1830s); Templecombe (1846); in Westonzoy, Middlezoy, Othery, Edington in the 1860s. Most of these were on the Levels, prone to flooding and also predominantly agricultural in occupation, hence attendance was good in the winter – some came by boat! – but poor in summer. It seems probable that these classes were attended by those already working and who perhaps had not had the opportunity of attending the still new elementary schools. An examination of rare registers of Sunday Schools – which usually focused on teaching reading (of the Bible) gives interesting insights. One from Stoke-sub-Hamdon shows several older students in the 16-20 age range during the 1860s, though this decreases by the 1880s. We also know their occupations – mostly labourers, glovers, masons and some other artisans (sawyers, thatchers, smiths).

Other Central area villages offering Night Schools included Muchelney, Long Sutton, Charlton Mackrell, with Barton St David's on Thursdays only, all in the latter part of the C19th. Stoke-sub-Hamdon and Somerton Boys School also held Night Schools over a considerable period of time. In the east of the county Night Schools were held at Corton Denham, Shepton Montague and Paulton – run by Joseph Cross the grocer, while at Hinton St George it was run by J Holland a paperer-glazier. Night Schools can be found in the far western areas such as Nettlecombe. The mining areas, too, had several Night Schools: Oakhill British School held classes in 1863 three times a week, for which the 21 attendees paid 3d per week. These were continued under Headmaster Bright who gave 'a lucid Science class' (with few attendees) and also wood-carving (much better attended). Writhlington offered English and Arithmetic, and also monthly Lectures on topics such as *Dawn of Life* and *Paintings and Painters* in conjunction with the Victoria Rooms in Radstock. Nearby in Coleford, there also seems to have been a combination of weekly classes and monthly lectures.

From 1903 a further flurry of Night Schools opened with backing from the new County Committee for Education in Thurloxton, North Petherton, North Newton, Ashcot, Aller, Pitney, Huish Episcopi and Montacute. These were held twice a week for 1d a month to study Reading, Writing, Geography and Singing – this last was popular in many of the programmes. At Cannington the Night School became a Technical Evening Centre for the surrounding area. We do not often have access to the details of what was provided, but we have details and registers from Somerton Boys School for almost 30 years. Classes included Book-Keeping, Commercial Arithmetic, Mensuration, Rural Arithmetic, Shorthand and Geography. The courses were 100 hours. Night Schools were subjected to similar Inspections as regular Day Schools and students could also be entered for examinations. After 1900, Needlework and The Science of Everyday Things were added. We find that classes were vocationally orientated and were seen as 'continuation classes' where secondary schooling was still not available.

We can gain an idea regarding the costs of such classes to the students. At Horsington the school earned an additional £4 0s ½d from Evening Classes, (1872) from an attendance of over 40 i.e. 10s per pupil, though we do not know over how many weeks, but perhaps 1s a month, though for how many classes, we again do not know. This was a considerable outlay for these older students but it also reveals considerable dedication and commitment.

We also know the cost of hiring the school rooms: for the Main Hall Coleford charged 1s 6d for hire, for its cleaning another 1s 6d, plus 9d per fire, while the Classroom cost 1s to hire, 1s to clean and 9d per fire. The School Hall could be hired out for the annual meetings and dinners of local societies, choir meetings or lantern shows. But there were often problems, as in Writhlington. The caretaker complained bitterly when the rooms were left in a mess and furniture was even damaged. It happened more than once: a mixed blessing and hardly worth the income earned.

Two other national educational movements also had some representation in Somerset, but neither is recorded as using local school buildings. **Mechanics' Institutes** appeared in the eastern mining and manufacturing areas such as Frome (1852), Rode (1861), Shepton Mallet (1880). There was also a network of **Literary and Scientific Societies** which began earlier in the C19th but which made little impact in Somerset except in larger settlements (Wrington 1860-70s, Cheddar 1860-90s, Shepton Mallet and South Petherton 1860-90s). They were known to offer lectures on 'edifying subjects' and tended to attract the more genteel audiences, including women.

Reading Rooms were a further educational venture. They were usually separate, community buildings, often funded by a local benefactor, often in larger settlements. Some started remarkably early – like the one began by Thomas Poole in Nether Stowey in 1813, while another was established in Muchelney 1833 (by the Vicar and the Lord of the Manor) and another in Wellington in the same year. In general they were low, single-storey buildings as can still be seen at Merriot and Hinton St George (1880s). On the Mendips, at Cheddar and Wrington, Reading Rooms began in the 1860s which lasted between 20-30 years respectively; south-west of Taunton at Wiveliscombe the **Mutual Improvement Society** opened Rooms in 1866, while nearby Milverton waited till the Jubilee in 1897, and Bishop Lydeard delayed till the new century.

The spreading network of **Workingmen's Clubs** also made great efforts to support members, many of whom missed out on schooling as children. These facilities often included rooms for reading, lectures and meetings, smoking and sometimes billiards and were therefore intended to attract working men who, throughout the later C19th, became more politically aware and active, demanding increasing access to learning as well as leisure. These were established in Wrington (1863-1910), Castle Cary (1875-1914), Stoke-sub-Hamdon (1883), Coleford – in the Temperance Hall (1870s), Pilton (1894), as well as Stogumber (1894) where the United Counties Reading Room also opened. The Victoria Rooms at Radstock, funded by Lady Waldegrave, was a two-story building which housed a large upstairs room for hire for lectures or social events such as dances and, later, film shows.

In the last quarter of the C19th **political parties** began to sponsor such ventures rather than a personal patron – though often from the same social group. On the north-west coast, towns like Williton (1872) and Watchet (1883) opened Reading Rooms, as did the Conservative Club in 1897 and Liberal Club in 1919.

Finally, there are just a few examples of other education organisations: a **Ragged School** in Bridgwater 1860; **Bluecoat Charity Schools** in North Petherton founded by John Slade, also in Wells and Frome, and a **Red Maids** School in Bristol; **Factory Schools** at Milton Mills (1825) in Milton Clevedon, Pecking Mills in Evercreech (1861); a **Workhouse School** in Wincanton (1836-9), in High Ham and Langport from the mid C19th and, finally, on the north-west coast, a Work House (with school for inmates) having an edifice grandly designed by Sir Gilbert Scott in 1837 in Williton.

Teacher's Houses: These are the final pieces in the jigsaw of buildings serving educational purposes in a village. The importance of accommodation to attract teachers into the scattered villages was recognised and encouraged early on, by none less than the Privy Council in 1839. Indeed, many schools, as we have seen in the diagrams above, were built with an integral Teacher's House, or one adjacent to the school with a linking building. Some schools were built with a house close by which was used by the Teacher, or, an existing house, perhaps belonging to one of the Managers, was rented to an appointed teacher. Because of such instances it is not easy to be precise over which schools could offer accommodation. Certainly, not all schools had accommodation to offer. It seems that perhaps 65% of Exmoor schools may have had accommodation on offer, and the Levels regions – also with small isolated villages – may have had 50% of their schools with accommodation. However, in Somerton and in the eastern region this dropped to only around 30% with accommodation easily available. It would be interesting to speculate on what effect this had on recruitment and retention of staff.

Although the school buildings are of interest in themselves it is the impact on the teaching and learning within them by which they should be judged. But first, we need to investigate the teachers who worked in these buildings and see what changes in pedagogy occur and how this was accommodated (or not) in the alterations to the buildings we have just outlined – whether the buildings restricted, reflected or released teaching potential.

Chapter 6

Who Taught in the Schools: Training, Teachers and Tenure

We have seen how, under Rev John Poole's modified Lancaster-Bell system, young monitors were the mainstay of the teaching enterprise. Thus, by the beginning of the C19th, the *monitorial system* was firmly established and was to last for 100 years. As monitors, young people could be appointed at 12 years old, having just completed a minimum of Standard IV (later, V) and could then be set to supervise, hear and test children of a younger age. For as long as the purpose of education remained that of instilling discipline, sobriety and (very) basic literacy, this arrangement might have sufficed – and was certainly cheap. It was an approach based on the inculcation of would-be teachers into the 'techniques of the system' which were to be strictly adhered to without deviation. It was thus believed to be 'foolproof' and therefore suitable for the general low-calibre of the monitors recruited. Further confidence in the system was derived from the fact that monitors could be overseen by a single master who patrolled the large school hall.

However, England was considered to be far behind her Continental neighbours (Rich 1972) and also Scotland. By the 1840s, David Stow's new '*simultaneous system*' of teaching and learning was gaining ground. Innovations in his Glasgow Normal Seminary [an establishment which aimed to set 'norms' for educational method and achievement] had tried an alternative. This new 'system' rejected the method of small groups and rote-learning led by young monitors, in favour of single classes of children (approx 40-50) all taught, together, by an adult. Thus a number of children could be taught simultaneously by its own teacher. Not only did this 'class-based' system have architectural implications (as we saw in the last chapter) but it also needed more and differently trained teachers. The '*simultaneous*' method came to be associated with 'chalk-and-talk' delivery and lasted well into the C20th. Stow also emphasised the need for developing the culture and skills of the teachers rather than just relying on inculcating any one organisation's 'techniques' for teaching and managing.

It was to this challenge of teacher training that **James Kay-Shuttleworth** (later made a baronet) turned on his appointment as the first secretary to the Committee for Education in the Privy Council. In his evidence to the Select Committee on Education he stated that '*teachers from Scotland appear to be preferable to any others I have seen*'. Not content with only viewing home-grown efforts, during 1838-9 he travelled across Europe to investigate other ways of training teachers and was particularly struck by the Dutch method. There, candidates were apprenticed from the age of 14-18: they assisted in school classrooms by day and received instruction in the evenings in preparation for State qualifying exams in all Elementary subjects and in the 'practice of teaching'. On his return to England he was determined to address the needs of teacher supply.

Pressures for education expansion during the third quarter of the C19th, were two-fold: political, as reflected by Robert Lowe's comment on the need '*to educate our masters'* – (especially around the time of the 1867 extension of male suffrage); also economic, as articulated by William Forster - introducing his 1870 Education Act - when he asserted that '*upon the speedy provision of elementary education depends our industrial prosperity*'. By this time, businesses increasingly needed apprentices who had better numeracy and literacy skills. However, in rural areas, there was still lingering doubt as to the need for any education at all. Indeed, several local farmers continued to be reported as believing that there was already too much of it around and were recorded as continuing to be suspicious of the 'ill effects' of education, which encouraged youngsters not to want to work as their forefathers had, but to have unsuitable aspirations. A local farmer quoted in Kingsdon's School Log (Kgd 1868) claimed to prefer to employ boys who had not been to school: although he did not mind reading and writing, he disliked too much education.

With the increasing numbers of elementary schools there was pressure to improve, first of all, the quantity of teachers and, secondly, the quality. At the time, quality referred in particular to the social class of recruits. Nevertheless, there was still a need to try to raise the standard of the teachers themselves, in terms of their educational attainment and their knowledge of teaching. Thirdly, there was a need to increase the general status and standing of teachers through increasing the attractiveness of the profession in terms of pay, conditions and, eventually, pensions. (In the 1840s a salary for an elementary teacher – drawn mostly from the 'lower classes of society' – was less than that of an able-bodied agricultural labourer.) These three elements were clearly inter-related: each in turn was targeted and re-visited in an on-going spiral over the next decades. Until changes occurred that no longer equated schooling with rote learning nor held cost as the main criteria of success, quality was always sacrificed to quantity. To tackle the quality, there needed to be a significant expansion of secondary education to raise the level of monitors and of trainee teachers. Many monitors saw their position as a way of obtaining an extended education: secondary establishments were few and invariably charged fees – a burden few could afford. The lack of a network of secondary schools continued to limit the recruitment of teachers throughout the century.

i. Quantity: The expansion of training facilities and the issue of their control. As we have seen (Ch. 4) pressure had been mounting to allow state funding to improve the educational facilities for the poor. Eventually, the principle of state involvement for the Education of the Whole People was contentiously agreed in 1833: government grants first became available to schools, and with state support extended to teacher training in 1839 a new era could begin.

Steps had already been taken by the two main Societies – in 1808 the Lancastrian (British) Society had set up **Borough Road Residential College** in Southwark for boys and another for girls (which moved to Stockwell in 1861). They added an Infants College with the **Home and Colonial College** in 1837. Also, 1840 saw the opening of the British Society College of **St Mark's Chelsea**, which was augmented by a **Central School** for training in **Wells**, Somerset. Bell's National Society responded with a Men's College at **Barrington Bishop Auckland**, near Durham in 1810 and, two years later, with **Baldwin Gardens** off Grey's Inn Road for Men (moving to Westminster in 1832) and in 1841 **Whitelands** for Women.

Following Sir James Kay-Shuttleworth's European visits, he founded a new college, **St John's Battersea** – a personal, private, experimental venture to implement his own ideas. St John's opened for trainee-teachers aged 13, for a three-year course of instruction in the training school, followed by two years as supervised pupil-teachers in a village school for 3 hours a day, then two years as an uncertified Assistant Teacher. At first, 24 working-class boys enrolled. If successful they would receive certificates to teach paupers in 'schools of industry'. Sir James Kay-Shuttleworth's aim was *to combine religious fervour, scholarly ardour, professional expertise and personal humility* (Dent 1977). Professor Maurice of King's College, London – who gave great support to girls' education in general and to Queen's College in particular which opened in 1848 – claimed, *'Teachers in a school aim to impart information; Teachers in a College must lead their pupils to an appreciation of principles'* (Kaye 1972). While in 1874 Joseph Payne, first Professor of Education at the College of Preceptors, declared, *'Education was first a science, a branch of psychology, which could be studied inductively or deductively and, second, an art which is efficient or inefficient in proportion to the educator's conscious knowledge of its principles'* (Gordon 1985). No wonder the students were sometimes accused of becoming cocky!

However, the goal of two- or three-year courses was an impossible expense for many students. Fortunately, another victory was achieved in 1846 when it was agreed to offer student maintenance grants. In fact most stayed only 3-6 months due to lack of funds, poor health and also the incapacity for sustained study, which they had never experienced. The young recruits had only ever known a life of rote-learning and had never acquired the habit of reading for study. There was little done to overcome this barrier till secondary education had expanded sufficiently – something which only began to happen in the C20th.

Rare exceptions of secondary schooling, for girls, who supplied most of the teaching positions, were pioneered by **Miss Frances Buss** at the North London College and, mostly for middle-classes ladies, Cheltenham Ladies' College whose Head, in 1858, was **Miss Dorothea Beale**. The latter College had a separate department for the training of teachers, mostly intended for its own students. From 1885 it developed into St Hilda's House, for Post-School Students wanting to train for Elementary, Secondary and Kindergarton schools. These institutions are mentioned by some of the Somerset teachers on their appointment to local village schools. In addition, the College offered vocational courses for Librarians, Sunday School teachers and Musician-organists, often with skills for conducting church choirs (Faithful 1924). These additional accomplishments were often required of teachers, especially in the smaller rural schools where such skills were scarce.

In passing, it is interesting to note that another form of teaching – that of being a governess – was also receiving attention through attempts to improve both quality and status. Since Governesses were associated with 'a better class of people', efforts to support them began a little earlier. The Governesses Mutual Association was founded in 1829, and the Governesses Benevolent Institution in 1843 with a fund-raising dinner the following year, at which the speaker was Charles Dickens. Also, from 1846, exams were introduced, supervised by the College of Preceptors (Kaye 1972).

Success in annual Training College exams could bring **qualified teacher status** with a certificate graded as First Class (Year 1), Second Class (Year 2), and Third Class (Year 3). Each year earned an increase in the basic salary. The Colleges were also funded by annual government grants – £20 for Year 1, £25 for Year 2, and £30 for Year 3 (Rich 1972). Further encouragement was also needed: for example, the Battersea College housekeeper accounts show £2 10s for wines and brandy given to students who were *'low and nervous'* at the time of the examination and inspection!

By the 1850s 30 colleges had been established: 19 were supported by the National Society, 5 by the British Society – including Bristol, Brecon (moving to Swansea), 2 Congregational ones in London, 1 Wesleyan College and, finally, 1 Roman Catholic one. The National Society opened Colleges in several Dioceses: 1840 Norwich and Chester; in 1841 **Salisbury** for Women and **Winchester** for Men, and St John's

York; 1853 **St Matthias, in Fishponds Bristol**, followed by one in **Exeter**, and an Institute for School Mistresses – later Derby Diocesan College. The closest colleges are often cited in connection with the teachers found in the Somerset village schools. [Ox-bridge were not (yet) interested in popular education or teacher training.]

Thus, provision for expanding the quantity of teachers was now in place but, whilst access to secondary education was limited, other ways of improving the quality of teachers were needed.

ii. Quality: Again, it was on Sir James Kay-Shuttleworth's initiative that a new 'pupil-teacher' training scheme was introduced in 1846. The major problem of the shortage of secondary schools from which a pool of possible recruits could be drawn for College training was to be partially addressed by this scheme. This could be done by bridging the gap between the educational level to which teachers should aspire and that attained at the end of their elementary schooling. But, as it often replaced secondary education it could be said that the scheme actually delayed its development.

At first, like the Monitors**, pupil-teachers** could be recruited immediately on completing elementary school, often at 13 years old. Unlike the Monitors (who could leave with one month's notice and were paid a pittance of up to 3s a week, the pupil-teacher began an apprenticeship of 5 years, whereby they were to teach up to 25 scholars in school for no more than 20 hours a week and were to receive up to 1½ hours of daily instruction from the Head Teacher – who was paid £5 for one pupil-teacher, £9 for 2, £12 for 3. Students were expected to keep a record book of both their own studies and the Master's instruction, which was checked by HMI who examined them. Some Heads preferred to employ pupil-teachers (rather than more qualified staff) so they could benefit from these extra payments. The Managers seemed to have preferred it, too, as it reduced the salary bill. The pupil-teachers were to be paid £10 in their first year and an extra £2 10s for each of the four subsequent years. Annual exams had to be passed by the pupil-teachers when the Inspectors called to examine the whole school. In 1848, at the first oral examinations, Inspectors were advised to be *'as pleasant as possible'* and *'by their nods and becks and wreathed smiles to entice reluctant pedagogues into the examination room'!* (Rich 1972).

When the apprenticeship was completed the pupil-teacher had three main options. First, the pupil-teacher could apply for a Queen's Scholarship to become a **candidate teacher** and then attend a Training College, with a grant of £20 pa, to become a **certified and trained teacher**. A second possibility was that of self-study for the same qualification but by taking annual written exams in all the *curriculum subjects* at local centres, with the addition of *Knowledge of Methods*, whilst continuing to work – and earn – as an **uncertified assistant teacher** in an Elementary school, and aiming to become a **certified** but untrained teacher. Thirdly, for those who could not gain access to a College, could not afford or want to, there was the alternative of becoming – and remaining - an **uncertified assistant teacher.** The results of these examinations led to teachers being qualified under a variety of different Articles which led to complex shades of differentiation in status and pay. These could be always be improved by further subsequent exams. Thus in-school training was a long-term commitment for those who wanted to pursue a career: others were content with the minimal uncertified assistant status.

To follow the efforts to develop and improve both the supply and standards of teachers we can turn to the **Newcastle Commission**, set up to look into the workings of the developing education system and find ways to expand *'a sound and cheap'* system of education. The eventual Report led to the **Revised Code of 1862,** already mentioned in Ch. 4. From now on the government would deal with schools only and not pupil-teachers. This led to each pupil-teacher having to negotiate their own pay and conditions with their own set of school managers, potentially leading to widespread abuse. Grants were paid to the school, not to the pupil-teacher. These were estimated on the basis of exam results, the number of 'special subjects' taught (over and above the basics), and the number of pupil-teachers employed (supposedly in order to encourage schools to take pupil-teachers but, often, employed *instead of* better qualified – more expensive – teachers). HMI Reports which encouraged Managers to employ more qualified staff to support a Head and raise standards within a school were often ignored (as revealed in several Log Books, particularly from Somerton Boys School). A common impact was that the number of pupil-teachers applying to Colleges halved (from 617 in 1860, to 371 in 1866), and Masters' salaries dropped (from £95 in 1860, to £89 in 1866) (Rich 1972).

The **Cross Commission** set up to review the effect of Forster's 1870 Act, found that 9 out of 10 elementary teachers had served as pupil-teachers and most had had little subsequent education, while the 1876 Committee of Council reported that 25% of pupil-teachers arrived at colleges without having received the required hours of instruction from their Head (Rich 1972). A break-through came in 1880 when new **Day Centres** were established. These Centres were usually linked to a local University, to which groups of School Boards were expected to send their pupil-teachers. This relieved the Heads of their duty to shoulder the full burden of training and, hopefully, improved standards. It was intended to give coherence to the 'science of education'. Heads in the focus schools never, with two exceptions, mention the training which they gave to their own pupil-teachers: perhaps it was not a priority. Log Books regularly mention their pupil-teachers having leave of absence to attend the local Centres - particularly for their annual examinations. Thus, instead of relying on Heads for tuition, student-teachers attended as part-time students, at Centres in Langport, Huish Taunton, Weston, Bridgwater, Bruton or Radstock which were linked to local Universities – Bristol University department from 1891, also Exeter College from 1902. Attendance was expected to last for 2 and then, from 1892, for 3 years. Inevitably, travel could be a problem for rural students, unless near one of a growing set of new rail-links. Students were also sent for 'observation periods' in nearby schools. For example, by the turn of the century we find that Somerton teachers could, by rail, reach Bruton School and Keinton School where they were sent to gain more ideas. For those in more isolated areas it was still a real struggle.

Simultaneously, the educational groundwork for any would-be student-teachers was also improving. First, the school leaving age slowly rose (to 13 in 1880, 14 in 1902) as did the starting age for pupil-teachers which was raised to 14 in 1877, to 15 and then 16 in 1903, but the number of years for their apprenticeship was reduced to four. Secondly, some form of additional education could be gained from the new Higher-grade Classes (Standards VI and VII) and also evening Continuation Schools. These were for older students who chose to extend their schooling and, also, for adults who had missed out in their youth. These were also part of the focus of the **Bryce Committee** on Secondary Education in 1895, which not only promised expansion of secondary schools per se but also retained the support for Continuation Schools as 'end-on' schools to supplement the lack of purpose-built secondary schools, particularly in rural areas. Standards slowly moved ever upwards. From 1907 all students destined to be Elementary teachers were required to have a secondary education – when Bursaries became available for student-teachers (the term pupil-teacher was officially dropped) between 16 and 18 years to enable them to stay in education and then train (Horn 1989).

The final break with the religious domination of training came in 1907 with the setting up of institutions to be run by the new Local Education Authorities.

However, by 1914 only 20 of the 146 LEAs had taken advantage of this. At the same time, in the denominational colleges, up to 50% of recruits were expected to be non-denominational. After 1923, a Secondary School Certificate became the new requirement for entry to teacher training, but secondary education did not become free till the **Butler Education Act** of 1944. By 1942 the 100 Training Institutions together with 11 universities were formally grouped into Area Training Organisations (ATOs), the Somerset one being centred on Bristol. This University had for several decades already been conducting annual in-service courses for local teachers in many outreach bases.

Further progress was made in 1951 when the entry qualification for teacher training required five passes in the new GCE. At the same time 'the Pledge' was abolished – this had started in 1911 whereby students were contracted to teach for a specified number of years in return for a four- year grant to train at a University Department of Education, thus giving security of grant and job. The extending of a Teaching Certificate from 2 to 3 years in 1960 was a potential deterrent for those with limited financial support. Yet money and opportunity became less of a barrier after the **Robbins Report** of 1963 which supported a massive expansion of higher education (from 11 to 21 Universities) with no fees and with the promise of maintenance grants. In the 1960s teacher training courses increased from a 2- to 3-year certificate and became an all-graduate profession in the 1970s after another shake-up. Finally, of the 160 independent colleges, 25% were to remain independent, 25% to merge with a local University, 25% with a Polytechnic and 25% with other independent colleges into larger units. This brought even more colleges under government supervision.

iii Social Status and Standing

a. Character and Class. Education was always considered a moral enterprise and teachers therefore needed to set a moral example. The teacher's qualities and character, not qualifications, were considered of greater importance. In the C18th applications for a teaching post had to be supported by 'local people of standing' to vouch not only for the good character of an applicant, but also for his or her religious attendance. As we have seen from the formulaic letters of application to the Bishop to gain a licence to teach (Ch. 1), the support was first about moral and spiritual suitability and, secondly, the merits of their teaching skill.

Kay-Shuttleworth, in planning Battersea College, wanted *'to inspire students with a sympathy for their own class; to implant ideas of honour in rescuing the poor from the misery of ignorance; to wean them from the influence of personal competition dependant on a commercial world which leads to sordid aims... and to seek to heal the mental and moral diseases of society'* (Rich 1972). In 1846 the officers of the **Whitelands** Training Institute for Women in London, believed that *'a young person is not fit for training unless there be reason for believing her to be influenced by religious motives'*. Soon afterwards HMI Rev Cook declared that *'elementary teachers were to be the educators of the mothers of peasantry, of domestic servants, of the wives and sisters of small shopkeepers and tenant farmers [therefore] their training should be of a thoroughly practical nature'* (Horn 1985). Several suspicions were harboured concerning these training-college girls: Pamela Horn (1989) quotes a view that *'a girl comes up to a training college* [from the lower classes] *and comes back exceedingly conceited'*, hence, *'all pretension is to be crushed and checked without mercy'!* Certainly, in the early days, the additional education received in these Colleges led to over 50% of trainees not taking up posts in the Schools for the Poor as intended, but either going to more middle-class schools or into non-teaching jobs (Rich 1972).

A second feature of the effort to improve the quality of teacher recruits was its class bias. The Royal Commission of 1887 suggested trying to recruit more middle-class teachers 'to raise the tone'. In 1873 Bishop Otter College in Chichester had been set up to attract entrants from the middle-classes, particularly daughters of the clergy, medical men, officers and some traders, but admitted that there was a high percentage of orphans, which led partly to a large drop-out rate (Horn 1989). However, any attempt to attract the more middle-class student did not necessarily mean that such students, when qualified, would want to teach the children to be found in elementary village schools! An observation in Mercy Grogan's book *How Women May Earn a Living* published in the 1880s, states '*I have no doubt that ladies would find the class of children they would be required to teach a great trial ... and in all probabilities* [they would] *prove a considerable shock to the sensibilities of those ladies who come into contact with them for the first time.*' She added, however, that teaching could offer '*opportunities for working-class girls to rise and to gain financial reward, the merit of respectability and some personal independence*' (emphasis added, quoted in Horn 1985).

b. Conditions. Being a low-status and low-paid profession, teaching quickly became dominated by girls and women. The argument for lower pay was based on the fact that women ate less than men and they could do their own domestic chores! They were therefore suitably inexpensive to provide the minimum education for the labouring poor and would remain so until the Equal Pay League of 1904 began its efforts to improve the situation (Horn 1985). Despite the efforts made to demand a higher academic level for recruits, the attempts to achieve the desired improvement in terms of social class were less successful. Nevertheless, improvements in academic quality did gradually help to overcome the low status from which teaching suffered in its association with specific gender, class and attainment.

Before taking up a teaching post intending females needed to know that even in 1902 guidelines for female teachers (in towns, but probably for their rural sisters as well) were very strict and included directives on the following lines:

1. *You will not marry during your period of contract*
2. *You should command respect from your pupils at all times*
3. *You should be home between 8pm and 6am unless attending a school function*
4. *You should not go beyond the town limits without the permission of the governors*
5. *You cannot ride in a carriage with a man other than your father or brother*
6. *You cannot visit ice-cream parlours*
7. *You will dress in plain colours of grey or black, and your dress must not be more than 1" above the ankles....*

Having survived the rigors of training, being a teacher in a small rural school could rarely have been any easier. Imagine the life for a young single woman, alone and without family or friends nearby. To overcome this several teachers moved to their post with a parent or sister. Socially, a teacher's status was very ambiguous. Certainly, the teacher had had a little more education than many of his/her neighbours, but they remained caught between two worlds in a 'socially inferior' position in relation to others who might wield some influence in a small community, such as the priest or the local landowners or even local farmers and businessmen.

Life must have been lonely and there are few examples of teachers leaving to get married. While in many occupations it was disallowed, or, at the very least frowned upon, there seems to have been some leniency in rural schools. A few cases are noted in the Log Books: amongst other examples, an existing teacher got married in 1887 and moved away with her husband (OkBr); but Miss Harrison became Mrs Eyers and continued (SmM 1917); another, in 1931, had to absent herself under the Married Women's Regulations while, in a later case in 1958 (Ctc) a teacher, having already worked for 25 years, married a Manager and left – though she probably gratefully retired. Gradually, changing social attitudes, enabled teachers to continue – even if married, owing to the shortage of men (particularly after the First World War when, according to Bagley (1969), by 1917, 90% of male training-college students had signed up).

However, we find that in rural areas expediency often took precedence over distantly designed regulations. Widows were accepted, as were wives of known respectable villagers (often the shopkeeper's, postmaster's or blacksmith's wife), who would 'step in' when other applicants were not suitable. Wives of the Headmaster were often employed as sewing mistresses, or mistresses of the infant class. This is particularly noticeable in more remote areas.

Extra duties were frequently included as a condition of employment and were thus sometimes an integral part of being a teacher, such as playing the organ or conducting the church choir. Some masters attended coroner's sessions, acted as jurors, and were secretary to local organisations. Even as late as 1891 an NUT survey found that a third of teachers were required to do such extra duties. Such duties were officially dropped in 1903 (Horn 1989). Many teachers even today undertake to run school choirs, clubs and sports teams in out-of school hours and it is 'part of the job', though clarity on contractual hours is streamlining the issues. Some may still additionally choose to be committee members in local organisations.

It was not only women who found life in the village schools difficult. Head James Cook at Blagdon comments, Sept 27th 1880, '*The labour of teaching boys and girls what they ought to have learned at 5 years is immense*'. (The Heads usually took the older children). When he resigned in May 1883 he notes, '*I observe from the papers, that a Master* [in rural Lincolnshire] *has committed suicide through over-strain and I can truthfully say that I and all the teachers in the neighbourhood are daily suffering from the same pressure. Teachers are expected to perform miracles*'.

From another rural county, Yorkshire, HMI Swinburne's *Memories* noted, in 1881, how in such areas '*Isolation prevented, in many cases, any advancement; teachers knew no other methods but their own; there was no meeting of teachers; no learning from one another*' (published c. 1912). For this reason he instituted a Library of Books for teachers to share. The books were sent from a depot and circulated for a month to each participating school which had paid 2s per year for the loan of 24 books: supportive wealthy individuals gave money for their purchase. This scheme was later imitated by the National Union of Teachers, originally founded as the union of Elementary Teachers in 1871 – in the same year that Maria Grey founded the Union of Women Teachers. These organisations emerged, in part, to overcome this very isolation and to provide a forum to share ideas, and also, to articulate demands concerning conditions. Just four years later, the Association of Head Mistresses began. Each of these organisations helped to raise the profile of the teaching profession and overcome some of the isolation. Around the turn of the century, some Somerset School Logs have entries concerning staff having permission to attend a local meeting of teachers, more often Sunday School teachers, but at least an opportunity to share similar concerns.

With reference to the nature of the training being offered to teachers, Swinburne noted in 1898, '*The prominence now accorded to methods etc. is fully appreciated by managers and teachers, who, recognizing that the so-called 'results' systems* [referring to the payment-by-results introduced in the Revised Code 1862] *has done its work, are now loyally advancing to the higher state of things now attainable... The new system which carries one step further the principle of self-help (the soul of true teaching) by practically making the teacher his own examiner*'. Later, he added, '*Deliver us from Fads*' - as he describes the rural Head needing to be a one-man-band, desperately trying to keep up with the 'methods' and 'crazes': '*A master, magnificent at military drill is black-listed ... because he is not up to date with the latest physical drill manual; or a mistress, splendid at her work, girds herself for double-digging'.* He makes a heart-felt cry, asking *'when will they learn not to cut the rural cloth with urban scissors'*?

iv. Training of teachers.
a. Theories and Methods.
Exactly which 'methods' were taught is difficult to pin down. It is evident that key reformers, HMIs and other public education figures, visited countries such as Holland and Germany in their efforts to search for answers to the needs for improved schooling. While they became familiar with western European ideas, only later did they become re-conversant with eastern European educationalists such as the C17th Czech Comenius (who had toured and given talks in England) and, much later, the Russian educationists such as Makarenko (1888-1939) or Vygotsky (1896-1934) whose works were not translated till the 1960s, but which then confirmed and extended ideas coming from Dewey in America.

Innovative ideas based on the methods of the German Froebel (1782-1852) had been introduced in the 1840s and the work of Swiss Pestalozzi (1746-1827) was translated into English in the 1880s - both focusing on Infants. At about the same time, the work of the German philosopher Herbart (1776-1841) came to be known and admired. The Herbartian 5-step approach was an innovation for school instruction (preparation, presentation, association, formulation and application) and his notion of the 'concentrated curriculum' (focusing on the basics) was also favoured by many. This was in contrast to a broader curriculum based on five 'areas of experience' as advocated in some 'radical' circles. However, these ideas were mostly only applied in the elite schools and training departments for example, pioneering Miss Beale (Cheltenham) – where some Somerset teachers were trained – and Miss Buss (North London School for Girls). Many new ideas were propagated in the inter-war years such as Montessori's (1870-1952) *Method for kindergarten Children*, promoted through a first Conference in 1919, Godwin-Curwin's *Sol-fa* system for teaching Music continued – already gaining ground in the 1880s, and Dalcroze's *Eurythmics* (music and movement) was introduced in 1923. The new century also saw interest in the work of the Swiss education philosopher, Piaget (1896-1980), whose classification of the stages of child development influenced the new child-centred approach for younger learners.

The range of texts with which trainees needed to become familiar for each class included *The Book Cards of Alphabet* which taught the combination of vowels and consonants in the lowest class; the *Second Book* which taught reading by the syllabic method at the second stage/class; and the *Bible* from which lessons were given on the Sermon on the Mount, Parables, Miracles and Discourses, as well as key stories from the Old Testament. Having watched a lesson at Stow's Glasgow Normal Seminary, the local HMI praised the 'inductive questioning', though felt there was too much 'simultaneous answering' [choral response] which 'dims individual responsibility'. Stow commented, *'The questions pump the water and the ellipsis* [final condensed summary] *directs its course. The Master is the filter who returns the information in a pure form for all'* (Rich 1972).

At Kay-Shuttleworth's Experimental College at St John's Battersea, in the 1840s, the **oral teaching mode** [lectures] dominated, as students had little idea how to use books for self-study and there were few books for them to use. He believed that the aim should be to provide moral education and professional training in the art of method and principles of practical teaching. He was convinced that the drudgery of teaching the lower classes could only be carried out by those with a strong vocation, but feared that a little learning would create empty pride and that intellectual training might sow seeds of discontent. Thus the cure was religious training and a Spartan life style. Kay-Shuttleworth claimed that the spirit of service was stronger on the Continent and that (as at Borough Road) the aim was to keep trainees busy from morning till night – with their studies, their classroom work, in the garden (where self-sufficiency was the goal), as well as in their religious devotions (Rich 1972).

Between 1840 and 1860, the new Colleges had already introduced the study of the **Science of Education** consisting of three key components: knowledge of human faculties and their development; knowledge of different systems and methods of teaching; and the history of education. Method lectures, however, often suffered the *'curse of formalism and terminology'*; students were forced to memorise chunks of lectures, using contrasting terms such as introduction / recapitulation, educe / deduce, synthetic / analytic techniques, elicitation and the Socratic mode, elliptical (summary) vs diacritical (comparative, showing distinctions). Let's hope they did not use these terms in class.

There was an ambitious programme covering child development, comparative studies of Continental and English schooling as well as details of the experience of the United Kingdom. All this was alongside the trainee's own education and classroom practice. Colleges differed markedly in the proportion of time devoted to **classroom practice**. This was partly owing to the lack of good 'model' or 'practice' schools and partly the sheer logistics of organising it. The Education Committee of the Privy Council, in 1855, reported the following diversity in hours devoted to practical classroom work:

Home and Colonial	340 hrs	Norwich	148 hrs
Whitelands	340	Brighton	178
York and Ripon	245	Cheltenham	80
Bishop's Stortford	240	Salisbury	70
Derby	no returns	Bristol	no returns

There were also attempts to evaluate the impact of training. Figures from the Newcastle Commission (1861) implied that the more *trained* teachers in a school the more chance of being *Fair*:

49% of *Fair* schools had trained teachers	39% of *Fair* Schools had none
27% of *Inferior* schools had trained teachers	58% of *Inferior* Schools had none

By the 1890s an account of a small training venture at Newnham describes 3 staff: a maid, housekeeper and one tutor who created a new course and taught psychology, logic, history of education, methods of teaching, theories of discipline and school management (with discussion of real problems), hygiene and speech production. One text book was available, by Fitch, which advised, *'Never tell a class what they can tell you'*. Students gave one half-hour practical lesson a week to 20 pupils followed by **The Criticism Lesson** (Hughes 1912).

b. Training in the hands of the Head. We can occasionally glean insights as to the training of the Pupil-Teachers from some of the school **Log Books** filled in by the Headteacher, each day. These Logs were kept very idiosyncratically and details are not consistent. However, Mr Hewitt, Head of Somerton Free School for Boys 1891-1900, gives us details of the lessons given, as well as some comments on the progress of his pupil-teachers! The lessons given usually covered two different curricula areas in each one-hour meeting: e.g.

> Algebra and Euclid, Scripture and History, Grammar with Analysis and Parsing, Arithmetic and Geometry, Geography of Britain and of N. America, Physiography, English History, Map Drawing, Recitation, General Exam Work, and, very occasionally, Knowledge of Methods.

The annual exams gradually covered each of these subjects. We do not know if the lessons were delivered in class lesson-size portions and thus served as a basis for subsequent lesson plans, or, as subject-based lectures for the students' further education. The Log Book reveals that pupil-teachers seem to have taken different subjects on the same examination date. Perhaps they could elect the order in which they took the subjects, or retook a subject to improve their marks.

These lessons given by the Head generally lasted one hour, before school from 6.45am. It seems some students must have complained to the HMI, for a subsequent Report from HMI suggested changing the time. Lessons then began at 7.00am! Later, during the winter of 1898, lessons were conducted after school hours. In June 1896 the Head recorded *'I now require Teachers to get ready before school hours, to prepare equipment and to do any writing on the blackboard for dictation'* [copying?]. He frequently bemoaned the fact of his own heavy teaching load and wished for a reduction so *'I could give more time to supervision'*, and *'I could do more if not tied to continuous teaching'*. He also complained of the *lack of effort* and *little punctuality* of his pupil-teachers. Once, he found that pupil-teacher Palmer was doing his 'private studies' during his class with the older pupils – who even helped him! He also found that some individuals were *slack at keeping their Record Books* – presumably their lesson notes and/or plans for the lessons they prepared and taught. Given that during the Headship of Mr Hewitt he was the only qualified teacher in a school of over 100 boys he clearly depended on the support from his pupil-teachers: twice HMI Reports remind him that *'Pupil-teachers should not teach more than 50% of the time i.e. for not more than 20 hours a week'!* There are also rare insights into his own methods and expectations of teaching. He often commented that classrooms are *too noisy*. This had a practical impact for there were multiple classes in the single large Hall: a partition was a much later improvement. He also commented that *'there is a need of keeping the interest of the boys'* in order to improve their work and behaviour – and therefore reduce noise. A very brief reference by another Head, at Blagdon 1897 merely recorded, *'I have written out the Lessons to be given by the teachers according to my notes'*. This was not what was intended as 'training', yet was probably far from unique.

In terms of pupil-teachers, Mr Webber of Coleford in the 1920s noted that monitors did not know how to study – another confirmation of the lack of training in reading for study and the skills of note-taking to collect, collate and use information. It was decided to introduce Criticism Lessons every Friday. Teaching skills were directly promoted by the next Head, Mr Selby, who demonstrated 'questioning techniques', and probably other 'method skills' too. These are the only clear indications of Heads undertaking their training role towards their pupil-teachers.

c. In-service opportunities: Qualifications could also be upgraded, during the teacher's career. Several organisations emerged to help and support teachers, which would also help to overcome the isolation and insecurity mentioned earlier. We find several examples in the mining area: Writhlington teachers attended The Radstock District Teachers Association on 1908, a Wesleyan Teachers' Conference was held in Frome in 1932 which Holcombe teachers attended, a Head's Study Circle met at Coleford in 1933. These are the only references to locally run professional groups found in any of the Logs, other than meetings for Sunday School teachers to which many of the younger staff also belonged. Thus permission was given for some or all staff, to attend such meetings (SmWE 1877, IsB 1897, 1900). These, as noted at Cutcombe (1884), were mainly summer social events, but at least they allowed teachers to get together and exchange common concerns, while enjoying an outing.

From 1890, teachers were commonly required to attend good neighbouring schools 'to get more ideas'. This was regularly made possible for those taking up a new post and also sometimes to 'refresh' or develop a teacher. It was a small step which might overcome the isolation of staff and encourage the exchange of ideas. It was not until the inter-war years that an extended period of practical school experience was a regular part of College training programmes. At the Somerton Boys Free School we find that from 1929 to 1959 several students from nearby colleges attended for their 'school practice': from St Luke's Exeter, Cheltenham Training College and the post-war Emergency Training College at Redlands, Oakley College and St Matthias Diocesan College in Fishponds – the last three were all in Bristol. The arrival of students, and sometimes their tutors, must have contributed to raising awareness and hopefully standards amongst the staff.

Another way of improving qualifications was by taking the *in-service* route with courses by post, or in person, whilst teaching. We do sometimes find mention of the Head taking a day off to attend an examination centre, or an HMI confirming a new status as a result of such studies.

More formal in-service training, for existing staff already in-post, began in the mid 1930s, in the form of annual Refresher Courses. This meant that the school had to be closed for 3 days while staff left for either Bristol, Taunton, Clacton, Weston or Bath. In addition, post WW II, in response to the many new initiatives being introduced, Heads reported going to meetings for information and discussion of the latest ideas, for example in 1949 the Cutcombe Head went to hear about Methods of Teaching Arithmetic in March and, in April, about Methods of Teaching Reading, with many more to follow no doubt.

v. Who were the teachers?

a. Individual Teacher Careers. Despite trying to create a 'career structure', pupil-teachers appear to have come and gone frequently. Some left in the hopes of better employment elsewhere, in factories, farms or as domestic servants. Some 'were needed at home' and returned to look after remaining siblings. Still others were withdrawn for medical reasons – severe deafness or difficulties with eyesight. Some just left, perhaps they got married or because they did not want to go on battling against the conditions and difficulties that teaching involved.

We can trace the fortunes of some of these aspiring teachers through the Log Books of local schools. Somerton, for example, had two parallel schools, the older Free School for Boys and the Monteclefe School for Girls and, also, the West End School for Infants. Some details gleaned from the Head's Log Books illustrate some successes and struggles of pupil-teachers in the following table:

1868 1873	Miss MA Hiscock	Pupil-Teacher Gains 1st class scholarship --> leaves to attend College
1871 1873	Miss Bishop	Candidate for Pupil-teacher Removed owing to deafness
1873	Miss Annie Bennett	Pupil-teacher, failed exam in Jan 1875 Allowed to re-try, but removed June 1876
1875 1880 1884 1885	Miss FM Richards	Pupil-teacher Qualifies under Art.79, in 1881 under Art.60 Assists in Infant Dept → leaves for College, to obtain Certificate... ← returns, sent to model school 'to gain ideas'
1871	D Stawell	Monitress → leaves because 'needed at home'
1876	M Granger	Monitress → 'brother decides she is required at home'
1882 1886	Miss A Giles	Pupil-teacher Qualifies under Art.50, 1887 under Art.52
1885 1892	Miss E Giles	Candidate for Probation (i.e. P-T) ...but, together with Miss Peddle, 'found to assist each other in the exam'. Miss Giles removed
1920 1920 1922	Miss Ellen Pinkard	Pupil-Teacher Candidate Monitor (now PTCM) Passes Yr 1 exams Fails Yr 2 Decides to leave rather than re-take.
1926 1927 1929	Miss Gladys Cox (17)	One year of unpaid work till 18th birthday Appointed as uncertified teacher → left for *Salisbury* Training College
1934	Miss D Harrison	Appointed for Infants, from *Cheltenham* College – but 'with no music'... Left, after 6 months

Perhaps the boys had it easier. Certainly, there were not so many conflicting domestic demands. The table below gives examples of the training paths of selected staff at Somerton Free Boys School.

1891	Pupil-teacher Atkinson	After 5 years, having passed under Art.50, left to be Assistant at Willesden school
1891 1895 1900	Pupil-teacher Williams	In July 1893 took the Queen's Scholarship Exam to enter *Battersea* College; Moved to *Exeter* Training College having passed a 'Teachability' exam; He then withdrew from teaching to work in ironmongery
1897 1903 1904	Monitors Reeves and Bowering Reeves Bowering	They both gave *great satisfaction* and were *very persevering* . Both qualified under Art.50 ...left for College on a King's Scholarship ...left to be Assistant Teacher in Maidstone
1905	Pupil-Teacher Holly	After only two years, left to be uncertified Assistant Teacher in Shepton Mallet.
1908	Monitor Strang	Left in 1910 to join the Great Western Railway Co.
1908	Monitor Gibbs	Progressed to Pupil-Teacher, and attended new *Instruction Centre at Huish,*Taunton
1910	Uncertified Mr Toller	Ex-student of *Bristol* University Dept.
1910	Uncertified Mr Stone	Called up for Military Duties in 1916 Returned, then in 1920 left for appointment in *Exeter* Training College; (in searching for a possible replacement, a candidate was rejected - *for being a nonconformist.*)

These examples were not unique to the Somerton area. In Coleford, in the mining area of the north-east, we find similar difficulties and conflicting pressures on young girls. In August 1881, Mrs Hix complains that unless more help was given, she would not allow her daughter to continue working as a monitress, as she was overworked. However, over the summer she had a change of heart, especially as the Head offered her daughter the chance of being a Candidate Pupil-Teacher, which would give opportunities for much better prospects, despite the continued hard work. However, a more serious matter arose two years later for another monitress, whose mother withdrew her from the school as she was not considered strong enough to make the daily journey during the winter. In this school two dynasties of monitresses seem to have emerged. The Turner family seemed to have had plenty of girls. As one completed a stint, or found another job (in service) another one stepped up to take her place: Alice, Isobella, Mabel and Edith all served as monitresses between 1883 and 1890. During the same period another dynasty of monitresses came from the Hamblin family who supplied Sarah, Olive and Jane. This may be the same family from which Kate Hamblin came, who was to become the Head in nearby Oakhill British School 1932-44.

Qualifications: It was the exception rather than the rule for Heads to have had any formal training at a College or Institution in the C19th. Kingsdon had many troubled periods, yet appointed a good proportion of certified teachers: beginning with the first Head, Miss Challiner, from the London *Home and Colonial College*, followed by another certified Head who only lasted 6 weeks. Soon after, Sarah Newport arrived in 1877, also having just had 2 years at the *Home and Colonial College*. The Managers, having had trouble with the previous heads, who could not manage the children, perhaps felt that another *Home and Colonial* trained teacher would be more successful: she stayed 4 years. A further 3 certified Heads followed after 1900, which made 6 out of 19 between 1877 and 1944 which was unusual for the period. In contrast, in nearby Somerton, another troubled school, Monteclefe, achieved just 3 consecutive Heads over 36 years which held things steady in the early years.

In Fiddington, Miss Vaughan came from *Exeter Diocesan College* (First Class Certificate, indicating she had completed the first year) and stayed 20 years, 1883-1902. In the west, only Mr Hand at Skilgate was Certified (1884-89), apart from one other who left very quickly owing to poor health. On the Mendips, Headmaster Westbrook at Blagdon was Certified from *St John's College Battersea* and stayed for several years. By contrast, on the Levels, there were no Heads who were certificated at Westhay or Isle Brewer's, and just one at Chaffcombe, while Chillington had two at the beginning of the century, 1907-10, 1910-24.

The eastern mining area (with strong evangelical traditions) had the highest proportion of certified staff. After Miss Wilkinson's 34 years, Writhlington had 2 out of 8 over the next 34 years – Mr Bolwert (1923-36) and Mr Biggs (1926-36). Coleford had a similar proportion, 4 out of 12 over 60 years: two from un-named places, then one in the Infant section from the *Home and Colonial College*, and the other, for less than two years in the Mixed school, from *Winchester Diocesan College*. Similarly, Oakhill British School had 3 out of 7 certificated Teachers: Isaac Mitchell from 1864 to 1899 – a stalwart 35 years, and William Toms who died in post after only a few years, and finally a 3-month temporary certified Head in 1908. However, two other Heads left to go to College when a later opportunity presented itself, as at Holcombe where one Head went to attend lectures at *Salisbury Training College*, and another left for a 2-year full-time course at *Cheltenham Training College*. Not a very strong record, but perhaps not all Heads wrote their qualifications in the Log Book, though it seems more likely they would have declared this when any qualification existed. The Managers' Minutes were often more likely to include such details on appointment, but there are fewer extant Minute Books.

b. How long did they stay?

So much for the training of the teachers. We can also discover details of the length of tenure and the origins of some staff. For this we can turn to the county Trade Directories as well as School Managers' Minutes. Again, such entries are not consistent and frequently lack the details we would like.

Tenure: most schools managed at least one long-term Headship: Mr and Mrs Butler – 36 years at Charlton Mackrell; Isaac Mitchell – 35 years at Oakhill; Ada Wilkinson – 34 yrs at Writhlington; John Westbrook - 31 years at Blagdon; Ada Taylor – 27 years at Montclefe; William Webber – 24 years at Coleford; and Miss Vaughan – 20 years at Fiddington.

Table 6.1: Percentage of Heads x Years of Tenure in the focus schools

Years of service	0-4	5-9	10-14	15-19	20-24	25-29	30-34	35-39	40-44	45-49	50-55
%	44*	14	1	1	8.5	3.5	12.5	6.5	2.5	2.0	3.0
Nos of couples/ family					3	1	6	4	1		

* nearly a third of these served less than 2 years (one only 2 weeks, several just a few months)

Clearly Headships which were short-term resulting in rapid turnover was the norm. Yet, the table shows some remarkably long-serving Heads! Other places, beyond the focus schools, also had long-serving Heads: Miss Elizabeth Taylor at Withiam Priory, 45 years; while at Farrington Guerney Miss Martha Hoskins was Head for 45 years, became Mrs Martha Pinney and then Mr Pinney took over for a further 13 years; Mrs Martha Long lived up to her name at Chilcompton and stayed 40 years, as did Miss E Jenkins at Wanstow, Mr and Mrs Northcombe at Winsham; several were in post for over 30 years such as Mr and Mrs Lewin at Radstock National School who were almost equalled by Mrs Goodwon at Radstock British School, while Limington, Barwick and Miverton all had Heads for more than 30 years; perhaps the prize goes to (the local) Miss Ruth Coomb at Doulting for over 50 years from 1861 to 1914.

Some schools also had stalwart assistant teachers who lasted decades: Miss Townsend (Monteclefe) for 21 years and Mr Luke (Somerton Boys) for 32 years, while at the same school, Miss Lacey began as Assistant teacher, then became Head of Juniors and finally Head of the amalgamated Boys and Mixed schools during a period of over 40 years; but this time the prize goes to Miss Copping of Charlton Mackrell who was at the same school for 53 years – first as a pupil, then monitress, then Infant Teacher. However, experiences were very varied and other schools had periods of rapid turnover of Heads, assistants and monitresses.

From the table it would appear that being a husband-and-wife (or family) team, sometimes 'steadied the ship'. Nevertheless there were many single women who were 'married to the job' and also served very long periods. Usually this meant that the school experienced years of positive stability, though of course, stagnation could also set in. After a lengthy tenure ended, it was common for the subsequent HMI Report to observe how the new teacher was breathing fresh life into the school.

It seems not unusual for a family dynasty of teachers to be established and to run a school for decades. In Cutcombe School on Exmoor, Mr John Hayes was appointed Head in 1877. His wife, Harriet, helped with the Infants and the sewing. They were joined, in 1896, by son Henry who was an Article 50 teacher and by daughter Hilda who began as monitress. Meantime, Mr Hayes died, so his wife took over from 1896 to 1899. After these few years – clearly a stop-gap measure – son Henry assumes the Headship having become certified under Article 68. Hilda now took responsibility for Infants and continued her studies, becoming an Assistant teacher in 1901. Following this she passed (with difficulty) as an Article 68 teacher – HMI noted *'approved with much hesitation'*. By 1926, however, brother Henry had become ill and was forced to retire, but the new Head continued to employ Hilda (who was given occasional time off to play the organ for funerals) until 1926 when she, too, retired as her eye-sight had seriously deteriorated. Thus, the Hayes dynasty ended – after 56 years. Each of these moves was approved by the Managers, who seemed to prefer the family they knew to the process of finding an alternative. Another dynastic example can be found at Horsington with the Hillyer family whose father, mother, son and daughter all worked in the school over a 26-year period from 1889.

Several teachers brought parts of their family with them who helped out in the school. For example, in Skilgate, Miss Wigley came with her father, who helped with the Boys' arithmetic to good effect (1881-1882). Miss Caddy came with her mother, who improved the standard of the Girls' Needlework which was commended (1882-4). Miss James came with her sister who was a paid Assistant on £10 pa, and in fact took over for six months when her sister became ill and had to leave. At Luccombe (1907) another young Head brought her 16 year-old sister to act as monitress, while at Kingsdon Miss Holdsworth (1872) brought two daughters who helped in the classrooms when needed, likewise Mr Thomas (1914) had both a wife and daughter who helped. At Montclefe Miss Ada Taylor (1903) brought her sister Florence who worked for years at the school before moving on to become Head of West End School. This last school also experienced a family take-over when Miss Mary Hiscock (1875-88) was followed by her sister Edith (1888-03).

In terms of support for teachers, it is interesting to note that in February 1872 Miss Sarah Fitch, the assistant at Monteclefe, was absent through illness, *'so her sister has taken her place'*. It is the *'so'* that is significant – the assumption being that if one member of the family was capable of teaching, so is another. In this instance, the sister may also have received some training, or the family may have been better educated and well-respected in the community, with the confidence, availability and willingness to interchange: we cannot know. A similar arrangement is also recorded in Blagdon in 1889: so, *'When Miss Ellen was ill, her sister took her place'*. Clearly the prevailing view appeared that teaching was often 'all in the family'. The same situation is evident at Coleford school. Without family, it would have been very lonely for young girls in such a small village.

Teachers sometimes had to leave for health reasons: a Head declared she had to leave, *'having caught rheumatism at the School House'* (Skg 1878), while another teacher had to leave, from Isle Brewer's, located amongst the frequent winter 'inundations'. She noted, in December 1913, *'This place does not suit me: I have been suffering from colds'*.

Recruitment Catchment Area:
The Head's Log rarely gives information about the background of any newly appointed teacher or monitress. This is occasionally available in the less common Managers' Minute Books.

It is quite noticeable that in some of the more remote areas, teachers were often recruited from amongst the villagers themselves – if one can make assumptions from shared surnames. Thus, in the far west of the county on and around Exmoor, we find many more married female teachers than is usual and many share surnames with local farmers, artisans and small businesses. Such teachers sometimes work for a whole year, sometimes for considerably longer. For example, in the moorland and western areas of Carhampton Hundred, we find the wives of a watchmaker, overseer and, also, of a grocer-draper. In Williton Hundred, we find wives of a farmer (3), sub-postmaster (3), auctioneer (1), shopkeeper (2), shoemaker (2) and of a wheelwright, mason, steam-thresher and a miller as well.

In Luccombe we find that, while not from the village, teachers are generally recruited from nearby, from amongst people who therefore know the area, the climate and conditions and are not too far from home: from Watchet, Sampford Brett, Minehead and Crewkerne, though two Heads were from Bristol, having qualified at St Mary's Redcliffe and a temporary Head from Bristol University – perhaps venturing out into the real world, briefly. This number of local recruits increases again in the central Levels (IsB 1879); in the east of the county around Binegar, Wootton and Lamyatt; and in the northern mining areas near Wellow, where we find a daughter of a cattle dealer, and wives of a farmer, 'postal receiver', blacksmith, dairy farmer, mason, shopkeeper, builder and Parish Clerk. These would probably all have been the more literate and numerate families, and of some social standing within the village. However, in the more central areas associated with larger urban areas like South Petherton, Crewkerne, Somerton and Glastonbury there appear to be fewer instances of local connections.

Apart from the grapevine and personal recommendations, we occasionally see that a school advertised in the professional National Press, *The Schoolmistress (*already gender specific), *The School Teacher or Guardian.* A very large number of newspapers and magazines existed through the century, with varying life-spans, indicating the mass media were also used as a means of circulating information.

By contrast, references from the 'cv's of two early teachers at Blagdon throw further light on recruitment. First, James Cook was a pupil-teacher at Montacute, then completed a period as 'acting teacher' in Chislehurst Kent in 1873, was at High Ham in 1897 before taking up the headship at Blagdon in 1880. It is unusual to see such geographical diversity – perhaps he had relatives in Kent. Secondly, John Westbrook, the son of a police constable, also seem to have had Kentish connections. He was a pupil-teacher in Tunbridge Chapel School before going to the Anglican St John's Training School at Battersea for a year. The next four years were not mentioned before he came to Blagdon as Head, with his wife. They must have liked the move, for they stayed for 41 years! During the Westbrook era several monitors were apprenticed for between 3 and 5 years at the school. The list indicates a considerable range of social backgrounds: daughters of a shop-keeper, estate gardener, farm bailiff, haulier, who were each employed on the annual salary of £10 with £2 10s increment for each year of service. Uncertified assistant teachers could opt to teach and simultaneously follow a correspondence course before attending a College 'to finish': Carmarthen College was attended by one.

Turnover: However, the opposite also occurred – and some remarkably short tenures are also in evidence. Kingsdon appears to have posed some severe challenges to at least two Heads: one stayed only a month and just a few years later, another for six months. Miss Hannah Mayhew, a Certified teacher, became Head on January 13th 1873 (an unlucky day?). Her immediate entry reads, '*I have been quite shocked with the unruly conduct of the children which has been beyond anything I have ever met with, in any School that I have ever set foot in as Mistress'.* The rest of the week wasn't much better:

14th Children not so noisy but still unpleasant;
15th Children very troublesome;
16th Small attendance, rather better order;
17th Children, many of them more teachable, but their movements still very noisy and distracting.

By the following Wednesday 22nd she writes, '*The most unsatisfactory day I have ever spent in any school in my life! Complete rebellion*'. The following day Miss Mayhew notes, '*School much interrupted by parents: a woman took her child out of the Infant School by force, a rude girl came to demand the two Lees, and the boy Pyke ran away*'. On February 7th she writes, '*My last day in Kingsdon School*'. She must have been so relieved!

The school was then taken over by a former uncertified Mistress who took charge for the whole year, followed by Hannah Holdsworth who became Head – and lasted 3½ years. In Aug 1875 Miss Isobel Dore took up the challenge: she only lasted till the end of the year. The replacement was Sarah Newport, trained at the *Home and Colonial Institution* in London. Perhaps, being used to tough London children she coped better – in fact for 4 full years. After the first six months the HMI Reported that '*The school is still far from satisfactory, Miss Newport has thrown herself into her work with spirit and will hope to be able to shew (sic) a very different result next year*'. In fact, by 1879 HMI reported of yet another Head, '*This school has decidedly improved and I hope that in another year, the Mistress will have made it a thoroughly good school*'. Well done the new Head!

This situation does not appear to have been an exceptional case. It was common to see fairly rapid turnover in specific villages during a sequence of bad years, which seems particularly to have been the case in some very small and possibly especially isolated places. The Levels areas, with their regular winter floods, seem to have suffered badly from short tenures: at Isle Brewer's, between 1877 and 1901 there were 10 Heads who mostly stayed only 1-3 years, with 4 lasting less than a year and, again, between 1909 and 1915 another 4 Heads; while at Chillington between 1924 and 1930 there were 5 Heads, although immediately before and after there were Heads who stayed over 10 years each and, then again, a series of short stays. Was it just the bad climate, or the high rate of irregular attendances and the 'backward' children, or the negative attitudes of parents and the pervasive sense of gloom this generated?

Some schools in other areas, around the Parrett estuary, also experienced a spate of very disrupted years: as in Fiddington in the 1880s:

1880 Feb	Miss Morris		
1880 Nov	Miss Deacon	£37. 10s + ½ school fees,	*2 months**
1882 Jan 16th	Miss Talbot	" " "	*2 weeks only*
1882 Jan 28th	Miss Norman	" " and to play the Church harmonium	
1884	Miss Vaughan, who stayed 20 years, starting on £50 and ending on £75.		

** told to resign with immediate effect. No full reason given.*

Salaries were a factor likely to influence tenure, particularly for the monitresses, especially where there were alternatives in nearby factories or businesses. Details are often hard to come by as they are more likely to be given in the (less commonly available) Managers' Minutes than in the Head's Log. School monitors earned very little and teachers were not well paid either. We have a few examples: Mabel was paid 1s 6d a week, Isabelle 2s and Olive 2s 6d – the latter after working two years in the school (Wrl 1888). By 1914 a monitress could receive £13 pa. The next step up was often an untrained Assistant Infant Teacher (Art. 68) who was paid £25 pa (Wrl 1903), while in a nearby British School a Certified Assistant Infant Teacher received £40 pa (OkBr 1908), and four years later received £60.

A Head obviously earned considerably more, especially if male. Above, we see that Miss Vaughan earned £50 in 1884, rising to £75 in 1902. After the war a male Head (certified) could earn what seemed like a princely sum of £360 pa and his wife (uncertified) £144 (Clf 1943). However, just two years later, national Burnham pay-scales were set which meant the wife was paid in her own right, not just given a supplementary salary as an adjunct of her husband. It also put an end to the large discrepancies in salaries paid by better off schools.

Comparing salaries between schools over periods of time is confusing as there are so many possible variables: gender (women, it was believed, needed less pay as they could perform their own cleaning and laundry and they also ate less!). Other variables included levels of qualification and experience, size of the school and age of the pupils to be taught, and other sources of income (e.g. such as from playing the organ, training the church choir) and Heads were also paid extra to train pupil-teachers. We can see from the list above at Fiddington, a Head's salary was not the only source of income. Managers often negotiated a multi-part income which included a portion of school fees or a portion of the grant awarded. This had two benefits: the Managers paid out less, and the teacher was motivated to win pupils and perform well. We also need to be aware of variable expenses: whether rent for a house or cost of coal was included. Finally, the salary depended on the wealth – and willingness - of the School Managers: some idea of rates can be gauged from the figures for similar-sized schools below:

Table 6.2: Different rates of pay between 1804 - 1948

	1804	**1848**	**1865**	**1899**	**1918**	***1948**
Head	Hd £31 (Ctc)	H+W £50 (NCry)	Hd £65 (Enm)	H+W £70 (Ctc)	£165-250 (KM)	H+W £393 (Enm)
Cert Assis			InfT £35 (Blg)		£ 60 - 80 (KM)	
Suppl				£5 10s (KM)	£ 40- 65 (KM)	

* in 1931, the Government cut salaries of all teachers by 15%, owing to the international crisis.

Linked to salaries, we might also find that **Staffing levels** could affect turnover. The typical small, single cell school would normally have had a Head, supported by one or two monitresses. As the buildings developed and an infant classroom was added, a separate Infant teacher would normally be employed, often an untrained and unqualified member of staff. We can find that many schools left the Head to struggle on with unqualified staff or even just pupil-teachers (as in Somerton Boys), however often HMI recommended, as a matter of urgency, that staffing should be improved. Kingsdon gives a typical example of a school, in terms of pupils' attendance and number of staff in the *smaller schools in 1886*:

single cell attendance 56 pupils Head with 2 Monitresses

This can be contrasted with Somerton Boys and with Somerton Monteclefe (Girls and Infants) which were *medium-sized* schools but with very different staffing experiences (average 'attendance figures' are given, and variety of staff - Head, Assistants, Supplementaries, pupil-teachers and monitresses). The Girls' school fared better: the Boys' suffered from an inadequate endowment.

Table 6.3: Comparison of staffing between Somerton Girls' and Boys' Schools

Girls' School	Boys' School
1873 124 av Attendance Head, 2 pupil-teachers, Monitress	1891 88 av Attendance Head, 2 pupil-teachers
1908 109 av Attendance Head, Senior Assit, 2 other Assit	1907 108 av Attendance Head, 2 Assist, a pupil-teacher
1921 107 av Attendance Head , 2 Assistants, 2 Supplementaries	1934 103 av Attendance Head, I Cert Assistant, I Uncert Assistant

Variable staff / pupil ratios and often low qualifications must have made the task harder. Some areas fared better. In terms of the 'quality' of Heads in the target schools we find:

	Heads	Nos. Certified	+family member / couple
Skilgate, Exmoor	16 Heads: 1879-1940	2	4
Isle Brewer's, Levels	17 Heads: 1877-1914	none	none
Kingsdon, Central	18 Heads: 1872-1940	6	1
Som Monteclefe, Central	10 Heads: 1867-1940	3	1
Coleford, Mining area	11 Heads: 1880-1940	4	1
Oakhill British School	9 Heads: 1863-1940	3	1

Thus the top two listed had the highest turnover and lowest qualifications. Yet, while Isle Brewer's had a very high turnover with no trained Heads, the troubled Kingsdon school also suffered a high turnover yet had the highest level of trained Heads, so qualifications would not necessarily the answer! It was in the mining schools (the last two listed) where staff had proportionally better qualifications and proved to be better 'stayers' – perhaps with a higher level of commitment.

Finally, the **Teacher's House**: This may well have been an important additional factor making a difference to conditions for the Head. Just less than half the schools seem to have provided accommodation, but not all houses were free. The alternatives of finding private lodgings or of lodging with the clergy, a School Manager or a local villager may not have made life more attractive. Not surprisingly, a considerable number of staff came with a family member for moral support and quite often for practical support in the school as well.

In the next chapters we shall see what went on inside the classrooms and find out more about the experience of teaching and learning in the village schools.

Part IV

Changing Processes of Schooling: Inside the Classroom –

Teacher Roles
Curriculum
Pupils' Experiences

To illustrate the core of village schooling we turn to the details of the Heads' Log Books. These reveal changing roles and conditions for teachers; changing expectations of the methods of teaching and learning – from memorization to discovery; with further change of content – from 3Rs to the addition of physical and practical subjects; changes in school conditions and attendance regulations – at last giving compulsory and free elementary education to all.

Fig. iv

	Key National Events	Somerset Examples
1858-62 1862	**Newcastle Commission Report** on the condition of education **Revised Code** *introduced by Robert Lowe* Sec of Board of Education, Payment-by-Results starts as a method of bringing accountability to the increasing grants given to schools.	**Annual HMI inspections** recorded in Head's Log Book. The Report, received several months later, was copied into the Log Book **Payments depended on** *exam results* (teachers and pupils) + *standard of facilities provided* and condition of buildings (managers) + *level of attendance* (parents). Logs record daily numbers
1864-68	**Taunton Commission Report** + HMI Arnold's Report on European. Ed urges wider curriculum+technical educ. (weakness shown up by Great Exhibition); more Secondary opportunities urged, based on Endowed Sch.	**Somerset Elementary Schools rarely add** more than Geography till 1880s/90s, when Drill and Nature Study also added. No village mentions 'secondary' schooling, though Evening Continuation Schools increase.
1870	**Forster's Education Act** empowered Boards to be set up to provide Elementary School where 'insufficient' available. Board Schools to be non-denominational + visited by HM Inspectors; grants continue to denominational schools; also, formalized **Infants sections** sanctioned in Elementary Schools.	**1870s Boom-time for school building** e.g. *East Pennard, Milton Clevedon, Pylle, Ditcheat, Henstridge, Kingsdon, Muchelney, E Chinnock, Chaffcombe, Merriot, Ilton, Fivehead, Stawell, Creech St Michael, Goathurst, Bishops Lydeard, Crowcombe, Chipstable, Exford, Brompton Ralph, Cutcombe .* Many new Boards formed and some existing schools convert to Board status.
1875	**Agriculture Children's Act** employment age raised to 10 yrs. Can only work from age 8 if for *parents* and on *their* land.	Children still frequently absent working in the fields in every school, especially *Isle Brewer's, Brewham, Horsington*
1876	**Sandor's Act** empowered Parishes to appoint Attendance Officers to enforce attendance of school age children	**Attendance Officers** appointed: could submit names of persistent offenders to local magistrates to be fined. This was very variable in different areas. AO in Monteclefe Somerton was vigorous, while in Brewham action was rare.
1880 1880-88	**Mundella's Act** compulsory school for all children 5-10 yrs **Cross Commission** set up to examine working of 1870 Act	'Compulsory' status had little impact on attendance!
1889	**Technical Instruction** to be provided by Local Authorities. Supported by government grants for wider range of subjects.	Spread of Cookery, Gardening and some Woodwork - where facilities allowed
1890 1891	**End of Revised Code**, change to block grant to schools instead **Free Elementary Schooling** funded from grants of 10s per pupil Payment-by-Results phased out by 1898	**Grants** calculated on several criteria, including Order, Tone and Discipline, (not just examinations) + quality of facilities + attendance 'Free' education filters through into schools so many schools **enlarged** e.g. *Cadbury Charlton Horthorne, Shepton Montague, Queen Camel, Pitney, Barton, St David, Barrow, Stoke-s-Hamdon, Ash, Winsham, Misterton, Donyatt, Bawdrip, Huntspill, Huish Champflower, Exton*
1893	**Acland's Attendance Act** School Leaving Age raised and exemptions effectively set at **11 years old minimum**	
1895	**Bryce Commission** also urges Secondary Ed 'for National Efficiency'	1894 **Sir Thomas Acland** (Chair of Luccombe Sch) visits with PM Lord Roseberry
1899	School Leaving Age exemptions raised to **12 years**	Children completing Std IV (later V,VI) could leave before SLA, but continued to attend for 2 hrs daily till required age, or, total days of attendance reached.

Chapter 7
How the Teachers Worked: Relationships and Contexts

To gather information on this particular aspect, we need to turn to the Log Books which were kept (almost) daily by the Master or Mistress of the individual schools. Not all survive. Some are to be found in the county archives at the new Somerset Heritage Centre, Taunton, while many others can be found in the schools – in lofts, cellars, storerooms, in the homes of ex-Managers or Heads. Sometimes the Logs have disappeared with a departing member of staff. Nevertheless, by examining a sample of those which are available, fascinating details are revealed on the daily life within the school. Heads are very different in the ways in which they record events, or even what counts as an event worth recording! The most frequent entries concern pupil absences and their reasons. This was vital information for the Inspectors as it was part of the data upon which grants to the school were estimated.

The Head's task of managing the school seemed to focus frequently on responding to the stream of visitors and helpers that some schools experienced; coping with the behaviour of certain pupils (and their parents); constructing the yearly programme of studies; preparing for the annual visits from the Diocesan Inspector and the HMI; dealing with smoking fires, smelly toilets and battling to get repairs financed; finally, ordering and receiving the equipment and books which were needed. More rarely, a Head records information about *how* the teaching was conducted (Ch.7), in addition to *what* was taught (Ch. 8). However, what was *learnt* and how it felt to be in school during this period is more difficult to estimate (Ch. 9). From interviews and recollections of school experiences, most contributors say least about what went on inside the classroom: stronger memories relate to what went on outside in the playground, on the way to and from school, or concerning the tasks done to help parents before and after school.

To trace changes concerning life inside the classrooms, we have already noted the character of the schools at the turn of the century, when the Lancaster-Bell 'monitorial system' was in full swing and that this system was the predominant mode until the 1840s when Stow's 'simultaneous system' grew in popularity. The Log Books mostly begin from the 1860s or '70s (when it became a requirement of the new Board Schools) and it is with this period that the chapter starts. The key periods of change within the schools appear to be first, 1860s-80s which includes the introduction of the 1862 Revised Code and the creation of Boards Schools from 1870. Secondly, 1890-1914 from the time when elementary schooling became free and a decade began of considerable curriculum development in response to the changing codes of 1880, lasting until the New Code of 1904, which saw welfare concerns tackled by the Liberal reform government that introduced school services and, in particular, medical care. Thirdly, the inter-war years which saw another burst of curriculum and teaching development (particularly in the arts and sports) and a significant increase in secondary education. Finally, the post-Butler Act 1944 period which will be the focus in the last chapter.

i. Teachers and Teaching
We have noted how teachers gradually became better trained and better paid, perhaps better motivated and better respected. However, in terms of staffing levels, it is important to remember that in the village schools, the most common situation, throughout the C19th, was to find a single Head supported only by young monitors and, later, by pupil-teachers whom he also had to train. Only larger schools could afford an assistant (other than the Head's wife who helped with the sewing and the Infants).

a. The Community: school helpers. In some villages other members of the community were very active as visitors and helpers. These often included the Rector's wife and daughters, the family of the Lord of the Manor or any other 'significant' person. Such benefactors and patrons were often very proud of 'our' school and brought their friends to visit and listen to the children singing or to inspect the needlework. In some cases the visits were very regular and of a more practical nature.

Vicars and visitors. In Kingsdon, Miss Challiner, began work as Mistress in January 1872 in the new school buildings (having only just completed her training at the Home and Colonial Institution in London the month before). On day two of her appointment we find the school was visited by the Rev GC Thornton, and the next day by Miss Neal and Miss Frazer and, on Friday, by the Misses Neal. These visitors were very regular, almost weekly, for a considerable period.

The Reverend took the upper section of the school for Scripture, while the monitress took the lower section for the same subject. In many schools where a Rector visited, it is rarely mentioned that he taught a lesson, rather he appears to conduct a Question and Answer session (to test). However, in this instance he definitely seems to undertake regular teaching. The ladies came and listened to the children singing – a favourite task: perhaps it was thought to provide a stimulus for the pupils to work hard at this subject and motivating to have an audience to whom to perform. In March, '*Miss Ada Neal attempted to teach the children to sing seconds by ear, but found this must be abandoned for a time*'. However, she was more successful and certainly much appreciated when, in February, the Monitress was ill and the Head had to take the whole school on her own. Miss Challiner notes that her throat was so sore as to be scarcely audible. The Misses Neal came to school and heard Standards III and IV read and a Miss Thornton came to take the upper section of the school. This was a real and substantial commitment to the school, above and beyond mere visiting and it can be found elsewhere in other school Logs, but not often as such a regular undertaking. Kingsdon and Miss Challiner were fortunate.

Unfortunately this relationship was not always maintained with some of the other Heads – who, as we have noted, experienced real difficulties at this school. In 1873 (after a very brief and disastrous interlude) visits recommenced with Miss Holdsworth as the new Head. In November, Miss Ada Neal began taking a lesson with a class of Infants on her visits, while in the following July Miss Eleanor Neal taught Standard I Reading and Miss Ada took Standard II for Dictation. This arrangement continued throughout most of the Autumn. In October, Miss Neal also took a Composition Class, while Mrs Holdsworth (probably the Head's mother) took needlework on Tuesday and Thursday afternoons and also heard children read. Gradually the Misses Neals' role declined to occasional inspections of needlework and distributing prizes.

Patrons. Meanwhile, in Somerton Monteclefe School for Girls and Infants, Lady Smith was an active patron. As in Kingsdon, within the first week of the newly appointed Mistress, Miss Parker, in January 1867, Lady Smith paid a visit and continued to do so almost weekly for a considerable time. In March the Head notes that Mrs Pinney visited and that Miss Pyne instructed the class in Scripture, while Miss Elton took Class I for Catechism. In the next year, with a new Head, Lady Smith's visits continued. Miss Pyne also continued to come and, in March, practised some hymns for the Juvenile Missionary Meeting. In September of that year, Lady Smith heard a Scripture lesson and stayed *'to see the discipline on the Gallery'.* A few months later Rev Grogan came to examine each class in Scripture and Catechism and the following year he is noted as coming to ask questions in Arithmetic. That year, Mrs Grogan inspected the Needlework and expressed herself as well-pleased.

From the 1870s, there are several occasions when the Head mentioned a cheque from Lady Smith for salaries (July 21st 1870 for £17 10s 7½ d, again in April 1871, and on some subsequent occasions). Similarly, Mr Pinney sent money: 7s 6d which is *'the school money for several children'.* Sponsoring some of the poorer scholars was a common practice and Somerton had more that its share of 'problem families' and there were few contributors to the school funds. The Somerton schools, all run by the Pinney family, seem constantly to have been short of money and always delayed responding to HMI's requests for spending on repairs, staffing and materials.

Yet the Pinneys and Smiths continued to be active supporters. Mrs Pinney sent a doll for the children to sew and dress in December 1870 and, in October 1892, she sent a piano. Miss Pyne continued to take an interest in the needlework. Lady Smith also seems to have established a Clothing Club: in January 1871 she called to give out Clothing Club cards. In June, she brought toys for the Infants, she supervised some carpentry work, in January she provided an excellent tea and magic-lantern show for the school. These visits are almost every other day! One wonders to what extent they were disruptive or supportive. In 1875, we notice that Lady Smith is also supplying materials for the school in the form of new books and slates, and again ten years later. In November 1884 a Miss Digby came to hear the First Class (top) children 'parse' during their Grammar lesson (she does not seem to have come again!).

However, in more remote Cutcombe there was a singular dearth of reports of such helpers, yet it was also the case in West End Infants on the edge of small-town Somerton. Location does not seem to be the prime factor, but rather individual inclination and opportunity.

b. Organisation of the school. Apart from details about who was involved in teaching in the classrooms, the Log Books also give us insights into how the school was organised. The usual pattern was for the Head to take the older scholars, usually in the main School Hall, and an assistant to take the younger ones, in a separate classroom. In larger schools more teachers would be employed, though these were often only pupil-teachers or even merely monitors as, of course, they were cheaper.

We have some clear descriptions of internal organisation. Skilgate (1878) recorded that the children were divided into three classes – Infant, Standard I + II and Standards III-V. The Head took responsibility for the older group while also supervising two monitresses working with the two younger groups. The average attendance was around 40 children with approx 12-14 children per class. By 1886 numbers had risen to 66, so one monitress was replaced by a more capable pupil-teacher, with approx 20 pupils per class. In addition, the New Code of 1882 had added higher Standards VI and VII for which the Head also took charge, so the typical division was Infants and Std I, Std II-III, Std IV-VII. This was similar in Cutcombe till the turn of the century when, in 1910, we find a Head with 50 children in Stds II-V in one room and just one monitress for the younger ones. In 1922 HMI recommended a second adult assistant, though in 1931 it is again one Head with 2 monitresses, but in 1959, with 47 on roll, it becomes a two- (adult) teacher school.

The usual deployment of staff was changed in two innovative methods, in different schools, intended to raise the attainment levels in particular subjects. In Cutcombe 1903, the HMI noted, *'The lessons for Arithmetic underlined in red are taken at the same time to allow more supervision'*. This gave a chance for some staff specialisation to take place. A similar idea prevailed in Somerton Boys where, in 1930, the more enlarged staff was encouraged to specialise and thus work to their strengths, by taking their subject across several classes. This was extended to the sister school, Monteclefe School for Girls and Infants. Thus Mr Luke took Science and Maths in the Girls' School, while Miss Powell took Crafts in the Boys. These, however, are unusual instances.

In Blagdon, 1890, we discover how their school day was used: the Head took 10 minutes of Drill to start the day and, to start the afternoon, Singing and Tables alternated with Drawing (for the Boys) on Monday, Wednesday and Friday from 2-2.50 pm. One wonders if most of the lessons were this long or only the Practical lessons. In Enmore and several other schools we find that some act of religious worship was performed at the beginning of the day, as we are told, in general, *'Secular teaching began at 9.30'*.

Further, we have an example from the returns made to the County Council Education Committee 1902 from Cutcombe of how much time was spent on each subject. This clearly demonstrates the priorities and aims of the schooling process:

Reading	5 hrs.	20 mins	Writing	2 hrs	10 mins	Arithmetic	2 hrs	20 mins
Stories		30 mins	Dictation		30 mins	Modelling		25 mins
Recitation		25 mins	Games		20 mins	Occupations		25 mins
Reproduction		30 mins	Drill		40 mins	Needlework	3 hrs	
of stories in pupils' own words			Singing		20 mins	'Observation'	1 hrs	30 mins

This already amounts to some 19 hours. As secular lessons ran from approx 9.30 – 3.30 with at least 60 minutes for lunch, over a 5-day week this might leave around 60 minutes a day for either Geography, History, Grammar, Cookery/Woodwork, Gardening/Handicrafts.

We also discover how the children were organised: we know from several Logs that the regular examinations which took place – sometimes monthly, sometimes quarterly - resulted in children being re-arranged and their order of seating changed according to their results. In Blagdon, 1895, we are told *'Children are eager for the exams, for they are given a new place in accordance with the marks gained'*. In Kingsdon, 1898, the children were *grouped* for the Class Subject, Grammar, at the HMI's suggestion. This novel approach appears to have been considered a success, so children were also grouped in the other Class Subject, Geography, in the following year. We can assume that the 'grouping' was done on the basis of ability groups. Whether this allowed the teacher to address the children together so they were *instructed as a group* we do not know. Or, whether they worked collaboratively, shared books and *worked as a group* the Logs do not reveal.

This latter technique seems to have been implemented elsewhere at the beginning of the C20th, when children are described as helping each other and working collaboratively, in Kingston Seymour. There we find one solution to the perennial problem of small village schools – namely a wide mix of ages in one class. HMI recorded, in 1922, '*By careful planning and private study for the two higher classes* [the Head] *keeps them usefully employed. Careful records of the children's progress are sent to the parents at the end of each term*'. A contributor recalled, "*We were in small groups and helped each other. The Inspector who came (in1934) was quite impressed with the work we were doing*". Further details about this were given by HMI who noted, '*Informal teaching methods are used with group and individual work carefully organised. The children make satisfactory progress according to their own ability*'. Such grouping was, however, a rarely reported detail at the time. Nevertheless, these are early signs of what came, in the late 1960s, to be widely used and regarded as 'progressive' methods.

ii. The Status of the Head.

a. Additional duties: A teacher, more particularly a Head - especially if male - was a person of some social standing and significance. In the mid-C19th, in a small rural village, the Head may be one of the few fully literate persons and could play an important part in Parish institutions. However, male and female teachers were also called upon to undertake extra duties: several Somerset teachers were called upon to be choirmaster and/or organist (1872 Evercreech and Pennard W, and Bradford on Tone, and in the 1870-80s at Blagdon, 1903 at Muchelney, and 1931 Holcombe).

Male Heads were found to be Secretaries of local organisations such as the Library (1870 North Curry), or the Reading Room and Workingmen's Club (Pilton 1889-19 and 1923-35). Another common task was to act as agent for the new Insurance Companies such as the British Life Assurance in Milverton (1861), at Croscombe (1861), at Barrington (1866). Even the task of Parish Clerk was sometimes given to the Head, as at Wayford near Crewkerne (1866). A few helped out in the local shop or post office, especially if it was a job shared with a spouse.

In some instances they played an even bigger role. The mining village of Coleford is a case in point. The end of the C19th was a troubled time for the pits and those who worked in them. In Spring 1891 pits were not working and, in the summer of 1893, a strike lasted several months. When school re-opened, the Head, Fredrick Close, gave the men dinner on Mondays and tea on Thursdays. By November most of the men had returned, on 15% less pay, but 150 failed to find employment. In the New Year the Head was involved in meetings between the miners and some of the mine officials – including Mr Batey, one of the school managers. It must have been a tricky meeting. He attended further Miners' Meetings in subsequent weeks, but there was little to be done: pits had closed and families were leaving. The Head calculated it would mean the loss of up to 80 children for the school. He was clearly supported in his endeavours by his staff, whom he warmly thanked and noted in the Log, '*I wish to acknowledge hearty support from the staff in all efforts made for the welfare of the school during this past year*'.

This Head also undertook further community roles in addition to the Headmastership: he was twice called to an inquest when men had been killed underground (1889, 1895) and he was called for jury work at nearby Edbury (1896). Nevertheless, he did not neglect his school duties and, in fact, increased those too. He gave his spare time to individual children. In December 1894 he tutored a boy for the County Scholarship. In 1896 he gave Saturday tuition to a pupil-teacher for six months. He also attended meetings regarding the Evening Continuation School, for those beyond the school age (always a separate establishment, separately funded and usually separately staffed). In addition he seems to have been keen to keep up his own level of professional knowledge too, for, in the summer of 1894, we find that he gained a studentship to attend a course for development at the centre in Weston-super-Mare: the school holidays were delayed a little to accommodated this course from Aug 2nd – Sept 1st. However, soon after, in 1898, he retired, on grounds of ill-health – and probably exhaustion. He left an important legacy to the school, the community and, not least, an inspired staff whose positive attitude was noted by his successor, Mr Bassett, who commented in July 1898, that *'The Teachers do not think it too much trouble to hunt up objects to illustrate their lessons and readily try new ideas. They shew (sic) interest in reviewing their work as a scientific effort'.*

b. Head, Parents and Staff:

Parents' relationships with schools was very variable, not only in the matter of attendance but also in relation to punishments. A few examples will serve to illustrate the dilemmas. The attitude of parents is very ambivalent. Some approved and even asked for caning to be used. Two boys were punished for truanting and the Head noted, *'One parent came to the school and asked me to do it'* (1894); but on another occasion a Somerton boy, having been caned, the next day brought a note saying *'If my boy is caned I will come hup …'.*

Heads clearly had difficulty in trying to instil discipline regarding attendance and behaviour: parents were not always supportive. The Horsington Head had a string of hostile encounters:

1871 June Kept in KG for disobedience and impertinence. His Mother sent and demanded him to be sent home. I complied as I have been abused by this woman before.
1871 Aug Mrs D accused [the Infant] *teacher of striking her child. I investigated and found it to be a complication of untruths.*
1889 Mrs D visited at 9 am on account of her son being punished. Her voice was of a powerful character and created a sensation for a short time. [Similarly in 1896.]

Two other girls were punished (caned) for bad conduct in Horsington, whereupon *'Mrs Watts* [the mother of one] *arrived and vociferously demanded her daughter. I ordered her to leave the room. She refused, whereon she was gently removed, uttering many threats'.* Two further pupils (boys) were punished for different offences soon afterwards, which both resulted in complaints from a parent. Nothing came of any of it and it seemed to have died down.

Twenty years later, another Head in Coleford, Mr Webber, saw himself having to do battle on several fronts, both personal and for the school. Whether it was his style of leadership or a series of misperceptions/miscommunications is unclear. It started in 1923 when a parent sent a letter of complaint to the Managers regarding what was described as bad behaviour towards certain children and of rudeness to one child in particular (the child of a Manager). A report to the Management was made in which only two of the managers registered their support for Mr Webber. He was asked to leave by the end of the year, the Managers added, *'They hoped that the Committee will see their way to finding him a suitable post elsewhere'.* But, in fact the Head stayed.

Another parental complaint was made two years later, followed by one from a teaching colleague five years after that. It appears that while that teacher was away on a course, Mr Webber set exams for the whole school (one way around the difficulty of being a teacher short). He asked his wife to help out with the marking of the complainant's class. On her return the teacher was furious. Eventually it was pointed out that the Head's wife had no more rights or privileges than any other parent. Clearly, this must not happen again. Was Mr Webber being imperious? Was he out of touch with possible shifts in attitudes to the exercise of his authority in the post-war period? What were the boundaries of the powers of the Managers? How often did Heads or Managers appeal to the higher authority of the County Education Committee to resolve serious disagreements? We do not find any further examples in the Logs of the focus schools.

Staff posed further problems on several occasions. Other cases appear in a variety of schools. Horsington had more troubles in the mid-1870s. A Head and his daughter took over the school from a previous husband-and-wife team which had been in post for three years. A year after they took over they were asked, *'If there is any charge against the previous Head and whether the wife gave satisfaction to the managers'*. This seems a curious opinion to request and nothing more is noted in the Log.

As is predictable, there are several cases of conflict between Heads and junior staff, particularly monitresses. At Monteclefe 1870, a Head had to forbid an Assistant teacher to use the cane (was she being excessive or was she exceeding her position?) Either way she appeared to have flounced off for the day, feeling slighted, with her authority undermined: the Head remarked she could do better without her. Further incidents involving monitresses at the same school (1876, 1892) related to them cheating in their tasks – one had correct answers to arithmetic problems but wrong workings, while on another occasion two were collaborating during an exam – their papers were dismissed and one left.

A further case, this time of serious inter-staff conflict, appeared in Skilgate (1905). The previous, well-thought of Head, Mr Stephens, after 7 years at the helm, was forced to resign as his sight was failing badly. It must have been a hard blow to accept. His wife, Mrs Stevens, who had worked alongside him in the school, continued in post as Assistant teacher. The new Head, Miss Harris (possibly a relative of the Rector Rev Harris) was appointed. After only six months, she recorded:

Mar 20th *'Mr Abrahamson has just told me to expect a visit from Mr Bottomly concerning my Assistant, and he has also told me of Mrs Stephen's clandestine malicious conduct with respect to myself – in circulating about the village a certain letter written by Miss Toller my successor at Holywell Lake, implying that I got on badly with my Assistant there. This is an entire fabrication. I do not hesitate to say she has tried to hurt my reputation ever since I took charge at Skilgate. I have been a Headmistress for 33 years and have never experienced this treachery, double-dealing and mischief. Since* [HMI] *Mr Leng's visit, Mrs Stephens and I have been on agreeable terms in school and I ceased to assert my authority as Head Mistress. My Assistant has formed the habit of tale-telling to the Rector's wife. The Rector has been away on a Mission to Russia.'*

Shortly after this, the Head was ill with bronchitis and must have given one month's notice, to terminate on April 18th. However, Mrs Stephens was not going to let her go quietly. The subsequent behaviour is more to be expected from children on a playground:

Apr 6th *'Mrs Stephens purposely made noises to disturb my lesson. When I remonstrated with her she became hysterical. Her husband too came up at playtime and forced himself into the School Room and was insolent with me.'*

Managers: A different kind of case is recorded, also at Skilgate. This time the affair showed staff solidarity in facing up to Management. In 1895 Miss Kirkham was appointed Head, with Miss Shepherd continuing as Art.68 Assistant teacher. In Oct 1896 there was a positive Report from HMI, then suddenly, on March 2nd 1897, we find, *'Miss Shepherd not able to come to school as she is much upset by the Rector and co-managers'*. A month later we read, *'Miss Shepherd has passed Second Class at the Queen's Scholarship exam and is now qualified under Art 50'*: She was clearly hard-working and keen to make progress. Suddenly this was followed, on May 28th, by *'The present Mistress and Assistant resign duties'*. No fuss, but no reasons.

Another mysterious, discreet case occured at Fiddington,1882. A recently appointed Head, Miss Deacon, was suddenly asked to leave in December, with immediate effect. No reason recorded. She was replaced by another Head who lasted just two weeks. Two months later, the Vestry noted that the ex-Head was asked, by Messrs Moor Solicitors, to attend the County Court summons at Bridgwater. However, Miss Deacon's replacement also did not last long: by September she was cautioned about striking a child and resigned soon after. What was the summons all about? No dirty washing aired: no hints dropped. A summons was also threatened in one other school where it seems that School Funds had been held in the Head's personal account and thus got 'confused'. Perhaps this was the problem here as well.

In contrast, reticence was certainly not in Headmistress Miss Isobella Reed's nature. This was another instance of Head / Manager altercation, (again) from Monteclefe (1934), where the battle lines are drawn (at first) regarding the school cleaner. The following entries in the Log show the mounting frustration felt by the Head:

Mar 9th *'Have pointed out to the Managers that the school is being cleaned by an uninsured person aged 15 assisted by two children aged 13 and 6. Have also pointed out that a Bye-law is being infringed.'*
Mar 27th *'Stove smoking again. Room uninhabitable.'*
Mar 30th *'Called attention to state of school and yard.'*
May 4th *'Cleared the school till 10.15 so that I could get the floors swept and place dusted.'*
May 7th *'Again, had to dust and sweep before starting work.'* (Repeated on 15th, 16th.)
July 4th *'HMI Moore visited. I called his attention to the dirt.'*
July 6th *'Mrs Pinney* [Manager and Patron] *visited. Ditto'*
July 9th *'The windows are not openable. Complained by letter again to the Managers.'*
July 16th *'Complained by letter to Mr Pinney.'*
July 18th *'Managers' Meeting in School to discuss this. The cleaner spends only 20 – 45 mins in the school and often leaves the work to her 15-yr-old daughter.'*
July 23rd *'Have complained again to Mr Pinney.'*
Sept 4th *'The underparts of desks still ingrained.'*
Sept 6th *'I sat in school while building was cleaned.'*
Sept 15th *'Mr Searle* [Manager] *came to sign registers. I pointed out cobwebs etc.'*
Oct 1st *'Mrs Abbott commences as cleaner.'*

So, it took six months of persistent complaints to the Managers, HMI, the Patron, in both oral and written form before finally an alternative cleaner was appointed. Why such a delay? Was one party being over-particular and another being over-protective?

Simultaneously, the same Head, was in dispute with the Managers over perhaps a more important procedural issue which she certainly felt undermined her authority and status – namely the appointment of new staff. The Head clearly believed she should be consulted and her opinion sought in such a professional matter, which affected the nature of the team of staff she was trying to develop in order to raise standards in the school. However, reading the Managers' Minutes from this and other schools, it does not seem that the Head was usually present at an interview or was formally involved. No doubt, in the past where relationships were good, a quiet word or two were probably exchanged. But, despite new regulations set in place for the new climate and conditions of inter-war England, by 1934 relationships between the Head and the old-guard Managers were already strained. We find the following entries:

May 29th *'Miss Rodford retired today after 41 years. We made a presentation of money and a gold watch.' 'Am told that an applicant is coming for interview on Sat. I have not seen the application nor been told any details. See Handbook Section 57, para iv and v, p 58.'*
June 11th *'I am informed by letter of the appt of Miss D Harrison of CheltenhamCollege (Credit History, French, Botany, Maths) as an <u>Infant</u> Teacher in this school. I did not attend the interview nor was asked to...'*
June 18th *'Miss Harrison knows no music which is awkward with Infant teaching. I am trying to arrange other members of staff to help her.'*
Sept 24th *'As Miss Harrison is unable to play piano, I have arranged with Miss Powell to relieve Miss Squire and for Miss Lidbury to take Percussion and Eurythmics for half an hour. It is by no means convenient but is the best we can do. Both Miss Squire and Miss Lidbury are supporting me.'*

During the Autumn term everything limped on despite the difficulties. One certainly gets the feeling that the Head's Log entries were made with a view to having written documentation to support 'her case'. Things got worse when the 'supporting' staff left at the beginning of the new year, 1935:

January *'Presentation to Miss Lidbury (a looking glass) on the occasion of her marriage.'*
Jan 18th *'Miss D Hallet arrives to act as temporary teacher in Std I+II. She has none of the qualifications needed.'*
Sept 30th *'Miss Powell is retiring. Neither candidate is appropriate but Managers decide to appt Miss Fredrick. Letter from County suggesting Miss Fredrick is not sufficiently experienced for Std III+IV. So shall have to rearrange the school so she can take Std I+II. County have not yet sanctioned this arrangement'. 'Meanwhile, no supply teacher has been organised for the interim, so have wired Miss Swanson.'*

Having taken matters into her own hands and gone behind the backs / over the heads of the Managers, the Head embarked on a lengthy essay in the Log on her views of working in *'one of the most difficult schools in the County'*. She pointed out the changes in the school population and therefore the different staff now needed, *' There are now 148 children on register, half of whom are Std V+ as against one quarter in 1929'*. She went on to outline all the problems with accommodation, heating, sanitation, inadequate and under-qualified staff, poorly organised schemes of work, lack of equipment and apparatus, lack of a playing field and proper playground. However, it was not all negative. She then put forward a plan for reform – a new policy of provision, staff and materials based on regular and open communications between Head and Managers. What the reaction to this amounted to we are not told, as the Log book ends with no response or resolution of these issues. What did the Managers feel? Were they angered or thwarted and did they react by stubbornly digging in their heels? Were they overwhelmed by this new-style female, confident and opinionated Head whom they had no way of handling? Or, was it a serious personality clash?

One further case, at Writhlington 1939, is also of interest, though rather sad. A new Head was appointed in April 1936 and all seemed to be going well for 2 years. Then some worries seem to have built up: first, in relation to *'the difficult world situation'* (Sept 1938), in response to which she read a message from the League of Nations at the Armistice commemoration and talked to the children about the need for World Peace. Meanwhile one HMI had criticised some aspects of the arrangements for music – the Head was a musician and viola player. January brought burst pipes and weather-related challenges. A second HMI visited, at the Head's request, and was more supportive and suggested to the Head that she *'was doing too much of the work myself, and he would come again to help direct the staff to do more'*. He seemed to be concerned. In April a member of staff left and the Head wrote in capital letters: *NO. ON ROLL 52, FROM 3 YRS TO 13 YRS 11 MTHS*... all of whom she now had to teach.

The problems increased. She noted,*' Much clerical work to County to arrange supply and appointment'*. She seemed to take upon herself the business of finding a teacher and wrote,
'Apr 24th *Have interviewed a lady from Taunton. Not keen as difficulty of lodgings. I sent her to Mrs Batt at 2 Seward Terrace and await her return'*. Later, *'Have interviewed Mrs Bakes of Yeovil then taken her by car to the Manager, but she says distance and lack of lodgings a problem (she has an invalid husband and baby)'*.
Apr 26th she noted, *'Mrs Parfitt [Manager's wife] came in the afternoon to help'*.
Concern about the Head seems to be spreading.
May 3rd *'Scholarship form to complete, report on school situation to HMI to be made, order coal, piano tuner visited'*. And on May 4th *'Most gruelling day'*. On the 5th, she wrote at length, *'My plan had always been to improve the standard of Infant Room and Juniors and thus wise bring the school more up to date as Seniors. I found the Most Poor Section at the Top (left till aged 9 yrs, in Infant section). I firmly believe one must start with Babies, work up through Juniors and thus get Good Seniors.*
[FEAR!! scrawled in the margin*]*

Her last entries became increasingly distraught, the hand writing deteriorated. The Rev refused to sign her last entry and she asked a deliveryman to sign it *'as true...'* [The Head seemed to have left suddenly without giving formal notice. Is this a nervous breakdown....?]

Tremendous social changes were afoot. Perhaps these kinds of problems were occurring elsewhere too, though the seriousness of the above is the only one found in the focus schools.

iii. The Role of HMI. When the Inspectorate began in 1839 there were at first only 4 Inspectors for the whole country. By 1851 this had increased, but their area of responsibilities were still vast: one Inspector covered Cornwall, Devon, Somerset and Dorset, with 156 schools and 17,510 pupils! Nevertheless their Reports and comments show what was expected by them and what they hoped to see during the Inspections. They also reveal their powers to advise, admonish or appeal on behalf of staff, to try to wring some improvements from the often reluctant Managers. The annual visit followed by a Report (which was carefully copied into the Log Book) often supported Heads in their battles with Managers to appoint an Assistant or qualified member of staff to raise the standards, improve the exam results and thereby increase the grant. Equally, it was important to improve the premises and provisions and to get repairs done, all of which Managers often seemed reluctant to do. The grants, under the Revised Code of 1862, were based on a combination of these elements as well as the attendance record of the children. This was intended to be a key incentive to sustain the quality of the staff, of the premises and of the regularity of pupil attendance all of which, as we will see, became a constant battle.

a. Advice
We find shifting fashions and expectations in both methods and objectives of teaching. These are reflected in the HMI Reports for individual schools. The ones from Blagdon and Kingsdon for this period are very detailed and worth quoting in full.

1904 New Elementary Code signalled a liberalising of the curriculum and teaching process. New aims were announced which were, in contemporary parlance, more child-centred. The goal of schooling, as now recorded in the Blagdon Log was, *'To ft a child practically as well as intellectually for the world of life...A teacher should know their children and must sympathise with them. He will seek to adjust his mind to theirs and draw upon their experience as a supplement to his own'.* For the girls, *'Household management courses should set a high value on the housewife's position and to understand that their work may do much to make a nation strong and prosperous'.*

In more concrete terms this was to be translated into practices similar to those described in Kingston Seymour above. However, we find HMI noted, at Blagdon: [underlining added]

1909 *'It is desirable for this class* [Std VII] *that a progressive scheme of work is needed which should aim to cultivate self-reliance and industry. Continuous readers, atlases and dictionaries for the top class are required'.*

1911 *'The children have not been trained in habits of order and carefulness. There is a lack of tidiness. The teachers lecture too much, the children are too passive and soon become restless. The general aim should be to achieve co-operation of the children in their work, train them to make their own observations and to express themselves orally and on paper. For the Infants, organised play could do well towards developing the mental power of these young children'.*

1914 *'Older children should be given independent work guided by definite written exercises. Coherence and purpose would be given if they kept a record of their own work'.*

1924 *'It is an opportune time to create a private study group at the top of the school. They would profit from a well-planned and well-supervised programme of work'.*

The New Code marked a significant change in both aims and methods. It must have sent shock-waves across each county as it swept the entire country. Meanwhile, at the far (southern) side of the county, a school received similar advice but worked under additional constraints. Does one size fit all? In Kingsdon HMI notes:

1912 *'The mistress works conscientiously, but few profit by the instruction because they lack self-reliance and interest in their work. With such small numbers of scholars there should be less 'class' and more 'individual' teaching. Elder scholars should be trained to study by themselves with the help of good texts... Children of all ages have been grouped for oral lessons (e.g. Nature Study). Instructions cannot be suitable for the two extremes of the class... Much of the Boys' Paperwork is careless, the composition shows little originality and few of the children hold the pen properly ... The mistress receives little help from the monitress* [Head's daughter!] *who shows little energy or aptitude for teaching'.*

Infants: *'The teaching lacks life and brightness. The Classroom is small. In fine weather these little ones should be taken outside for games and physical activities... An effort should be made to train these Infants to speak distinctly and correctly and obey readily. Much of the Kindergarten work consists of amusement without a definite aim'.*

1914 *'The* [new] *Headmaster has now had charge for 5 months and has considerably improved discipline and attainments of the children. There are still weaknesses in detail... Senior children should have special work which they should largely do for themselves from books.*

The Head was advised to submit a new scheme of work for approval and to keep a record of lessons taught. The work of the monitress should be carefully supervised'.

Infants: *'The new teacher has done good work. The older Children have made excellent progress in number and they read well. Attention needs to be given to classification ... as the number in the room is becoming rather large...and the younger children cannot receive proper attention'.*

1921 *'The Head has a difficult task of teaching 27 children of all ages with no assistance except that of a young monitress. The few Infants appear to have a dull time. They need more speech training and more movement'.*

This new need for a spirit of autonomy in children reverberates in a comment from Enmore 1940, where HMI appeared to feel that the school had not maintained its previous *avant garde* status and had failed to move with the times, *'There is too much emphasis on remembering isolated facts. More opportunities are needed for children to work things out for themselves'.*

Each of these extracts clearly show how HMIs' comments changed over the years and reflected their new expectations. In the previous century *'quiet and obedient', 'quick to answer', 'accuracy of answers'* seemed valued. Later, *'bright and responsive', 'interested and lively'*, and still later, *'able to discuss and to apply to their own lives', 'shows initiative and self-reliance'* appeared more commonly. Now, however, phrases like, a *'progressive scheme of work'* with the objective *'to cultivate self-reliance and industry'* occurred more regularly, as did *'less class teaching and more individual work'*. With this went the need for *'careful individual records'*, and we begin to find references to reports being sent to parents.

This changing perception of the purposes of education was evident in the debates occurring when major pieces of legislation were being introduced during the period under study: while Forster, in 1870, proposed that the need for elementary education was because on it *'depends our industrial prosperity'*; Chief Inspector for Elementary Schools, Edmund Holmes, in 1899, commented that *'The Village School has a national not to say imperial role, for its business is to turn out citizens for the battle of life to be fought in any part of the Empire'*. Nevertheless, it was not until 1931 that we see much official concern for the classroom processes of education: Hadow's Report on elementary schools expressed the principle, that *'teachers should take as a starting point the experiences, curiosity and interests of the child'* – perhaps echoing Comenius, Rousseau and others from a much earlier age. Hadow's statement is closer to current child-centred practices and was a far cry from the dominant C19th reliance on passive repetition and rote learning.

b. Admonishments. Many individual staff were singled out for praise or blame. HMI also had the task of examining the pupil-teachers and unqualified staff who were working to upgrade their status and thus the Inspectors made decisions on the pass or fail status of a candidate. Sometimes the whole school was found to be at fault and serious criticisms raised.

Even Heads came in for individual criticism. One HMI description of a Head read, *'Though the Master bears a high character he is wanting in his power as a teacher. Discipline is weak'* (SmM 1850). While in another school HMI stated, *'The issue of a Certificate for Miss Holdsworth is deferred for better results in Writing and Arithmetic'* (Kgd 1877) but, two years later, *'Kate Perrot passes but must attend to History to qualify under Article 60 and 79'*. Such examples are numerous across the schools.

Whole schools could go through difficult times: Kingsdon was certainly one which seems to have had a troubled history. In1893 the HMI Report was damning: *'Reading and Writing were fair. Standard III and IV have done fairly in Arithmetic, but by V and VI there is absolute failure. The results of Singing and Geography do not justify any grant. The school would benefit from the Organising Inspector of Bath and Wells Day School Association. At present the school runs a serious risk of being warned of inefficiency'.* This is a devastating summary of the year's work and sounds as though the school was destined for 'emergency measures'. When the Chief Inspector, arrived six months later, the Log recorded only that he examined the Registers. What else happened or what was actually said we shall never know, but at least this shows that back-up systems were in place for dire situations even if, from this Log, it appeared ineffective.

Cutcombe had a troubled time at the turn of the century, but preferred to rely on its own resources. It was the Manager's representative who was instructed to undertake the delicate task of "talking to the Head" with a view to identifying what needed to be done to pull the school round – successfully as it transpired.

By the inter-war years, HMI could also offer individual support for struggling teachers: it became common for staff to visit other schools to gain ideas, sometimes for a day, sometimes a month. Whether this would have helped a new teacher in Blagdon is uncertain: in 1930, HMI states, *'The new teacher must be described as not sufficiently experienced to be in charge of the Infants. She does not possess the temperament and she lacks animation'.* A visit to a nearby school was advised.

c. Appeals to the Managers. In addition, a further role played by HMI was to make regular and repeated appeals to the Managers for more staff, many of which seemed to fall on deaf ears. In this respect they really were the teachers' friend – sometimes the only one they felt they had. But, a recommendation, a suggestion – however strongly worded – did not always lead to action and such appeals frequently went unheeded for a long time.

Somerton West End Infants School, 1883, was considered to suffer from a weak staff. HMI comment, *'Managers do not appear to pay for a competent Pupil-Teacher, burthened (sic) as they are with a rent of £30 pa, an amount higher than I have ever encountered for the accommodation afforded'.* [The building, originally a barn, was bought and converted into a school by the Pinney family, a very prominent family in the area. Captain, later Colonel, Pinney was also the Chairman of the School.]

Similarly, at Somerton Boys School (1898) HMI urged reluctant Managers to improve staffing levels and add a qualified adult rather than rely on (cheaper) pupil-teachers and monitors. Managers received strong reminders of their duties from HMI. The annual Report for 1893 noted, *'This school has done creditably well considering the irregularity of attendance caused by the ineffectiveness of the School Board and the recent attack of epidemic added to the distinct weakness of staff. An Assistant should be provided and the neglect of the Board met, in some measure, by the establishment of a night school'.* The poor Head was struggling to cope with only one pupil-teacher to assist in a school with 126 pupils on the books. The pupil-teacher helped with Standards I and II while the Head took all remaining Standards (III-VII). This criticism resulted in another pupil-teacher being appointed, but still no experienced adult. Again in the 1895 Report HMI commented, *'The Master would do better if he had an efficient Assistant, his staff being decidedly weak'.* Nothing happened to improve matters and, in May 1898, a special HMI visit was made and the subsequent Report stated, *'It is impossible for Mr Hewitt to keep up the efficiency of the school unless some addition be made to the present weak staff. The appointment under article 50 in place of a Probationer and Monitor would best meet the case'.* In subsequent months nothing more was mentioned about staffing. The problems continue for the long-suffering head. Clearly money, or lack of it, was at the root of the difficulties. In January1899 HMI Report recorded, *'The Governing Body of the School think it not unreasonable to expect a larger amount of Subscriptions to the school. My Lords hope that these will be raised in the coming years'.* Meanwhile, the school received Grant Aid of £20, for equipment £5 (books, objects, pictures), for Repairs £15 (sanitation, floors and painting), but nothing additional for staffing.

The pressure was still on. In 1899, HMI stated, *'The Master's efforts are sadly hampered by a weak staff'* also, *'A pupil-teacher is now recognised under Article 33, but he must not be employed in teaching for more than half the time the school is open'.* Clearly the temptation to use the pupil-teachers as though they were Assistants must have been great. By 1904, the Head was still suffering. When both pupil-teachers complete and leave he was forced to close the school for at least a week. Soon after, we learn, *'A 14-year-old boy, Albert Victor, commences as a Probationer, and the Head's wife commences as a temporary teacher'.* This was hardly a long-term solution to a perennial problem. Only at the beginning of the following year did the Head finally get an unqualified assistant, a pupil-teacher and a monitor to support him – still not a properly qualified staff. [All three Somerton schools, though each with their own Board (on which the Pinney family predominated) were managed by using a considerable cross-over of personnel.]

Not only were Managers slow to respond to appeals for better staffing, but also for repairs and building improvements as witnessed by the long time-lag between HMI suggestions and Managers' response. This was usually due to lack of sufficient funds (or lack of will) within the school. Grants, from 1862 were dependent on the adequacy of the premises, the regularity of attendance, as well as good pupils' exam results, which in turn related to the quality of staff. It was much more than just 'payment by results'. So much rested on the existence of supportive and wealthy patrons and benefactors, also on the generosity of church members' contributions at collections, and the level of local education rate set. Managers seemed strapped for cash, or just reluctant to spend. The extracts below make this clear.

Table 7.1: Time-lapse between action recommended and completed.

Date	HMI Comment	Date	School Action
Blg 1887	Ventilation + toilets need attention		
1893	Again, more accommodation needed	'95	New classroom + cloaks added
1895,1899	Still overcrowded (after 'free education', 1890s)	'08	New classroom provided
Kgd 1907	Urinal buckets to be emptied twice a week	'55	Flushing toilets installed
1919, 1920	Room not warm		Not improved till post-1944
1935	Overcrowded		Only 'resolved' by falling numbers
Ctc 1893	Closets should be attended to	'98	Many repairs, but no closets
1900/01/03	Staff should be strengthened		
1903,1908	Closets, Ventilation, Heating needed attention		
1910/22/23	Head has 50 chdn in a room, needs support	'24	Supplementary T appointed
1912/35	Temperature 41° at 3pm		
1939	Letter re fumes (to Manag/Vicar/CEd Sec)	'37	Closed for heating refurbishment!

As we can see, it was often a battle to get repairs completed – particularly for the proverbial problem of stoves and toilets. All strings needed to be pulled in order to secure basic improvements. Cutcombe, being at the edge of Exmoor and the highest school in the county, often suffered from *'wet and rough weather'*, *'very wild winds and hail which broke some panes'* and, of course, smokey fires throughout the winter months from November to March. Low temperatures in the *40° F* range were regularly recorded. In March 1935 the Head spoke to the Managers about the frequency of problems with fires, and again in May. In October she wrote to the Vicar, who is also a Manager. In January 1936 she wired the Secretary for Education in Taunton, no less. This was rewarded: by April of that same year when the buildings were closed for heating repairs, but to no avail. It took further letters in Jan 1938 and in 1939 before the repairs were finally resolved.

iv. The contexts and provision for teaching

As already noted, the condition and suitability of the premises were also criteria for an application for a state grant under the 1862 Code. Again, despite frequent recommendations from HMI, money (or lack of it) was the key to whether squalor or stimulation was the characteristic of the learning environment.

a. General maintenance

In addition to the endless difficulties reported about heating, lighting and ventilation there was also the constant need for general repairs from wear and tear, as well as the need for cleansing and re-decorating. There were also new ideas about 'modern' features: wall-fitted blackboards, rather than a board and easel; cupboards became needed for the greater amount of books and equipment teachers were using. Finally, out in the playground, the school Flag Pole came to be a regular accessory once Empire Day was instituted in 1903 and, later, when Armistice Day was regularly commemorated.

At Somerton Boys, the Head noted in September 1895, that the ceilings and wall needed attention and that once a week was not adequate for sweeping the floors. This was reiterated in the HMI Report at the end of that same year. The end of year Report for 1898 did acknowledge that the general aspect of the premises had been greatly improved and expressed hopes for further enhancement. The summer holiday had to be prolonged by over a week as the workmen had not finished the painting and general repairs. During the summer holidays of 1904 many of the sought-after repairs were done: the main room floor was partly re-laid, the ceiling repaired, a new tortoise-stove installed, walls coloured pale green, battens fixed to walls from which maps and pictures could be hung, offices lime-washed, two basins and taps provided, guttering repaired and playground asphalt laid. Unfortunately only six months later HMI again complained about the state of the playground (previous shoddy work?) and described it as '*too rough for Drill work*'. Poor lighting was also still mentioned.

The purpose-built school at Keinton Mandeville, only commissioned in 1902, had no Gallery – they were already becoming old-fashioned. Yet the order for furniture is an interesting reflection on what was in fashion and helps us to visualise how the classroom looked and imagine the conditions in which teachers worked. The traditional long desks were still ordered, despite the fact that some schools were already changing to dual desks:

8 Infant desks (each 8' long) with sloping desk top, joined to long benches which seat 6 pupils	£6 0 0d
2 square folding easels	£ 8 4d
1 Abacus	£ 4 3d
1 Blackboard rules for music	£ 13 0d
3 dozen sets of rhythm thumb-bells	£ 6 6d
2 cocoa exercise mats	£ 6 6d
2 window curtains	£ 6 6d
8 dozen picture/map hooks	£ 6 6d
3 large Windsor chairs for teachers	£ 13 6d
Also, Head's Desk and Mistress' sewing table	
Insurance for buildings and contents per year	£800 0 0d

Blackboards were another innovation which was spreading through the county, this time larger ones fixed to the walls, rather than small ones on a portable easel. Kingsdon School was one of the first to use them, in 1904, while Blagdon followed two years later. Enmore, in 1906, ordered 2 frames for the boards at 4s 0d and 4 brackets at 3s 6d in order to fix the new blackboards to the wall, while Somerton Boys ingeniously fixed black linoleum to the wall to serve the same purpose.

b. The classroom environment and materials

As more equipment was now being used in schools, storage space had to be found. Shelves and cupboards were fixed in available corners. Blagdon ordered cupboards in 1899. These were also installed in Somerton Monteclefe and elsewhere. The cupboard in West End was also used to shut 'naughty' children inside. A contributor recalls, "*When a girl was shut in, the boys would all start being naughty, too, in the hopes of being shut in with her....*"

At Monteclefe, where overcrowding was becoming a problem, the Head noted, '*The room called a Library has been cleared and a class sent there, but there is still insufficient room*'. HMI added his voice and asserted, '*The Managers need to relieve the overcrowding by building a new classroom*'. In 1909 HMI again pressed the case for additional accommodation and noted that one room only was available for Infants which was quite unsuitable for the three existing Infant classes (46 children aged 5 and over and 23 under 5 years), also, the playground needed repair.

The annual HMI Report for Somerton Boys (1909), also emphasised that the buildings were still very overcrowded, lighting not satisfactory and that the Gallery should be removed. Again, in 1911 the Report stated, '*The work of the school is carried on under great difficulties. Three classes together in an undivided Hall; the only classroom is poorly ventilated, lighting inadequate, and insufficient desk accommodation.* Pupils had been pushed into unsuitable areas. In this instance, instead of focusing on separate classrooms for the younger ones, HMI reported, '*The Headmaster is advised to make a separate class of the best boys*' – in the top class. By October of the next year, a folding partition was installed, a classroom enlarged and better offices built. At last, a year later HMI was able to say, '*Accommodation is now good*'. Being squashed into corridors, cloaks and cupboards is obviously nothing new!

Text Books for the 3Rs.

Log Books frequently quote the orders for materials which were periodically submitted by the Head for approval and supply. These frequently arrived by carrier and, later, by train, and would then be fetched by the Head or a Manager.

New Reading Materials are also mentioned during these years. Unfortunately the titles are not always given and the publishers rarely. Examples include:

1874 new books were received for Standards I-III [no titles given] Kingsdon
1871 *New Standard Readers* were introduced at Monteclefe Girls School
1874 Collins *New Code Readers* arrive at Kingston Seymour.
1876 Nelson *Royal Readers* were first used in Charlton Mackrell and still being used in the 1890s.
1877 Chambers *Primers* were used in Skilgate and in Coleford,
1882 *Imperial Readers* were used at Horsington
1892 *Royal Readers* were chosen at Somerton Boys School
1890s *Blackwood, Star,* and *Century Readers* were all tried at Horsington
1903 Nelson *Royal Readers*, and (hopefully titled) '*Reading without Tears*' used in Kingsdon
1912 *Press Forward Series* was introduced at Kingston Seymour

And, in 1913, an HMI advised N Curry School '*to get some Primers with long vowels*'.

Despite the many alternatives, *Royal Readers* seemed a firm favourite. This list shows a very wide range of books which were available on the market – it must have been a growing sector. Copies of these titles were well-worn and well-used: not many examples are readily accessible. Thus we do not know how the nature of the content changed, what style of illustrations (if any) existed, or what teaching method was incorporated as the changing fashions for teaching reading evolved. It is only from the interwar period that it becomes easier to find old copies of *Beacon Readers*, with its post-war update *Kitty and Rover, Happy Venture Series,* or *Janet and John.*

Arithmetic Text Books were less frequently and less fulsomely mentioned. Examples include:

1875	*National Arithmetic*	Skilgate
1882	Collin's *Arithmetic*	Skilgate
1898	*Answers to Blackie's Arithmetic*	Kingsdon
1898	*Ajax Arithmetical Test Cards*	Kingsdon
1899	Lock and Collard	Oakhill British School
1936	Wheaton's *Parallel Arithmetic*	Keinton Mandeville

No indication of the style of contents of these books was given in the Logs. It is only by chance that it is possible to come across any of them on second-hand stalls.

To get an idea of the breadth of materials which any one school might order on any occasion we can look at the list from Charlton Mackrell (1891). A very full list was given for the opening of the school in September. The order indicated the numbers attending and also gave insights into the 'what' and 'how' of classroom lessons. It was important, too, in that the list revealed the curriculum subjects: Reading, Drawing, Writing, Practical Science, Geography (of which many details are given throughout the Log). For the first time, History gets a mention. That very August, the Rector had arranged for History to be taken instead of Grammar!

1 ½ doz Citizen Readers	
1 doz Stories of Chilor's Pets	Std II
17 Royal English Readers for	Std III
13 " " "	Std IV
12 " " "	Std V
1 ½ doz Stories and Fables	Std I
1 ½ doz Westminster History Reading Books	Std II
1 ½ doz Gill's Standard Geography of England	
1 doz Moffett's Geography	Std IV
3 doz Whitehall Drawing Books	
1 doz National Society Drawing Books	
3 doz copybooks	
1 doz ink-wells	
T- square	
1 Mariner's Compass	
3 Wall Maps: England, Scotland, Ireland	
4 doz Bacon's Memory Maps: United States and Scotland	
6 pictures from Royal Agricultural Society	
2 doz Home Seasons Books	
2 Whitehall Drawing Demonstration Sheets	
1 Green's Spelling and Dictation Exercises	

As the History Book is a Reader, perhaps it is of the genre of stories about brave British heroes rather than lists of dates and facts – it would probably be used for Home Lessons and then tested in class. The Geography syllabus covered England, then Europe and the World: it included physical features such as rivers and mountains and, also, economic features.

Library facilities: A very few schools with innovative Heads, such as at Cutcombe, Coleford, Keinton and Somerton Boys, looked for ways of widening reading opportunities for their children. They had begun by collecting subscriptions to try to start individual school Libraries. It was a very modest beginning. We find other schools trying to extend their range of reading materials, as in 1892, when the Head of Somerton Boys sent for a list of Reading Books for Infant's private studies and, in 1919, the school started a Library where books for pleasure could also be included. 1908 saw Cutcombe swap *Robinsoe Crusoe* for *Tom Brown's School Days* with nearby Winsford in their own library exchange system.

While the 1850 Library Act had given access to books in the towns, these opportunities had not reached the villages. A new service was started, in the 1920s, by the County Council. This provided a travelling Library van which brought boxes of books to rural schools to use for six months before being exchanged. This was a wonderful chance to widen reading opportunities in literacy-poor areas and a significant change from which hard-pressed Managers, Head, parents and children could benefit.

This at last could go some way towards providing the books needed for the 'self-study programmes of work' intended to encourage 'self-reliance and industry' which HMI were urging upon the schools (as we shall see in the next chapter). Somerton Boys' joined the Rural Libraries Scheme as did Writhlington in 1919, followed quickly by Keinton in 1920, soon followed by other schools at Brewham (1923), Kingston Seymour (1925), Cutcombe (1927) and Westhay (1928).

The new century's reading books were chosen for their strong and motivating content as a stimulus to want to read. HMI, too, suggested that in addition to the variety of text books indicated above, a diet of more Literary Readers would encourage greater reading. Hence, some schools adopted Nelson's *World at Home* series which included more classic texts from the English canon as well as classics from abroad - within the literature of the English language and therefore reaching only to America, rather than going beyond into translations of classics from continental countries.

c. Equipment and Education Media.

Some of the new equipment was bought with funds raised by the schools themselves through concerts, plays, country-dancing displays and poetry recitals. Other fund-raising events included sales of children's work made in the needlework, woodwork, gardening and cookery classes and even fetes where entrants had to guess the number of pips in a marrow, as at Charlton Mackrell in 1906 (the answer was 470!).

Three new oil lamps were hung in Blagdon in 1895, giving 100 candle-power for only £4, which must have greatly helped in the close work children needed to undertake. In Somerton, Monteclefe Girls had gas lights installed in 1885, while the Boys received the same during the summer holidays of 1913. The real breakthrough came with the arrival of electricity to outlying villages, making a significant difference to the range of resources which then became available. Electricity came to Cutcombe in 1961, to Keinton and many other villages. It was similar in Coleford, and only in 1968 did Enmore join the grid. Thus by the end of the sixties Somerset was criss-crossed with power lines providing consistent light by which children could work.

Once electricity arrived, hot dinners could be considered, wireless and even tape recorders and film-projectors suddenly became possible. Horizons grew with immediate impact for teachers, pupils, Managers – and budgets.

Table 7.2 Acquisition of new Equipment in a variety of Schools

Piano	SingerSewing Machine	Wireless	Records/Tapes Film Projector	TV	Swimming Pool
1898 from Mrs Pinney (SmM); 1909 harmonium (Chl) 1920 (ChM); 1920s (Kgd); 1926 SomB gave a piano concert; 1926 (Blg); 1936 piano(Wrl) (reconditioned)	1927 (Blg) 1928 (Ntc) 1929 (Skg) 1930s Barton	1927 (KgS) 1928 (Skg) 1930 heard King address 5-Power Naval Conf.(KgS) 1931 Vicar brought radio to hear Armistice service (Cte)	1924 A teacher brought in a gramophone to hear the King's Empire Message		1935 KM uses flooded quarry '*Lido*' as swimming pool
		1954 bought from funds raised at the Christmas Festivities (KgS)	1952 Film Strip Projector (Blg) 1959 Tape Recorder (Blg)	1950s B/W (Enm)	
				1975 TV (colour) for *Watch* - a Nature Prog (Kgd)	1965 (NCry) 1970s (Kgd) used Strode Pool, Street

The introduction of broadcast wireless lessons was significant for small isolated schools, which often had very few staff with a limited range of skills between them. To be able to tap into top quality specialists, through the wireless, must have significantly enriched the curriculum experience for pupils.

At first, wireless was used for important national events such as to hear the Armistice service, or a Royal broadcast. Soon, the special School Broadcasts were used and incorporated into lessons. Kingston Seymour, 1927 having listened to a music lesson from Sir Walford Davis, found "*It was a wonder to many.*" Much taken with the new medium, the following January the Head recorded, "*History and Nature Lessons are now taken on Mon and Thurs afternoons. The children listen to a wireless lesson, notes are written on the board and each child follows in a textbook. The lesson is afterwards recapitulated with teacher's aids. Readers are used in conjunction with History, Spelling, Composition and Drawing which are all correlated. The first batch of compositions were sent to the BBC Education Officers. The subjects of the essays were Winter Sleepers or Creatures which Hibernate.* Feb 2nd *We received information that James Powell's essay was praised.*" By 1938, the school was also listening along to *Music and Movement* with the wireless.

Another experiment was encouraged by the wireless, which, in 1928 linked History and Nature Study. A further use of wireless, also for History Lessons, was in Oakhill British School (1935), with a course which started with *Ancient Britain.* This would seem to be a more traditional chronological approach. It is unusual in that it is a first attempt to teach the earlier stages of the British people, while most-quoted syllabi focused on the post-Tudor period. Perhaps this was precisely why the broadcasts focussed on what schools often avoided. Meanwhile, Charlton Mackrell got carried away with the new medium: the Log recorded that two lessons a day were based on the wireless. Thus they used broadcasts on History and Folk Stories, Nature Studies, Music, Literature, Geography.

Teachers found the advantage to be threefold: it managed the lesson plan, motivated the children and made monitoring easier, as the teacher could concentrate on watching the children rather than trying to conduct the details of the lessons. During a series of visits to schools using the new broadcast lessons Miss Mary Somerville from the BBC came to visit Charlton Mackrell in 1930 and commented, *'A jollier school I have never met'* !

Commercial Companies: It is also a period when commercial enterprises began to offer free items and became involved in sponsoring materials: **Coleman of Norwich** gave starch-blue and mustard to Cutcombe (1903), **Ovaltine, Cadburys, Horlicks and Anglo-Swiss Condensed Milk** are all reported as participating in school-based 'health' schemes (SomB 1929, KM 1936) as did **Lever Bros** in the ***Clean Hands Scheme***. Somerton Boys won a real football (1927) having collected 2,400 **match box tops**, while **Shell Nature Posters** were much sought after and are remembered at Kingston Seymour (1950s).

Further facilities like improved sanitation, heating and electricity must have made a huge difference to the daily battle to overcome the physical shortcomings of the buildings. And the introduction of the telephone must have been a delight – Coleford had theirs installed in 1965, as did many others around the same time!

The above insights into specific relationships and the resultant atmosphere of the school, together with the general details of the books, opportunities and resources available begin to give an idea of what it was like for teachers in village schools. It also shows us something of the curriculum being taught over these years. So we must now turn to the next chapter where this is outlined with rich details from the School Logs.

Chapter 8
What was Taught: Curriculum Content and Materials

There was a dramatic change in the **content** of the curriculum during the C19th, away from exclusive attention to the 'core', or 3 Rs plus the added 4th R of Religious Instruction, to a broader conception of 'education'. Through government statements at key moments we can trace shifts in aims: from the early C19th focus on moral and religious training (on grounds of national concerns of political necessity and, later, industrial expediency) to a consideration of the child. This appeared in Morant's claim (announcing the New Code, 1904) that, '*The purpose of public education is the forming and strengthening of the character and the development of the intelligence of children to assist boys and girls to fit themselves for society...and to instil the habits of industry, self-control and perseverance*'. In order to achieve this, more and more subjects were added to 'what' children had to learn – including Drill and Sport, and Health campaigns.

Significantly, 'how' pupils learned changed too: away from reliance on teacher transmission and pupil rote memorisation, towards private study and needing to think as well as to use imagination. After the implementation of the **Revised Code in 1862**, 'schemes of work' became ever more important and teachers had to stick to them ever more rigidly. This led to enormous pressures to teach to the tests and restricted any experimentation. Gradually, from the 1890s, teaching methods became more flexible again and curriculum changes were introduced to meet the new perceived needs of society: the needs of the individual were acknowledged later, in the inter-war developments.

The Log Books kept by the Heads, from the last quarter of the C19th, show the schemes of work which had to be approved by HMI (then copied into the Log). They also reveal how the Head had to seek permission to deviate from the timetable which made the slightest change difficult. The increasingly complex system of grants for different subjects, the levels of attainment and other criteria already mentioned (Ch. 4) all gave the schemes of work a still greater importance. In the most remote areas, some adjustments to the standard options were encouraged to suit the rural conditions, particularly from the 1930s.

i. The basics: 3Rs – reading, writing and rekoning
a. Reading

Learning to read had consistently been the central purpose of schooling. The teaching of reading, however, underwent many transformations. We can see that, in the time of Hannah More, the emphasis was on 'syllabification'. Texts were presented to children in graded sequences: the first-year texts contained words of just one syllable, second-year texts with two and so on. So the children were asked to read texts such as '*Do not nod on a sod*', or '*Let Sam sip the sap of red jam*'. These texts are barely intelligible! It is a real challenge to write interesting texts with just one syllable words, especially if the texts also have to be 'morally instructive'. But then, children did not need to be motivated, just obedient. Such texts must have been difficult for children to read: because they were so contrived in content, the narrative would be hard to predict; because words had to be monosyllabic, they were not necessarily easy to decode, including as they did, phonetically complex words such as 'straight'. Catherine, in Austen's *Northanger Abbey* (Ch. 14) bewails the torturing of children and their teachers when she says, *'If you had been as much used as myself to hear poor little children first learning their letters and then learning to spell, if you had ever seen how stupid they can be for a whole morning together and how tired my mother is at the end ... you would allow that to torment and to instruct might sometimes be used as synonymous words'.* This must have been a similar experience for many a class.

A first detail from the examined Log Books, was in 1872, when the new Head at Kingsdon, Miss Challiner, aged 25, (straight from her training at the Home and Colonial Training Institute, London), in only the second week, conducted her first lesson on the **Phonic System of Reading**. It was a bald statement, with no follow-up, no further comment. What transpired we do not know.

In the 1870s Blagdon Logs revealed that children stood in a circle and each read one sentence aloud. (Many can remember doing this in the 1950s! One contributor recalled reading individual letters, and also syllables, which were then combined from the board and chanted e.g. 'c-a-t makes cat', and 'sup-and-per makes supper'. The policy for more phonic training has returned in the C21st with 'new' Literacy Hours). In 1878, ***Reading Cards*** were recommended by HMI (with individual letters and, also, perhaps consonant clusters, syllables and words to learn). The Head soon taught 'The Power of the Consonants' to the Infants. A decade later, another Head taught 'Letter Sounds and Syllables' to the Infants. In 1888, a ***Box of loose letters*** was used for word-building with Infants at Isle Brewer's while Chaffcombe children make letters with strips of card – a more tactile medium.

In the 1880s there appeared to be a shift in the favoured method for teaching reading. In August 1885, at Somerton West End Infant School, the Head noted that new ***Reading Sheets*** had been received. Perhaps these were word lists for children to help learn the common but phonetically irregular words, by shape, in the manner of the **Look and Say method**, for, in October the Head noted, *'The Pupil-teacher understands Look and Say method and is able to handle her class with more power'.* In November, the Head commented that she had examined the first class in Reading and there was some improvement: *'They are greatly given to notice the matter* [content] *rather than to acquire* [skills of] *reading'.* Was this a compliment on their comprehension of *what* they read, or a criticism of *how* they read – with interest favoured over accuracy? The next time that the method of teaching reading was mentioned was not until 1902, when HMI reported, *'A fuller development of the Phonic method of reading is strongly advised'.* In the following May, the then Head noted that a combination of Phonic with the Look and Say method was to be adopted. Somerton Boys' showed a determination to raise reading standards by the purchase, in 1902, of *The English Method of Learning to Read* by Sonnenschein and Meiklejohn, although no comment was made as to which method. There were also *Readers* to go along with this teacher's book, as we find at Holcombe Wesleyan School in 1910.

In terms of the expectations of reading, HMI commented, of Monteclefe in 1884, *'Reading is rather timid'*, but in the following year, *'Nice expression evinced in Reading, but mechanical answering as to content of the book'.* While in Holcombe 1908 HMI commented, *'Reading is practised not taught'*, perhaps a reference to a mechanical, rote-reading performance where the children did not really know how to read for themselves. Only once do we find reference to the value of silent reading

(Clf 1908) - an important element of independent study-reading. Even in 1959 (Cte) we still find HMI expressing concerns that there was not enough training in extracting information from books and producing an account of what is read.

Children who did not have the advantage of a literate home – as many did not - often struggled to read. In Infant classes I and 2 (SmWE 1870) half the children were not able to read and four months later only 6/18 could read without considerable assistance. At Kingsdon 1885, *'but* [only] *15% of children passed their reading exam'* when the Inspector called. Were already disadvantaged children at a further disadvantage of inappropriate methods of teaching without individual attention? At the same school HMI commented, in 1912, *'Two classes should not be reading aloud at the same time'*. (It saved time for the teacher - children were evaluated for fluency whilst assuming this also meant accuracy and understanding, in the belief that as long as they kept reading they must be doing it right. Examples of such multiple simultaneous readings were still evident in the 1970s.) At Kingston Seymour in 1934, a contributor remembered, *"The **Sentence Method** was used. Our books were very brightly coloured. We were in groups and helped each other. The Inspector was quite impressed"*. In 1965 Coleford adopted the very new experimental approach of the **Pitman *i.t.a.*** [Initial Teaching Alphabet] script as a method of learning to read, as did Keinton and nearby Charlton Mackrell for over ten years from 1970. There was no comment about the adoption of this method nor why it was later dropped. Another experiment was tried in 1978, when Kingsdon reports that teachers attended a talk on the **Colour Coded Reading Scheme** by Bridie Raban and Cliff Moon, both attached to the Reading Reading Centre. This system related to the 'natural' approach, 'learning to read by reading', or, 'whole language approach'- which relied on an ability to predict from context (text and illustrations) as a key strategy in reading: books were graded and coloured for children either to have read to them or gradually to read by themselves.

Reading for pleasure was also encouraged, but books were expensive and hard to come by. In remote Cutcombe we find HMI, in 1878, advising that at least two sets of reading books for each class should be available to extend the reading experience. Other ways of encouraging reading was by using ***newspapers*** in class, such as *Somerset Journal*, *Tit Bits, Great Thoughts* and *Pearson's Weekly*, as at Coleford 1891. Here, Headmaster Frederick Close found, *'Children take great delight in reading them. I fear their opportunities of finding reading matter are few. It is to encourage the love of reading that I have these interesting papers, and not just to read anything'*. To pursue this further, in 1893 he began collecting subscriptions to form a School Library to be opened half an hour before and after school. The books arrived, were numbered and prepared before borrowing began. The same Head noted two years later, that *'Varied occupations and the judicious use of periodicals are the best Attendance Officer possible'*. Clearly he found positive motivation more fruitful in attracting children to attend than the fear of punishment. A similar spirit was to be found at nearby Oakhill British School, where Newspapers were also used at the turn of the century, and Horsington in 1908.

b. Writing

Developing a 'good hand' was considered essential. We noted that Rev Poole, in 1810, had had sand trays in his school, in which children could get the feel and shape of letters. They were also mentioned in Somerton West End Infants' School (1905) and can be found in the Victorian Schoolroom at Radstock Museum (Plate 11). We gain a detailed insight into how handwriting - together with reading - was taught in Coleford School in 1878. A new Head arrived at the Infant school and she recorded the progress: First, *'The children are taught to recognise their alphabet letters'*. This takes about three weeks. Then, *'The Infants commence with strokes, then curves, before making small letters'*. Three weeks later *'The children are joining letters'*. By November, *'They can copy letters from the slate board, but not yet from memory'*. In January, *'The children are using* (word) *cards for reading'*. In February, *'The children can write dictated letters from memory'* and by May *'are reading several words*'. It is not until October that Capital Letters are mentioned. So, after 15 months, all the Infants in the first Class *'read Chambers Primer II fairly and distinctly, and spelt correctly a portion of the words from memory, and copied from the slate board'*. In the second and third classes of younger children, *'10 / 15 read very creditably and copied letters from the slate-board'*. A subsequent Head at the turn of the century in the same school also supplied details on teaching Handwriting: *'Today capital D was analysed, also the joining of certain letters was introduced, and other letters performed to practise parallels and turns'*, as:

bfghjklyz *and* *mmuunn*

Handwriting and spelling were generally of greater priority in C19th schools than the notion of 'free' expressive writing is in our current primary schools. Dictation, too, emphasised the 'secretarial' features of writing. Plenty of copying from the board in all subjects also required a habit of accuracy. To assist in neat writing, HMI suggested, at Cutcombe (1883), *'Infants should write at desks, on suitably ruled slates'* (Ctc 1883). Again, HMI advised, *'Slates should be properly ruled for Handwriting*' (SmM 1882). Soon we are told, *'Children are improving in the freer use of their fingers, owing to more frequent drill. Varying the children's position is bringing more finger power and better eye-hand coordination, but the writing in the third class is apparently hopeless as yet'* (SmWE 1885). An interesting insight is revealed at Blagdon (1899), when HMI declared *'Make an end to spitting on slates in favour of a sponge in order to avoid spreading diseases*'. Also in N Curry (1901) HMI declared, *'The practice of spitting on slates must stop'*. Later, at Monteclefe, there is an instance of a child being punished for stealing the substitute sponge. A contributor remembered the first knitted item in the Infant class was a cloth for cleaning your slate. Slates continued in use till the turn of the century. The style of handwriting taught in school seems to have changed, too. In 1903, the Monteclefe Head complained of poor handwriting: she intended changing from *Forster's Bold* (a very round and sloping style) to *Nelson's* upright style. In 1938, Writhlington adopted the *Cursive* style, while residents at Keinton remembered the *Marion Richardson* books.

Functional skills were considered more useful: at Horsington 1872, children wrote the notices for the Vestry meeting. At Monteclefe 1903, the Head bought envelopes and note paper as part of a project to teach children how to write letters, while at Coleford 1935 the children were encouraged to write letters to other children in different schools. What better motivation could there possibly be than when the children of Kingsdon decide to write to His Majesty in 1907, *'to ask if he will come to their village on his way to Glastonbury. Eve Chapple wrote the letter as she is the best writer'* (Nov) and, in December they got a reply *'which will be kept in the School Museum'*.

Writing ('writing out') often consisted of writing a summary of what had been read. The innovation of 'Free composition' was introduced only to upper classes in 1871 (Blg) but it was not clear what this comprised and was not often mentioned in other schools. Perhaps an example from Coleford (1899) may be typical: the Head set a composition, *'first giving a subject for reading up'*. Nevertheless in the new century the emphasis seemed to have changed a little. An indication of the restricted role of Composition may be gleaned when a Head decided that *'Dictation from unseen books will be substituted for Composition'* (Clf 1890). It would seem spelling was more important than expression, and reproduction more important than creation. Cutcombe set a different trend: in 1905 we find a syllabus which included Simple Composition for Stds I+II *'based on local sights and events'* and for Std III+IV compositions were *'based on the children's experiences'*. This was a very expressive and modern-sounding approach.

Yet, in an environment when the teacher's comments were more likely to suggest *'neatness needs to be improved'*, there may well have been little incentive or opportunity to write imaginatively. But some attempt at originality was also expected – along with neatness and correctness. A typical mixed message comment comes from an HMI report which stated, *'Much of the paperwork is careless, the composition shows little originality and few children hold the pen properly'* (Kgd 1912). In an effort to develop composition skills Somerton Boys' purchased a copy of *English* published by Schofield and Simms which *'has made decided improvement on Composition'* (SmB 1903). Sadly, no further details were given.

In a rare reference to Composition at the turn of the century, and an early example of commercial enterprises becoming involved in education, we find children from Oakhill British School being commended for essays written for a competition organised by **Lever Bros** of Port Sunlight on the Wirral (the topic relating to Hygiene and the use of company soap), and the results in another competition achieved by two further children were commended in a 1916 issue of *The Teachers' World*. However it was not often before the 1930s that we find compositions being a regular part of school life, for the senior classes.

Essay competitions came to be organised in Health Week, by the RSCPA, RoSPA and other such organisations, which would also probably not require a creative or imaginative style but be grounded in fact. The **Bird and Tree** competition was very popular in some schools, where they did very well and regularly won prizes, especially at Skilgate, Chaffcombe and Chillington. Essay titles such as *Night Life*, were intended to encourage close observation of local wild life and the children seemed to have responded well. The **Lifeboat Society** invited children to imagine they were in command of a boat on call-out in rough seas! Yet, relating to writing, HMI remarked, *'The children have good imaginations but do not know how to express themselves'*. Around the same period Westhay began to encourage the idea that, *'Composition with preparation before writing is advisable'*. Again we do not know if this was oral preparation and discussion of possible ideas, or a process of written drafting. An interesting comment emerged at Kingston Seymour in 1932, when HMI remarked, *'The freedom with which infants and juniors compose orally is most unusual and is an excellent foundation for subsequent work in English. Most children are restricted to Recitation in elaborate phrases which does not inform their ability to express themselves or converse in ordinary conversation and discussion'*.

Another specific reference to oral speech was at Chaffcombe (1912) where HMI commented, *'Some children do not use their organs of speech properly. Vowel sounds need attention'*. Perhaps he could not understand the local accent! While at Isle Brewer's, a list of Conversation Lessons was given with a comment on voice training, enunciation and expression – possibly in the form of prepared speeches. Coleford (1883) also noted Conversation Lessons for which, ten years later, records were kept for such oral work, but whether for content or delivery we are not told. When Horsington (1896) refered to Conversation Lessons, a title was given – *Man Know Thyself* – for discussion perhaps. For the rest we know nothing.

c. Rekoning, Mensuration, and Drawing

The younger ones were concerned with learning to count and to write their numerals while the other classes acquired the four basic rules and then more complex calculations. Much of the Infants' work was done orally. Materials to help the little ones increased during the period. The abacus style ball-frame was common (Ctc 1877) and later Fairfax bead counters (SmWE 1894).

With this equipment in place, there was a sharp reminder, *'Counting on fingers must stop'* (OkBr 1892). We gain an insight into the possible detail of Infants' Lessons when we find the Programme of Work for Class 1 included *'Notation 1-100 and composition of numbers 1-20,* and Class 2 should know *'Notation 1-50 and composition of numbers 1-18'.* While the little ones were expected to familiarise themselves with number properties and to manipulate them confidently it seems HMI often found the process to be too artificial: in 1936 HMI at Writhlington were still bemoaning, *'There is a tendency to formalise with the younger ones, but the upper classes can now think for themselves'.*

For the Standards, Arithmetic was also divided between oral mental arithmetic and paper work. The syllabus in the Standards progressed by the 'logic of the subject' (Kgd 1870s), starting with the four basic rules of addition, subtraction, multiplication and division. A detailed syllabus was not recorded, but random remarks from the Logs help to fill in some details:

Std I	Subtraction with borrowing	1885 Chf
Sd II	Multiplication with 3 digits	1872 Kgd
Std III	Square and long measurements and weights (Troy, avoirdupois)	1880 Chf
Std IV	Long division of weights and measures	1864 OkBr
Sd V,VI	Commenced teaching vulgar fractions	1878 Kgd
+ VII	Reduction of Money, Method of Unity	1895 Chf
	Proportion, Compound Division, Addition of Fractions	1901 Kgd
	Metric and decimal calculations, including recurring decimals and Graphs, % discounts, stocks and shares	1910 Hlc

In terms of teaching method, HMI 1912 commented, "*Too much time is spent on simple rules, while in the lower class, only mental arithmetic given*". More practical Arithmetic was urged for the Girls at Monteclefe by HMI, and their results then improved (1912). But this was not always successful: HMI commented, *'An attempt is made to make Arithmetic practical but the children do not show much readiness in attacking questions calling for the exercise of thought'* (Hlc 1910). While in 1928, HMI commented, *'Arithmetical method of working rather than just neatness and accuracy must be demanded'.*

Examples of maths problems set the children in 1866 included some then topical issues:

A tradesman bought a chest of tea containing 24½ lbs at 3s 8½d per lb.
He sold it on at 4s 4d per lb.
How much did he gain on the whole?

A farmer at a fair sold 3 oxen at £15 12 6d each;
A horse for 30 guineas; and a score and a half of sheep at 32s 9d per head.
His expenses were 9s 10½d. How much money did he carry home to his wife?

Tell me the difference between 11 x 98 and 18 x 9.
Find the difference between 12 x 17s 4½d and 4 x 3s 8½d

Two more examples relate perhaps to rather higher aspirations in life style:

The sum of 2,500£ is to be divided between two sons, in such a manner that the one may have four times as much as the other. How much must each have?

A fortress has a garrison of 2,600 men, in which there are nine times as many infantry and three times as many artillery as cavalry. How many are there in each?

The main complication was in using non-metric quantities, where children had to remember how many shillings make a pound [£], and how many ounces to the pound [lb]. The ultimate test was in calculating time, as in the question:

We know the school was opened at 11.15 on May 6th, 1858
How old is the school, tomorrow, at Morning Prayers 9.00 on June 3rd, 1902?

In addition, local adaptations were included to take account of the particular 'customary' land measurements which prevailed in Somerset. The exercise book (Plate 11) shows a drawing of an irregular shaped field, the area of which had to be calculated (1930s) in both standard measurements and in 'customary' measurements – for these differed in several parts of the country. It seems that when using *Acres, Roods and Poles,* instead of the standard 22 poles to a rood, in Somerset there were 24 poles to a rood. This was the case in the two other west country counties of Cornwall and Devon, and also true of such diverse areas as Staffordshire, Lincolnshire and Lancashire.

Drawing as a 'technical' subject, was introduced in 1890 and made compulsory for Boys. It was rarely offered to girls, who usually did their compulsory subject Needlecraft at the same time. Drawing was linked to the arithmetic and mensuration curriculum and included surveying. Once Drawing commenced, specialised equipment usually followed (Kgd 1892):

1898 3 pkts of Drawing Cards received.
1899 compass, rulers, protractors were received, and Drawing Charts.

Few schools give details of the Drawing syllabus, but we find HMI Gefferton, Inspector for Drawing (1903) gave advice to a school as follows:

Freehand: Use common things freely, teaching by demonstration. Full page copies to be made
Practice curves in Std I and II, do not use copies of 'things', draw as seen not as elevations
Free-arm: Practice concurrently with Free-hand
Memory: Practice regularly by ref to common things
Scale work: Take less squared paper, more plain
Use actual size of objects
Geometry: try taking patterns based on Problems worked earlier
Illustration: accompanying Circular on Primary Drawing (1901) must not be used on copies.
Date all work.
Also, Std I: drop slates, use paper instead
Infants: discard slates and square paper, use plain instead.
Use copies of common things, not elevations, just straight lines and curves
Coloured chalk on brown paper may be used
Half-Hour Lessons in Stds too short.

Cardboard modelling was also often an adjunct of arithmetic, in particular, geometry. It started in many schools in the second decade of the C20th (SomB and ChM in 1911, Kgd in1915). Later, cardboard modelling materials were recorded at Blagdon and in Cutcombe (1930s). Cardboard modelling allowed children to make 3-D shapes of increasingly complex natures. Further, it also provided materials for Geography, in making 3-D maps by building cardboard locations according to contours. As a practical subject it seems to have been welcomed. In fact sometimes there were complaints that '*Too much attention is given to problems relating to Cardboard Modelling and Woodwork*' (OkBr 1914). Perhaps this was feared as reducing time spent on more 'formal' arithmetic.

Good achievements in the 3Rs were vital to the success of the school and to its level of grant. It is difficult to estimate the standards of the schools, other than through the pass-rate when HMI came for the annual examination, in which the children were carefully drilled. Below are some examples:

In 1871 at Horsington, 59 children presented:
  56 passes in Reading, 52 Writing, 36 Arithmetic
In 1872 at the above, 42 presented:
  105 passes, plus 7 in Geography; 30 Infants all pass.
In 1875 at Churchill, 32 children presented:
  27 passes in Reading, 25 Writing, 21 Arithmetic.
In 1885 at Blagdon 85 were presented:
  73 passes in Reading, 68 Writing, 71 Arithmetic.

What we do not know is how many children were *not* presented. In all cases the pass-rate was deemed acceptable - it would be interesting to compare these with modern League tables.

In passing, it is revealing to note that on a number of occasions HMI compare Girls and Boys, always to the disadvantage of the Boys: *Boys are inferior to Girls in Arithmetic* (Clf 1894), *'Girls read well, but Boys read badly'* (Chl 1895), and *'The Boys pronounce with less vigour than the Girls in their Reading'* (OkBr 1910). Yet in several schools, during the lessons, teachers drew the opposite conclusion and refered to the difficulty in getting any responses: *'There are several immovable older Girls whom I have tried to interest without success'* (Clf 1894). However, when it mattered, in front of the Inspector, the Girls could perform and outshine!

ii. Recitation: Poems and Songs

This part of the curriculum has a high profile in the Logs: visitors came and heard the children recite and sing. As concerts became part of school life, it became an opportunity for children to perform. In fact, a book of poems was in the first order for school materials made by the new Cutcombe Head in 1878. These would include Action Songs, such as *The Chinaman* (Kgd 1905). A glance at the poem titles to be learned shows a rather solid diet of patriotic verse by the established authors of the day. It provided a grand basis for a history-through-heroes approach for children 'in the Standards', while the Infants were given a lighter sample of poems often relating to Nature. As the children got older, they were expected to achieve considerable feats of memorisation of the longer pieces. The titles below are typical of what the Logs showed. Kingsdon Head, for example, noted in February 1883 that Std IV started learning the poem *The Deserted Village* by Goldsmith, set for the examination in the Spring – so, they had several weeks in which to learn it and earn the grant that went with it. By 1894 a full syllabus for all classes – starting from the Infants to upper Standards - was copied into the Log:

Table 8.1: Range of Recitations

	Infants	Lower Division	Upper Division
1894	*The Children's Hour* Longfellow	*Inchcape Rock* Southey *Battle of the Baltic* Campbell	*Burial of Sir John Moore* Wolfe *Ye Mariners of England* Campbell
1901	*Jack's Letter*	*The Birds* *Battle of Blenheim* Southey	*The Solitary Reaper* Wordsworth *The Armada* Lord Macauley
1902	*My Doll's Tea-Party* *Carry your Box, Sir?* *My Monkey* *Shake hands, Doggie*	*Storm Song* Taylor *Excelsior* Longfellow	*A Spring Morning* Wordsworth *Evening in Paradise* Milton

Other favourites which appeared regularly included:

Beggar Man	Lady of the Lake	Shakespearean Dialogues: *Henry and his son*
BethGallert	Fakenham Gost	*Hubert and Arthur*

These titles or other similar ones are common across all the schools. A few particularities relate to local circumstances, specifically, *The Collier's Child* in the mining area of Coleford – a very mournful account of the death of the child.

HMI often commented on the quality of Recitations. They seem to have been looking for *'clarity and good delivery with attention to meaning'*, and thus avoiding any *'monotonous and indistinct speech'*. There was never any mention of a 'rural accent' or of 'non-standard forms' from the children, nor of the need for 'elocution' – the bane of many an aspiring working-class child. What the policy was on this is not recorded. There is occasional mention of needing to train the children to speak distinctly.

Singing was also a serious business and required exercises first before a melody was sung. The most popular method of teaching singing was to use **Sol-fa**, a pedagogical technique which became the dominant method for teaching sight-singing, rather than learning a song 'by note' (rote). Invented by Sarah Glover (1785–1867) of Norwich, it was later popularised by John Curwen who adapted it from a number of earlier musical systems. It uses a system of musical notation based on movable 'do'. All the schools seem to have used it, though it was introduced at different times: Rev Hansell commenced teaching it at Kingsdon in 1874. At Somerton exercises were recommended (SmWE 1891), but at Monteclefe, the HMI stated, *'The Singing was not in good tune but the necessary exercises were correctly rendered'*. Solfa was also mentioned at Charlton Mackrell (1890), Churchill (1892), at Somerton Boys and Isle Brewer's (1900) and North Curry in the 1910s.

Many schools had to sing unaccompanied as there was no harmonium or piano. Part-singing and rounds were included. Problems were experienced, as we have seen with part-singing with Miss Neal at Kingsdon. Rounds were tried in Blagdon (1895). Songs even changed keys. A Head (SmB 1891) was *'much gratified by progress'* when the boys managed to shift from Bb to F and back to Bb! Another major challenge was acquiring a harmonium or piano: these were sometimes donated (Lady Smith at SmM 1899), or bought (a reconditioned one at Writhlington 1932). It was something for which the children often worked hard to achieve through fund-raising activities such as concerts and sometimes though the efforts from the new Parent Associations which began to spring up in the inter-war years.

Song titles are frequently listed, often a new song every month, especially for the Infants. It must have offered a little light relief during a day of static lessons. A few of the many titles are listed:

All Day Long in the Cornfield so weary
O'er the foaming Billows,
The Fearless Boys of England
The Fire brigade are a famous host
The Railway Train is Ready to Start
Buttercups and Daisies,
The Months,
The Apple Tree
The Boy and the Rose-bud,
Which is the fairer?
Isle of Beauty

Singing hymns must have also figured strongly in the lives of the children, though there was no mention of doing this in school-time. Most pupils would have been regular Church- or Chapel-goers. In very rare instances, a school visitor came to practise some hymns for an upcoming Missionary meeting. As already noted, several teachers were also organists in the local church and the school regularly attended special services. As far as we can tell from the Logs, morning assembly usually included a prayer, but may have added a hymn as well. Certainly, in the denominational schools children were frequently taken to church for services on special days and would have been expected to attend every Sunday. Several of the children were in the Church choir – and took leave of absence on Choir Treat Days. By the inter-war years many schools attended Choral Festivals and several were regular prize winners. Soon the general Music curriculum was also undergoing changes. However, in 1908 HMI remarked, *'It is regrettable that the school has no musical instruments'.* None of the examined Logs make any mention of instruments other than some percussion ones for Drill purposes.

iii. Object lessons

These were introduced in the late 1860s, compulsory in 1890 and lasted for four decades. The idea of the object lesson seems to have been to focus on something familiar to the children and which would be *of* interest to them as well as *in* their interest. It appears that a Head could select from a core list of possible items, for the Logs show many similar but different examples. The objects were intended, at first, to be familiar and thus motivating: the exotic was added later. Below is a sequence of lessons planned for Infants during the Autumn term (SmWE, 1883)

Table 8.2: Sequence of Object Lesson Topics

Animal		**Object**		**Phys Act**	
Sept 11th	The Beaver	Sept 18th	Water	Sept 19th	Lighting a fire
Sept 25th	The Cat	Oct 2nd	A clove	Oct 3rd	Setting tea things
Oct 9th	The Horse	Oct 16th	Animal clothing		
Oct 23rd	The Squirrel	Oct 30th	A potato	Oct 21st	Washing
Nov 6th	The Camel	Nov 13th	Salt	Nov 14th	Making tea
Nov 20th	The Owl	Nov 27th	Glass	Nov 28th	Carpenter's actions
Dec 4th	The Elephant	Dec 11th	The Seasons	Dec 12th	Making a hairbrush
Dec 18th	The Mouse				

The categories of lessons from which the Head could choose, in 1885, were as below:

Table 8.3: Alternative Topics for Object Lessons

I Animal			**III Natural Phenomena**		
Bat	Squirrel	Toad	Clouds	Brass	Floods
Bee	Fox	Rabbit	Stone	Rainy Day	Silver
Eagle	Sparrow	Hen	The Moon	Coal	Summer
			Copper	Night & Day	Salt
II Vegetable			**IV Domestic**		
Apple	Orange	Pepper	Bread	Soap	Sponge
Coffee	Date	Rice	Chain	Lighting a fire	Starch
Cabbage	Potato	Tea	Spade	Candlestick	Candle
			A garden	Looking glass	Knife & fork

The list offered to schools varied year to year, with an increasingly eclectic mix of familiar and exotic, which was continually evolving. What the children made of this is hard to tell. Also, how much a 'townie' teacher might be able to add to what the village children already knew about a fox, hare, or bat is difficult to imagine. By the 1890s it included:

> animals (lion, elephant, donkey, camel, goat, mackerel, beaver, crocodile, hare, owl, bat);
> vegetable (cotton, fir tree, turnip, clove, oatmeal, grass, rice, India-rubber);
> natural phenomena (thunderstorm, rainbow, frost, dew, seasons);
> natural materials (lead, chalk, coal, leather, slate);
> domestic items (the tea table, rooms of the house, a pin, money, straw hats).

Nevertheless, some very imaginative lessons clearly took place when teachers were able to respond to items in which the children were interested. For example, a Head from Charlton Mackrell recorded in the Log for 1881 that, having noticed the children playing with a magnet, he placed a steel pen-nib on a floating cork and introduced ideas about a mariner's compass. This was with a Master who was particularly interested in science and was able to spot the potential. Such impromptu lessons must have sparked real enthusiasm. We cannot assume that most teachers in most schools were doing everything by rote and according to the pre-set lessons plans, but neither can we assume that this kind of inspirational teaching happened very often amongst the majority of poorly educated teachers.

In addition, at Somerton West End Infants, the Head noted in 1885, *'The Colour lesson developed into a lesson on dyes and dying with a few facts upon dye-stuffs (indigo, madder, cochineal, garriboge), mineral dyes and dyes from refuse of gas-making fairly comprehended by the children'.* One wonders if they ever got to 'have a go' at dying in class, or whether they rushed home and disconcerted their mothers with their experiments! Much later, in 1900, the Head was reminded that one hour a week was not enough.

In general, 'object lessons' earned a poor reputation. The idea was parodied by Charles Dickens in *Hard Times* with the infamous Mr Gradgrind, whom we meet in the second chapter appropriately entitled 'Murdering the Innocents', where he asked for a definition of a horse:

> *'Very well. You describe your father as a horse breaker...Give me your definition of a horse'*
> *(Sissy Jupe thrown into the greatest alarm by this demand.)*
> *'Girl number twenty unable to define a horse! Girl number twenty possessed of no facts... Some boy's definition of a horse. Bitzer, yours.'*
> *'Quadruped. Graminivorous. Forty teeth, namely twenty-four grinders, four eye-teeth, and twelve incisors. Sheds coat in spring; in marshy countries sheds hoofs too. Hoofs hard require to be shod with iron. Age known by marks in mouth.'*
> *'Now, girl number twenty' said Mr Gradgrind, 'you know what a horse is.'*

Sissy Jupe, of course, worked with circus horses trained by her father and knew all about horses. A further extract, from Dicken's *Nicholas Nickleby,* is between Mr Squeers and his new teacher:

> *"This is the first class in English spelling and philosophy, Nickleby.*
> *Now, where's the first boy?"*
> *"Please Sir, he's cleanin' the windas."*
> *"So he is to be sure. We go upon the practical method of teaching.*
> *C-l-e-a-n clean, active verb, to make bright, to scour.*

W-i-n win, d-e-r der, winder, a casement.
When the boy knows it from the books, he goes out and does it."

This example demonstrates both the reading method using phonic letter sounds and syllabification, as well as illustrating the Master's (mis) pronunciation – as in the spelling of 'window'.

Examples of a Victorian Object Lesson can be commonly found. The one below demonstrates some of its use for vocabulary development: definition, composition, character, function, derived words.

Give me an example of a ruminant?	*A cow*
What is another word for ruminant?	*An animal that chews the cud.*
What is the derivation of ruminant?	*Rumi .. meaning the cud.*

However, the character of these lessons changed over time: we find children being encouraged to bring in specified items to describe and explain. Not quite a modern 'Show and Tell', but certainly less formulaic than the above.

By the 1890s a different categorization was used:

Table 8.4: Alternative Categorization of Object Lesson Topics (1890s)

	Colour	**Form Shape**	**Measures**	**Quality I-III Minerals IV-V**	**Domestic items**
Stage 1	White/Black	up/down/leaning straight/bent/crooked Square,Oblong		Rough/Smooth Hard/Soft	Basket of Veg. Table and Chair
Stage II	Red,Yellow, Blue	Triangle, Diamond	Length, Weight	Transparent/ Opaque	Egg, Milk, Cheese etc
Stage III		Hexagon, Octagon	Liquids	Soluble/Insoluble - alum soda, starch	Cork,Leather,Chalk Sugar, Camphor
Stage IV	Shades and Tints	Circle, Sphere	Dry Goods	Salt, Coal, Iron	Pins and Needles Paste, Gum, Glue
Stage V	Mixing colours	Prisms,Cylinders,Cones	Time	Rust, Casting	Textiles Bricks, Ceramics

The continuing evolution of the 'Objects' seem to reflect everyday things, as was demonstrated in a Scheme of Work at Cutcombe (1901), which included The Railways, The Use of Steam, The Letter and Postal Service. In this dominant curriculum area of Objects staff later were urged to introduce the **Science of Everyday things**, though few took up the challenge.

An exception was Mr Bright at Coleford 1909. HMI praised his programme where '*Experiments were successfully carried out and children taught to observe, record and illustrate*'. He also introduced Science into the Evening School where HMI regretted that 'O*nly 6/20 attended a lucid Science lesson, but that there were only 3 absences from the Woodwork Class*'. He also gave evening lectures on Blood Circulation and on Nursing. Having been called up during WW I he returned safely and reinstated his science work, *Conducting Experiments on Air and Water to introduce simple Physics and Chemistry'.* With his departure, the science classes went too.

iv. Addition of Special, and Class Subjects

To get an overview of the way in which school studies developed beyond the initial 3Rs to include a wide range of subjects which we would recognise as an elementary curriculum, we can start with the Infants, remembering that 'Object Lessons' were originally devised for Infants and then spread throughout the whole school.

At the turn of the century, an **Infant Programme** is given for Kingsdon School which seems to reflect much of the approach during the previous 50 years. While the focus is for children from under 5 to around 7 years of age, 'Infants' could also include what became subdivided into the new category of Kindergarten, as well. Thus:

Reading the alphabet, Word-building, Reading Cards and Primers
Writing the Alphabet, lead pencils on paper [as opposed to slates]
Arithmetic: counting, breaking up digits, adding two numbers
Needlework: learning plain knitting, needle and thimble position
Drawing: chalks and brown paper
Recitations, Singing notes of a chord, Nursery Rhymes and Songs
Drill and Marching Songs, and Model Course Drill
Object lessons
And, **Infant 'Occupations'** or crafts. [These were also a strong tradition – many of which appear very varied and highly imaginative.]

To get a general idea of curriculum content for the **Standards Programme**, we can look at the plan for all classes during the summer, as outlined by the Head at Kingsdon, in 1883. The increasing richness of the subjects offered is clearly evident in the 'plans of work' set out for the remainder of the school. This was achieved through a combination of the 3Rs and Object Lessons, with other subjects which could be selected and, if passed, could earn additional grant. The most common Special Subjects were Geography and Grammar. Singing also attracted a grant. History was a less common option. In general, First Class referred to the highest class, or top class, rather than the one first entered, so, in order to see the progression, we begin with the lowest, Class 3:

Table 8.5: Syllabus of work for Classes 1-3

Class 3	**May 28th**	**June 3rd**	**June 10th**	**June 17th**
Object Lesson Gallery	Idea of Rough and Smooth,	Idea of quality 'Tough'	Idea of 'Hard and Soft'	Idea of 'Light and Heavy'
Animal Lesson	The Hen	The Duck	The Pigeon	The Swan
Geography	A River	Recap	Parts of a river	continued
Grammar	Verb 'to be'	Recap	Verb 'to have'	Express subject quality

Class 2				
Object Lesson				
Animal				
Geography	England	Recap	Islands of England	continued
Grammar	Idea of a Verb	The pronoun	Exercises on Pronouns	Exercises on Noun, Verb etc

Class 1				
Object Lesson				
Animal				
Geography	Europe	Recap	Rivers of Europe	continued
Grammar	Case of nouns and parsing	Gender of nouns and parsing	Verb tenses. Simple sentences.	Parsing and analysis

We can now examine these additional subjects – Grammar, Geography, History – in more detail to get a clearer idea of what was being taught and how. These subjects were never central to the curriculum and did not always get as much attention. At Cutcombe, both Grammar and Geography subjects were assigned as Home Lessons, in 1877, where the tasks seem to have been based on *text books* in each subject, which were to be read and learned at home. Several instances soon follow where pupils were punished for neglecting their Home Lessons. (William Burroughs seems to have been a frequent target, but then he did have a particularly long walk home each day.) Other children who did their work carelessly were kept in to rewrite it (ChM 1890), for they would need to memorise it for the Inspection.

a. Grammar
This was taught in a very formal way using Latin as the model for sentence analysis and parsing. Infants were introduced from a young age to the basic parts of speech such as nouns and verbs. Increasing complexities were steadily added.

We find at Kingsdon, in 1876, the Head gave a class on *Transitive and Intransitive Verbs* to the First Class (top class). Other Logs also sometimes note a lesson on Adjectives, The Noun, Making a Sentence. The syllabus above, shows the range of topics to be covered over a short space of time. The programme of work, however, included plenty of repetition and revision. Perhaps children found it hard to grasp the abstract concept of grammar. Local speech variants must have added to the difficulties. A Somerset rhyme illustrates potential challenges in the classroom:

Us will not go back to she
For her does not belong to we!

Little mention is made of Grammar in the Logs. On rare occasions, HMI suggest the syllabus should partly be based on the mistakes of the children. Again, details were not recorded. Inadvertently, the distinction between Grammar and Writing/Composition was sometimes blurred. Composition work is said to result in *'Expression suffering from too much formal sentence-building'* (OkBr 1914), but a year later the report notes the opposite, *'Composition is too free – the sentences are too short and abrupt. It needs lessons in linking and paragraphing'*.

The policy of corrections in both oral and written composition lessons also blurred this boundary. Attempts were made to base Grammar on the children's errors and to apply it to their compositions (Ctc 1905). We also find programmes of work (OkBr 1915) stating:

Std I and II	Corrections of oral compositions
Std III	Forming of sentences
Std IV and V	Correction of oral errors

This increasing emphasis on expression, meaning and context was even reflected in HMI's 1928 advise that *'Written corrections should be done in complete sentences'* thus giving context and meaning, rather than doing corrections as random single words.

b. Geography
When Mr Hayes was newly appointed at Cutcombe in 1877, he was given a set of Maps of the World from Mrs Russell, the wife of a Manager. It was a good start. Many other schools waited years while HMI impatiently urged Managers to acquire maps. More than half the world was coloured red; The Empire, on which the sun would never set, was in full swing; Queen Victoria was Empress of India. It was a glorious time for school maps.

Drawing free-hand maps seems to have been a common activity. A Kingsdon Head noted, March 1873, *'Children in the First Class drew a map of the Eastern coast of England very nicely'*, and in September, *'Children drew a map of Ireland very creditably'*. Meanwhile the lower classes focused on Britain – often this provided an opportunity for local Geography: children drew maps of their own village (Clf 1895), or went on walks to familiarise themselves with the geographical features of their locality (Wrl 1938).

Meanwhile, in terms of content, the Geography syllabus seemed to treat the whole world as a natural resource for British manufactured goods and it was about them that children had to learn: what came from where. In terms of teaching-learning method, Geography was frequently a subject for Home Lessons and therefore self-taught from Readers. Hence text books were vital:

Horn's *Geographical Reader*	(Skg 1975)
Midland Geography	(Kgd 1898)
Geography of British Possessions	(Kgd 1902)
Britannia's *Geography*	(Skg 1903)
Arnold's *Home and Abroad*	(Ctc 1904)

Other inter-war text books used in Somerset schools, include

Over Lands and Seas – a Geographical Reader	
The Columbus Regional Geographies Junior Series	London University Press
Human Geographies: In the New World	Philip and Son

Text books for younger children appear to have adopted a device still common today: giving information about the country by telling the story of a child from that country. Thus, the second title above approached Geography through stories, as from Children of Many Lands: it came with four colour-plates and several small engravings; and used a narrative 'faction' style still in use. The last title, first produced in 1919, is more formal, with figures, diagrams and maps relating to one physical geography feature at each level – rivers (III), winds (IV), seasons (V) – and then focusing on each region and its produce, in the Americas.

1899 HMI recommend Geography for the Upper Standards, so in 1900 'Object Lessons' for these scholars were devised and included:

Cardinal Points	A plan compared to a map	Shape and size of the earth
The Seasons	Mountains of England & Wales	Hills compared to Mountains
Hills of England & Wales	Mountains and their uses	Rain and Clouds
Rivers	R.Thames & *R.Severn*	Rivers of England & Wales
Peninsulas and Capes	Coastline	Oceans, Seas,
Channels, Islands	Lakes, Valleys, Plains	Coal and Iron of England
London and Liverpool	Black Country	The Potteries
Woollen Manufacture	Cotton Manufacture	Care of Petroleum Lamps
Salt-mines of Cheshire	Battlefields of England: *Sedgemoor*	*Somerset*
Voyage from *London to Bristol*	Cargoes of ships bringing things to / from another country	

Lower Division: Geography of the *Neighbourhood*
Outlines of England
British Possessions, reference to Interchange of Goods

...and, in 1901, the school received *Geography Reader Vol II* – from which they *'talked about Exeter and R Exe'*, as well as the *Geography of British Possessions.*

This was the most detailed Geography syllabus mentioned in any of the Logs and gave marvellously detailed content. It was also significant in that adaptations were made to include local studies. For the Lower Standards, the focus was on Britain and on the details of which cities manufactured what products. This was sometimes offered in a 'catechetical', Question and Answer format which so dominated the belief about what made learning easy. An example from a 1829 text, *Simple Geography for Young Ladies*, at Milverton illustrates this:

> *Name the five south-western counties.* – Dorsetshire, capital Dorchester; Wiltshire, capital Salisbury; Somerset, capital Wells; Devon, capital Exeter; and Cornwall, principal towns Launceston and Bodmin.
>
> *What is Wells?* Wells is the capital of Somersetshire, one of the 52 counties of England.
>
> *What are the chief towns of Somersetshire?* Bath, upon the Avon, is a beautiful city and famous for its medicinal waters and strict police; Somersetshire supplies lead, copper, *lapis calaminaris*, and its manufacturing towns make bone-lace, stockings and caps.

Examples of a practical approach to Geography can be seen in the detail concerning the Rector at Kingsdon 1901. The Head noted, *'Received sand from the Rector for Geographical lessons and gave lesson on Hills, using sand to illustrate'.* A contributor from Tintinhull recalls, *"We collected labels off packets and tins of food and had to find out which country they came from and then put them on the map. It was mostly red"!* Other schools used lace from Chard, carpet from Axminster, horse-hair from Castle Cary to pin on their maps.

Local adaptations were suggested at Cutcombe in 1908 where an open-air Geography lesson was conducted on Dunkery Beacon which included Nature Study as well. Such cross-curricular work was praised at Somerton Boys (1908), Isle Brewer's (1910) and, in Kingston Seymour (1922), a HMI commented, *'Thoughtful association of Drawing, Composition and Nature Study'.* At Tintinhull, walks often combined History with Nature Study. This latter subject gave a chance to go outside on a good day. Cutcombe, Kingsdon, Keinton Coleford and Oakhill each took children for Nature Study Walks. The 'open-air classroom' became something of a fashion in progressive circles at this time. It was part of the reaction against the appalling health discovered amongst the recruits for the Boer War which so shocked the political circles into introducing campaigns for more drill, more sport, more health projects and, also, for more out-door education. Charlton Mackrell (1905) took advantage of their locality by taking children to the local carpenter's workshop and forge when studying 'occupations' and, also, to the quarry to search for artefacts where Romano-British burials had recently been found. However, in 1912, HMI Stacey commented of Blagdon, *'Nature Study, hitherto does not seem to have been, in any perceptible degree, of any use to the children'.* Perhaps 'out-door classrooms' were treated too much as a nice outing!

c. History

This was traditionally considered as one of the subjects within *'English Studies'* and it is perhaps for this reason that it appeared less often as a separate Special or Class Subject. Some content of History was absorbed through extracts in the Readers, which frequently featured daring-do tales of explorers and colonisers, and also through the poetry for Recitation which again included many stirring tales of long-ago bravery and endurance.

History, when it became a separate subject was, like Geography, taught through *Readers*, though this custom of reader-dependency at the expense of instruction was criticised by HMI as being too passive. History was reserved for the older classes, starting only with Std IV or V, by which time many children had already left. Maybe this was partly because there was such reliance on *Readers*: children had to have reached sufficient competence in reading to be able to manage. In general it seems to have been very passively taught, though one active example was where cards with dates, events and people had to be matched to the coloured 'century-cards' in order to sequence them correctly (Faithful 1924).

We have few examples of a syllabus outline for history, but we can discern a split between the biographical and the chronological approaches. For example, when embarking on History for the first time, a Head planed the following – monarchical – approach (Hlc 1910). Another school (Kgd 1902) chose a chronological approach:

Std IV	House of Lancaster, York and Tudor
Std V +	House of Stuart, Orange and Brunswick

Two years later, he ambitiously began the next year with 'Earliest Times to the Battle of Hastings'. Another school (1902) following the textbook *History of the West of England* chose:

Stuart Period, with special reference to the Monmouth Rebels and the Battle of Sedgemoor
Reign of Queen Victoria.

Again, it is interesting to note the 'local adaptations' made, the Sedgemoor area and its associated villages and churches - each with tales to tell of the Monmouth rebels – being a prominent area of the Somerset Levels. Presumably, younger classes tackled earlier periods, again incorporating local traditions, in particular, King Alfred hiding in the western marshes before his eventual victory beyond Penselwood on the eastern uplands of the county, also the Glastonbury legends, and the West Countrymen's contributions to Queen Elizabeth's naval successes against the Armada and in the New World.

In fact, one school took localism to its logical conclusion and embarked on writing their own Village History (OkBr 1864). Perhaps it was a one-off, but the teaching of History continued for another fifteen years before being dropped from the curriculum – perhaps after a change of teacher.

An alternative biographical approach (Clf 1901) is evident in the following example, Stds IV – VII

A. Raleigh, Bacon, Buckingham, Guy Fawkes, Pym, Coke, Shakespeare
B. Cromwell, Wentworth, Hampdon, Prince Rupert, Laud, Clarendon, Lord Falkland
C. Monk, Ireton, Blake, Penn, John Milton,
D. Monmouth, Titus Oates, Russell, Sidney
E. Argyll, Father Petre, Jeffrey
F. Sir Isaac Newton, John Locke, Tynconnell, Dundee
G. Marlborough, Bolingbroke, Walpole, Christopher Wren.

Here we have a mixed grouping of people, in rough chronological order, who perhaps were thought to represent their age. This format was supplemented by walks to the nearby church of Holcombe, '*which is a splendid relic of Saxon and Norman Architecture*' and a trip to Tintern Abbey, both of which would have given plenty of opportunity for further historical discoveries.

Examples of History Readers used in local schools in the 1930s include:

Nelson History Readers	used in 1883
Britannia History	used in 1903
Great Deeds on Land and Sea	Blacks Supplementary Reader (Seniors) 1911
Builders of History (to Bk VI)	Edward Arnold (c1900)

The third tells the story of great British Victories from Waterloo to the Crimea, while the fourth is equally full of brave deeds but is more biographical: Bk VI tells the story of great Victorians such as Prime Minister Sir Robert Peel, Soldier Sir Henry Havelock, Nurse Florence Nightingale, General Gordon, Explorer David Livingstone and Writer Charles Dickens. One contributor remembered their text book in which the chronology was illustrated as links in a chain.

These inspiring tales were intended to generate the Pride and Patriotism which was fundamental to Victoria's reign, only to be soon so brutally tested by the two global conflicts of the C20th. Raising the Flag in the playground (first mentioned at Blagdon in 1909) and later on every May 24th to celebrate Empire Day (first mentioned in 1916) helped to reinforce these values.

In a remarkably early example of innovation in the *what* of History teaching, a Head tried a novel approach of blending Geography and History for the top class, which was highly commended by HMI on their annual visit (Blg 1881). Another change can be discerned in terms of expectations of *how* children were to learn when HMI pointed out, '*It is advisable to release Stds VI and VII from their leading reins and leave them to their own efforts and resources'* and, also, '*Children must be taught to think'* (Wrl 1908). This may have been a reaction to the passivity of depending on Home Reading texts, but it also signalled a recognition that pupils needed to learn to read for study purposes, not just for memorisation. Greater initiative also had a practical advantage in a small mixed-age rural classroom. HMI commented, '*Training for self-reliance and private study frees the Teacher to be able to attend to the younger ones*' (Hlc 1925). So, it was a strategy for classroom management as well.

This area of the curriculum was particularly ripe for an interesting experiment which took place in West Pennard (1926) and in Cutcombe (1932), where the **Dalton Plan** was introduced. This was a new and very innovative approach developed in America which involved integrating and thus crossing subject boundaries and allowing individual children some freedom to choose their work. The Head hoped '*It will show the children's strengths...*'. The Dalton Plan was the precursor of the topic-based teaching method which became so popular in the late 1960s and 70s, only to fade at the instigation of the subject-based approach shaped by the National Curriculum from 1989.

In connection with this change, HMI also suggested placing the desks in groups, and arranging the children according to age rather than achievement '*so there is steady progress through the school'*. All of this was a probable response to the difficulties experienced in small rural schools with a wide age-range, huge ability-differences and very few teachers.

While **Citizenship** was not noted in any examined Log, text books were issued for this subject. The concern about the role of the Empire, of Britain, of every citizen was often highlighted in both the Geography and History classes and, of course, on occasions such as Empire Day. Somerton Boys tried a cross-curricular combination of subjects in 1924 through its *Empire Studies* which integrated History, Geography, Song and Literature. Empire Day invariably brought out speech-makers on the theme of duty to King and Country. No doubt much of this innovative programme would have done the same. The New Edition of *The Citizen Reader* published by

Cassell and Co, even had an original preface from WE Forster (the architect of the 1870 Education Act) and a new preface from Mrs Arnold-Forster in the 1930 edition. Other examples of this wider interest in world affairs comes from Horsington (1900) when a Lecture was given on the Origins of the Boer War and, in 1902 a half-day holiday was given when peace was declared. In Writhlington (1929) the Society of Friends gave a talk on the League of Nations and, in 1938, a Message from the League was read out on *How to keep the Peace*.

Only one school, in fact one Head, Frederick Close of Coleford engaged in Civics. He was very involved with his local community and heavily engaged in supporting the men made jobless during the pit closures in the 1890s. Perhaps this gave him the desire to help his charges know how to fend for themselves. In 1894 with the strike over, he embarked on a Civics Programme for Std V. This included a study of the,

> House of Commons, Representative Government, The Press, The Parish Council.

Also, Rates – Why and Who, Water Supplies, Infectious Diseases and Simple Remedies.

Headmaster Close also introduced Shorthand, for those Boys who showed promise, and Domestic Economy for Girls (not mere Cookery which was only just taking off – where facilities could be found – but a course to include home-making as well as food preparation). Whether this included budgeting and household management we do not know, but he was clearly concerned to give a vocational emphasis to this additional input. Later, Cottage Gardening was also added.

One other school came close to introducing some of these ideas in a more modest fashion. Cutcombe (1897) introduced topics in the highest Standards which included:

> Ways of Investing Money, Ways of Spending Money, Roads and how to mend them, Footpaths and rules of usage, Recreation by Games and by Change of Air.

v. Home Lessons

This appears to have been a regular feature of schools. So much so, that Bags for Home Lesson Books were sewn at Kingston Seymour (1878), where they must have been a regular part of the needlework curriculum as well.

Some indication of the nature of Home Lessons is first mentioned in the Logs of Kingsdon (1883). They seem to have caused strong reactions. The following example seems to indicate how much some pupils disliked Home Lessons. The Head recorded, '*Monday. This morning Joshua H refused to pick up bits of paper which he had flung away after tearing up the copy book which I had given him to take home. He was absent this afternoon. I find that many are encouraged in this by their parents. Tues: Rector came and complained that the playground was untidy. I pointed out Joshua H and the Rector corrected him and stood by him whilst he picked up the bits of paper.*

Further, Blagdon (1890) recorded, '*Previously the only Home Lessons set were words to be learnt – 7 each night, of 4-5 letters* [this sounds like spelling lists], *or a little Geography to be learnt by heart. Now the Upper Standards do some writing in Exercise Books and do it fairly well'.* The Head also recorded, '*One mother has burnt the book* [of words] *in protest'.* The Log does not tell us the outcome of this episode!

vi. Practical and Physical Activities: Crafts, Domestic Skills and Sport/Drill

This area of the curriculum very much depended on the handcraft skills of the individual teacher and reveals a wide variety of opportunities. Of course, the materials used were not re-usable and therefore incurred considerable expense. A grant for needlework was available – if the standard was sufficiently good – from the 1860s, for this was a valued activity as it provided girls with skills for their domestic futures as well as a possible way by which to earn a living. To cover costs, sales-of-work were arranged to try to raise money. Perhaps some of the 'ladies of the parish' came to such events, as they had some spending power.

Infant 'Occupations' became ever more varied: most involved coloured paper which was used for plaiting/weaving, while West End Infants (1886) took up paper-twisting and 'daisy-mats', bead-threading (using individual tin trays to hold the beads), basket-work and hat-plaiting in 1901. A very common Occupation was 'stick-laying', but no details were given. Coleford (1896) added paper-folding, cork-work, ball-making (with wool?) in Class 1, while the younger Class 3 engaged in 'ravelling', matching coloured wools, brick-building, bead-threading in twos or threes. The Kindergarten at Kingsdon (1898) took two Occupations - basket-making and embroidery, and felt mats were ordered for 'piercing' embroidery with skeins of silks. Many of these are recognizable activities used today.

Even Infants started sewing**.** The Head at Kingsdon (1877) reported, '*Have been attempting to teach 3 yr-olds Needlework but not with brilliant success – they generally succeed in losing their needles and breaking their cotton.*' But, in 1882 a subsequent teacher found, '*The smaller children are knitting very easily*'. In Kingston Seymour the Infants are recorded as finishing a quilt in February 1879 which was started in September, six months earlier.

Needlework: Older children also did Handicrafts. For the girls this was predominantly needlework, knitting and some embroidery. Needlework quickly became a compulsory subject which had to be examined for grants to be awarded. Some details are glimpsed as to what the girls made: at Cutcombe reference is made to the girls knitting their own woollen gloves and scarves for winter; in Blagdon a sale of children's work was organised as early as 1892, and in 1899 we read of 12 year-old girls sewing Samplers with alphabets and the school receiving a parcel of cotton prints and needles. Later, with better state funding, the children's craft work was more varied and sometimes were used as Christmas presents for the family.

It was, however, clear that needlework was a source of income for the school. Sometimes petticoats, shirts or linen items were made to order – there is a sudden rush and the girls take extra time from other studies to finish their work. The Needlework items were also used to raise money through sales of work either for charity or for School Funds or, later, for the War Effort.

A detailed invoice of needlework materials is included (ChM,1898):

1 doz yds flannelette	I ½ doz yds flannel
2 doz yds calico	2 doz yds prints
1 doz yds apron linen	1 doz yds muslin
1 doz yds lace	1 doz yds white fancy material
½ doz yards of tape	2 ½ lbs of wool
6 pkts of needles	3 pkts of knitting needles
2 doz reels of cotton	1 ½ doz thimbles
1 yd canvas	½ doz cards of buttons

We can imagine the garments and undergarments which could be made from all this and we can see from the list of items in the given illustration from a Sales of Work Book (Plate 4).
The Log goes on to list the skills to be developed:

> plain sewing followed by darning, knitting with 4-needles, patching and mending, finally, making patterns for cutting and sewing garments.

Schools report starting with thimble-, and knitting-pins-drill, hemming a handkerchief, seaming, also knitting hats, scarves and mittens, making shirts. Elsewhere (Hlc 1908) items listed include:

Std I + II	Brush and Comb Bag, Pillowcase, Brown Holland Pinafore, Knitted Cuff in plain/purl work
Std III+IV	Child's Flannelette chemise, and petticoat Knitted mittens, and Man's sock
Std V + VI	Girl's plain drawers, Nightdress Knitted vest

Girls' handicrafts were always intended for vocational benefit. They provided training for possible future employment and certainly for domestic duties. During the inter-war years, Singer sewing-machines began to be used in schools, which updated the girls' for modern demands on seamstresses and dress-makers.

Boys also did crafts: one respondent at Somerton Boys' remembers making leather purses with scraps from the nearby Clark's shoe factories, another remembers knitting his cloth for cleaning the slates. Boys at Coleford (1883) did Netting and one '*cut his finger on the twine…*'. This activity taught the boys to make nets for many agricultural purposes – whether for hanging hay for feed, assisting with hunting, shooting, fishing (or poaching), or as a general method for carrying items. Boys in the Infant First Class were taught to sew and to knit. Only when Drawing was introduced and made compulsory in 1890 did this begin to die out – though in many schools it continued and experienced several revivals, especially, as adults for those joining the Forces.

Cookery, Woodwork, Gardening.
Each of these subjects was a possible candidate for grant as additional Special Subjects. The great drawback for rural schools was finding access to the facilities needed for such subjects. Cookery was introduced in those schools which could manage from 1890. Cutcombe came up with the ingenious temporary idea of going to the nearby *Rest and Be Thankful Hotel*. Somerton Girls' started Cookery classes in 1883 and began by making porridge. It is clear that Cookery morphed into something with greater 'civilising' aspirations, to include home-making with a distinctly genteel flair: Lady Smith came to watch girls learn 'to lay a cloth for dinner in which they showed much interest' (SmM 1870). Later they were taught to make porridge and pancakes and, in 1890, they served diner to the gentlemen Inspectors and visitors, '*for which they were much praised*' – the way to a man's heart is…In fact Lady Smith sent along her own butler – whether to learn, to teach, or to encourage is not known.

Charlton Mackrell (1892) sent their children to the next parish, Blagdon began Cookery classes in 1904, Kingston Seymour first sent children north to nearby Clevedon (1913) and, later, (1925) east to Yatton in an effort to reach facilities. Chillington girls tried to get to Hinton St George for their Cookery lessons, but were often unable to attend '*owing to the state of the roads on which horses were unable to travel*'. Transport was also a problem in 1922 for Chaffcombe girls who were offered Cookery classes in Chard, but several mothers refused to send their children saying the 2-3 mile walk was too far. At Keinton the girls could cook in the Church Rooms next door, but had to collect water from the nearby Manor Farm House to do the washing up! Many schools, had to wait till the railways came to their area, allowing children to go to larger nearby centres where facilities were available. Kingsdon went to Somerton on the 'bucket train' from 1916.

Other domestic courses became available later: Writhlington girls went to Radstock for Laundry classes in 1911, Brewham girls went to Bruton in 1918, and North Curry noted its own Laundry course in 1933. Photographs exist showing rows of girls, each in front of their own enamel bowl, washing garments – which they must have been doing at home from an early age.

The same lack of facilities caused difficulties for Woodwork, the introduction of which was severely delayed in many schools. Some had their own facilities (Bgd 1914) or, later, could reach others by bus. Somerton boys travelled by train to Langport 1926**,** Keinton to Castle Cary, by train, in 1937. Cutcombe had to wait till 1950, when boys eventually found a place in Minehead.

Gardening for the older boys usually fared rather better, though again it depended on a local land owner donating some land for this purpose. Thus Lord Winterstoke gave a plot to Blagdon (1904) and a Rector gave part of his own garden (ChM 1905). Kingsdon received land in 1915 and, in Somerton, the boys had a temporary plot and worked it successfully. In 1917 Keinton pupils were very pleased with themselves when they recorded harvesting 2 cwt of their own potatoes which were sold for £1 2s 1d. Cutcombe also recorded a sale of produce (1930). In 1933, the Coleford Head noted, *'The Girls expressed a desire to grow flowers, while Boys set about growing vegetables on the other side of the playground. They brought their own manure'.* North Curry boys were very ambitious: they started biology and bee-keeping in 1933.

This led to some practical courses which were useful for domestic as well as vocational purposes. Hence we find Butter-making, Cheese-making, Bee-Keeping Classes, and even Teazle-growing and -gathering (IsB 1895). Charlton Mackrell Dairy Classes, in 1928, included learning to milk a cow – using filled rubber gloves as a substitute for udders! Dairy Classes also started in Chedzoy (1894) and Greinton (1920) and elsewhere (Blg 1905, KM 1928, OkBr 1936), while basket-making and poultry-keeping were noted in Creech St Michael (1903).

Somerset launched a major experiment in a new style of Agriculture Course in 1927. In September discussions began on the possibility of giving the curriculum a more 'agricultural' bias. Blagdon was chosen as one of eight schools .

Structure: A new experimental 2-yr course for those of 14-16 yrs, after leaving school, who were encouraged to attend Evening Continuation Classes.

Content: Scheme includes study of plant and animal life, meets the demands of Teaching Biology in New Elementary schools, visits to farms, dairies, apiaries, poultry-runs (one such outing each month).

Staff: Experts from Cannington Agricultural Centre would advise. The School Garden was to be enlarged and *agricultural crops* grown in addition to *cottage ones*. The Norfolk 4-year rotation system was to be used.

Organisation: There would also be meadow, pasture and woodland sections. A company would be formed for the animal side and scholars encouraged to take out shares. Poultry houses and rabbit hutches would be made in woodwork classes. No further details are given.

Physical activity did not figure in the curriculum at first – after all many of the children had a long walk to school. Nevertheless, long hours of sitting on forms must have taxed the attention of many a child. For educational reasons, HMI begin to write of *'needing a more active approach'* especially for the *'little ones'* and, on another occasion commented, *'The little ones often fall asleep in the afternoon'*.

Later, for practical reasons, which intensified by the time of the Boer War when the often shockingly poor state of health of the recruits became a national scandal, new and strenuous efforts were made to improve the physical condition of school pupils. This was developed through lessons in Drill – frequently led by ex-Captains and Majors. Interestingly, a section of **Drill Exercises** appeared weekly in *The Schoolmistress* journal, to help teachers not familiar with the new approach.

At Blagdon, the Head commenced the day with 10 minutes Drill, while Music with Drill was offered to the Infants. In 1899 dumb-bell exercises began. Other practices were adopted:

1886 Swedish Drill (SmWE), 1890s Musical Drill (ChM), with tambourines (SmM 1893)
1894 Infants have Drill with Singing of Marching Songs (Kgd)
1898 HMI record a preference for 'Infant Drill' rather than 'Swedish Drill' for younger ones

Having introduced Drill, several school playgrounds were found to be in too poor a condition, so it sparked a round of requests to have playgrounds levelled and drained.

There were a few instances where a sporting Head introduced organised games for other sporting pupils. Thus, at Oakhill, during the summers of the 1860s, the Head and his team were off playing cricket, often twice weekly. Sometimes he was invited to play for a local team himself – an offer he never seemed to have refused. Football was first mentioned in the examined Logs in Oakhill British School in 1920s. A farmer gave a bladder for a football. 'Sport' or athletics was rarely available till the inter-war years, but was soon taken up enthusiastically. Where possible, inter-school competitions, area sports and county championships were then encouraged. We find a sports field was used (NCry 1912) and several schools acquired the use of a neighbour's field for an annual sports event. Examples of these developments are noted below:

HMI suggests a cricket field, and supplies footballs and ropes (KSey 1923)
inter-school competitions are held (KM 1926)
Annual Sports Day is inaugurated (KM 1927)
football jerseys are ordered (ChM 1927)
children travel to Taunton by train for a Tug o' War (ChM 1928)
children attend an area Olympic Sports (Ctc 1931)
Major F. conducts ball games with the boys (Blg 1932)
A Challenge trophy Shield is presented to the winning House (KM 1934)

Gradually equipment, transport and organisation developed to enable sport to take-off and be followed with enthusiasm. Of course, such activities assumed an adequate number of children and a school close enough to make competitive sport feasible. Keinton and Charlton Mackrell were near each other – and on a rail link – to the Somerton Schools, so perhaps this is why it seems to have become such an active area.

By the 1940s the village elementary schools were offering a wide curriculum to all pupils, but expectations had once again outstripped practical possibilities. The

Hadow Report of 1928 recommending more Secondary Education began to have an impact on the traditional all-age 5-14 schools. This heralded another immense re-organisation, particularly of children reaching the age of 11 years and, consequently, a new re-distribution of children around the area schools.

Before we touch on those issues, we should look inside the classrooms to try and recreate the experiences of the children themselves.

Chapter 9

What Pupils Learned: School Experiences – Context, Content, Behaviour, Attendance, Welfare, Treats

So often we are told that school days are the happiest of our life. Yet in examples from literature we find mostly adverse pictures painted, whether genteel middle-class ladies in Austen, dire private schools in Dickens' *David Copperfield* and *Nicholas Nickleby* or in Hughes' *Tom Brown's School Days*. The following poets illustrate a mixed set of reactions. William Blake (1757-1827), in the *Song of the Schoolboy,* does not seem to have enjoyed his school days:

To go to school in a summer morn
Oh! It drives all joy away;
Under a cruel eye outworn
The little ones spend the day
In sighing and dismay.

...while William Shenstone (1714-1763) in the extract below illustrates a common – and sad – image, in *The School Mistress:*

In ev'ry village mark'd with little spire,
Embow'r'd in trees, and hardly known to fame,
There dwells, in lowly shed, and mean attire,
A matron old, whom we school-mistress name;
Who boasts unruly brats with birch to tame.

... but DH Lawrence (1885-1930) holds a more golden view of the teacher's experience in an extract from *The Best of School:*

Very sweet it is, while the sunlight waves
In the ripening morning,
To sit alone with the class
And feel the stream of awakening
Ripple and pass from me to the boys
Whose bright souls allay for this little hour.

However, Sherlock Holmes was also more positive and, after viewing some new Board School buildings from the train, is purported to have remarked to Watson:

Lighthouses, my dear boy! Beacons of the future. Capsules with hundreds of bright little seeds in each, out of which will spring the wiser, better England of the future.

The truth, as so often, lies between these extremes and was very different for each individual.

To excavate the children's experience is much harder: they did not write them down, or not until years later when memories may have changed. Nevertheless we can try to imagine their life at school from the details documented in the Head's Log Book, the HMI Reports and the views of contributors in both oral and written evidence.

i. The Context – Caged, Cold and Overcrowded

The discipline and rigour of schooling must have made demands with which it was difficult for young children to comply. Many of the 'scholars', as they were termed in the censuses, were as young as 3 years-old: it seems common that, as soon as the next baby arrived, the penultimate child was sent out to school. Various attempts to raise the age at which children could attend were made, as in 1905 and again in 1923, when it was declared that no under-4s should be accepted. However, as long as there was deemed to be the physical space, exceptions were made – to help hard-pressed, working parents. From 1944, alternative pre-school, Nursery or Kindergarten classes were formed which made it legal to accept such children again.

Older scholars, at the beginning of the C19th, did most of their learning standing up in groups along a chalked mark on the floor - toeing the line - around a monitor, by a sheet of paper on the wall which needed to be read, memorised and reproduced. Those standing took turns with those seated for written work. Where desks did exist they were usually 8' long, at which 6 to 8 scholars sat. Seating was on backless benches, or forms.

A relic of this 'standing' tradition which survived into the C20th was reported in Blagdon, where the Head noted, '*A ring of children stand around the teacher, read aloud one sentence at a time*', or, as contributors recalled, "*Children read from different books, read aloud simultaneously. So long as you kept going, with conviction, it was assumed you were reading correctly. Anyway, the teacher knew all the books by heart*".

For the Infants, it soon became the fashion, even a practical necessity, to install the tiered 'gallery' seating already mentioned in Ch. 5 (Plate 9). Unusually, Cutcombe never seems to have had a Gallery. These seats were not just restricting but were also a back-aching experience. Whilst from the 1870s HMI were urging their installation, thirty years later they called for their improvement. Recommendations were made to make the gallery more comfortable: backs to the tiered seating were suggested (SmWE 1882, SmM 1883, Blg 1892), desk-boards on which to write were encouraged (ChM 1884, OkBr 1886, SmWE 1896). This may have been a flat ledge, at writing height, fixed to the backs of the row of seats immediately below on each tier. It was part of the move away from 'slates on knees' to using copybooks which needed some kind of support.

By the turn of the century, almost every HMI was urging the removal of the gallery and its replacement with desks to allow more space and freedom of movement for the little ones. HMI noted, '*These children sit nearly all day confined to desks, and free movement and games which should form an important part of school life are impossible. The provision of a separate classroom is most desirable if these little children are to continue to be admitted to this school*'. The next year, HMI still commented that the school was not suitable for more than 2 classes of Infants, and the desks for under 5 year-olds should be moved so that more floor space was available (SmM 1909). Ideas were changing and the gallery had outlived its function. Most galleries were removed in the first decade of the C20th (SmWE 1905, Kgd 1908, ChM 1909 where it was described as used by the 3 and 4 year-olds). East Harptree seems to have been the last to remove its Gallery, in 1930. For the children, it was the end to many long hours seated in these tiers which usually had a handrail at the sides to prevent falls. It must have seemed like a pen, or the village pound, from which there was no escape.

New expectations related to the seating for children in the Standards as well. The common 8' long desk and backless form, or bench, (which Keinton even ordered for their new-build Hall in 1908) came to be seen as unsuitable and, *'not giving access to individual children'* (KgS 1924). In a few schools the innovation of dual desks came early (Skg 1881), while other schools campaigned for improvements by means of adding backs to the forms (Clf 1893-8). Most schools only achieved the modern form of dual-desk in the new century.

These long desks are still on view in the Allerford Museum School Room. A contributor from Tintinhull vividly remembered the classroom layout: *"Each age group sat in a different row with different desks of approximately the right size. The older ones at the back had a flat top desk with wrought iron ends to hold their books up. The next group had flat desks with a shelf underneath for their belongings. The Infants had an open fire and the others a smokey stove".*

Dark, dank and draughty. Apart from the furniture of the school, the school room was often large, high – extending into the A-frame rafters – and therefore very cold in winter. Children suffered from inadequate heating, smokey fires and mal-functioning stoves. Ventilation was not efficient – either a howling draught or a very smokey atmosphere. Lighting was also often poor. The windows were deliberately high (so nothing outside could distract), but this resulted in dark interiors, lit only by paraffin lights – which were also smelly and smokey. Many schools – and villages – were not connected to the national electricity grid till the 1960s. (Some isolated churches, in the C21st, are still dependent on candlelight alone.)

The conditions at West End Infant School, which came in for heavy criticism about poor space, light and heat in the HMI Report in December 1901, were resourcefully resolved by a parent. By May 1903, HMI suggested that the best plan was to do away with the Gallery on the west wall and for it to be replaced by *groups* of Infant desks, and asked *'Why shouldn't the lower part of the north wall be glazed?'* The north, street-facing wall had the traditional high windows, to prevent children from being distracted by passers-by. In December 1904 HMI again commented, *'No provision of artificial light exists. The children cannot see to draw so their work suffers'.* In fact, a parent in the demolition and reclamation business was able to supply a large ecclesiastical-styled window which was eventually positioned high in the west wall. Improvements were begun in 1905, but in 1912 HMI also suggested creating a covered area along the outer south wall, for protection during play time but, in order not to further reduce the day light, the veranda was constructed with translucent panels opposite each window through which to let in light. These features still exist today.

The smokey fires and unreliable lighting affected both teachers and children. For example, Needlework was suspended as the linen became dirty owing to the smuts from the fire (Clf 1907), no Needlework could be done on foggy days (IsB 1906), and Writing could not be continued as it was so dark (Skg 1910). Instead, Heads did Singing – where words were already memorised and probably performed unaccompanied as there was often no harmonium or piano. Contributors can still recall windy days when the draughts blew out the oil lamps, so what else was there to do, but Sing! As we have seen (Ch. 7) the gradual introduction of oil lamps, then gas lights and finally electricity from the 1930s to the late 1960s in Enmore and Keinton meant that there was, at last, consistent light by which to work.

Yet even worse, for the children, was the cold. Several schools report that the youngest ones often didn't attempt the path to school during the winter months –

on both the Moors and down in the Levels. For those who did brave it, they often arrived to find the fires unlit, the coal supply delayed, the stove unfit and the temperature so low that children shivered and cried from cold (Skg 1912 and SmWE). Many Heads recorded temperatures in the Logs – in fact it was a requirement to have thermometers in each room. One Head entered, *'The children marched and sang it was so cold'* (IsB 1888), while elsewhere a Head noted, *'38°F The temperature was so low no work could be done'* and other schools recorded, *'42°F. The children ran round to keep warm'* (Chl 1917, 1919) and in 1932 Chillington recorded only 29°F, while in 1946 Cutcombe children did Country Dancing to keep warm.

Unusually Coleford (1889) records that in the classroom (not the large Hall) there was no heating at all and a stone floor. Perhaps this was an example where the added room shared a chimney with the main Hall and was supposed to gain heat from that, the money having not stretched to an additional fireplace? HMI advice to overlay with wooden flooring was not acted upon. Whilst there were no legal minimum or maximum temperatures, it is interesting to note that in 1910 the Head at Writhlington was advised to keep the room at 60°F. This was also very close to the legal minimum temperature for an office environment in the 1970s (61°F or 16°C). From this we can see just how cold it was for these children.

In Monteclefe School, Somerton, the February daily temperature was recorded in 1904, as *43-55°F* at the start of the day, and *44-57°F* by afternoon. In March, the weather continued cold (*40-43°F* in the mornings, and *40-49°F* by afternoon). In November of that year the HMI Report commented, *'The school is not sufficiently warmed'*. The next year, the same message is repeated, *'The school is insufficiently heated'*, and again the following year when the end of 1906 Report firmly stated, *'The warming of this school is very defective. The attention of the Managers has been repeatedly called to this point in past reports. I am to enquire what steps will be taken to remedy this'*. At last, in February 1907 the elderly Colonel Pinney visited to see about fixing the stoves (he died in March 1909, before solving the problem). In 1911, children were again sent home in February as the classroom was only *35°F*: Daisy Cabble died, of pneumonia. Gradually the installation of the more modern free-standing 'tortoise stoves', as at Blagdon (1926) either supplemented or replaced the open fires. Only post-WW II did the comfort of central heating, mostly by oil, become available.

Then finally, the sanitation, or lack of... As we have already seen, the 'offices' were a constant headache for the Managers. Children must have dreaded the run out to the stinking, slimy, unlit, freezing outdoor toilets and tried to get back as quickly as possible into their room again. As we have glimpsed from the 1956 Sanitation report (Ch. 5), until the 1960s many schools were still without flushing toilets or running water. Now, thankfully they are warm, dry, with mains sewage and water 'on tap' – a far cry from the previous dark smelly holes.

These conditions were recognised as concerns by Inspectors at the turn of the century when expectations regarding health and comfort rose and the level of standard requirements were raised, but it was often not till after the newly formed County Council Committees of Education took over responsibility from the multiplicity of School Boards that any action resulted.

All in all many schools did not present an attractive, welcoming, much less healthy environment in which children could learn. From the exterior, the typical stone buildings stand solid and proud, but the interiors were far from practical, comfortable or effective as learning environments.

ii. The Content - Monotonous, Meaningless and un-Motivating

We have already noted how, even at the level of teacher training, much of the instruction was given orally, as students did not have experience of using books, or, of self-study, nor were there enough books available to allow this. We have already noted the lack of study materials and facilities in school which contributed to the difficulties in implementing the new self-reliance urged by HMI from the beginning of the C20th. We have also noted the distances from Public Libraries and other learning opportunities faced by rural children.

Thus, the child's task was to listen, repeat, memorise and reproduce, and then be tested in Question/Answer sessions by the teacher, a visitor, a Rector and, of course, the Inspectors. Mental arithmetic was conducted in this fashion, facts delivered in the object lesson were learnt by rote – as the Gradgrind example illustrated – and much of the information imparted in Geography and History lessons was similarly transmitted.

From the time of Hannah More, text books had often been compiled in the Q/A or 'catechetical style'. This was the method of the Prayer Book Catechism - the one method of learning all (Anglican) children knew. This tradition took a long time to die out! It was also considered to be pedagogically positive as it divided large amounts of unwieldy information into simple manageable bite-sized portions and, through the interaction, it engaged the learner. The whole experience of teaching and learning, however, must often have been mind-blowingly boring and real drudgery for most of the children. Even story-time came with a sting in its tail: a Kingsdon Head (1874) commented that while a visitor was taking part of the school for Dictation, '*I was able to find time to read to the children... which they were then required to reproduce*'.

One feature of such memorisation which might have been more enjoyable was the importance given to learning poetry by heart, for Recitation. Many of these were long ballads, often heroic, often about English heroes in battle, exploration, or other feats of endurance. A later Kingsdon Head (1903) commenced the introduction to a piece for recitation with an inviting, '*Oh! I'll tell you a story...*'. Many adults still remember the poetry they learned at school before the war.

Poems were not only recited, they were also stitched, in the girls' samplers. A few such samplers are displayed in Allerford, and Radstock School Museums (Plate 11), while others are in nearby locations including Wells City Museum, a large collection at the National Trust property at Montacute near Yeovil and, also, in Dorset Museums. Quaker schools were particularly known for their detailed samplers on which children had to stitch many alphabets (both upper and lower case) in a wide variety of fonts. We can see the development of the alphabet: 'u' became more commonly distinguished from 'v' in upper and lower cases, around 1800, and 'j' was added around 1810 to complete the modern alphabet – although the new letters reached various parts of the country at different speeds. Many beautiful examples from Quaker Schools are kept in Bristol City Museum which also includes several lengthy texts about topics which could be associated with Object Lessons and with Nature Study, such as 'Dew' or 'The Bee'.

Gradually, the domination of the oral mode gave way to less dependency on oral repetition and greater use of copybooks (aptly called, as children were required to copy from the newly installed blackboards, or to take dictation before learning texts by heart). Memorisation continued to be considered a powerful tool to learning. Blagdon Log (1880s) tells us that the children were taught '*hooks and hangers*' to help them remember. This is tantalizingly ambiguous. Perhaps techniques of 'association' were used, or rhymes employed to remember facts such as

Birkenhead, Barrow and Belfast for Beautiful British Boats
(sadly, most of these shipyards have since closed)

or chants for the monarchs of England:

Willy, Willy, Harry, Steve,
Harry, Dick, John, Harry III,
Edward I, II, III, then who and so on, to *Victoria.*

Although there was an overwhelming emphasis on memorisation, a high priority was also given to developing '*a good hand'*. Learning to write – after using sand-trays – was done on slates. These frequently formed part of the Head's list of ordered materials (Skg 1876, Clf 1880, Hsg 1896). However, we also find slates being blamed for handwriting defects (OkBr 1906) and thereafter discarded, as at North Curry from 1906.

Copybooks had been used by older children for many years, as we can see from the items ordered which included numbers of dip-pens with nibs, holders and ink – often as powder to be made-up, but sometimes ready-made, by the gallon. The desks – whether long- or dual-type – came with a hole for the ceramic inkwell. It was a chosen pupil's task to refill these at the beginning of the day. The dip-pen would drip on the pupils' work and ink-stained fingers make blotches everywhere. It was a messy business right into the 1950s when some older pupils with good enough handwriting were rewarded with the possibility of using the more expensive and privileged fountain pens. In poorer schools, especially for younger children, pointed sticks were initially used rather than steel nibs and holders. Nowadays, few children understand the phonic charts which may still show 'i' is for 'ink'.

Nevertheless, as we noted in the previous chapter, we have found delightful examples of interesting and exciting activities with teachers who really worked hard for their children in often very difficult circumstances. Given the burdens of what the children were expected to do in school hours and out of school hours at home, and the alternative of the hard physical work they would probably undertake for the rest of their lives, school probably did provide 'the best years'.

iii. Moral Purpose of Schooling: Literacy in order to read the Bible

Character was often seen as of greater importance than achievement. Morality and literacy went hand in hand. As though to emphasise this, in Leicestershire, the typical five (Standards) classes were sometimes referred to by the kind of texts to be read: *primer, battledore, bible, testament* and, finally, *psalter* (Gill, in Simon 1968).

As we saw in the terms of several of the Charities set up for schooling, the purpose of the teacher was to ensure the children could read their Bibles. Thus Religious instruction was fundamental to the school's existence. It was also an immensely contentious area. As we have already observed, it was not until 1870 that state grants established non-denominational Board Schools, at national and local rate-payers' expense, rather than predominately at the cost of one of the two main religious organisations, with the support of a local religious establishment – whether church or chapel – or an individual philanthropist.

Boards were allowed to decide their own policy on religion – principally, whether to read the Bible with or without doctrinal commentaries and notes. Eventually a list of non-controversial passages was provided and the suggestion was made to use 'narrative' sections as these were less contentious. Thus children would go home knowing about the story of Noah, Abraham, Moses, Jonah, Samson, David, Solomon and other biblical heroes. Another issue concerned the role of prayer in the school day: the practical issue was whether children should start and end their school day with collective prayers. Many argued against using public money for overtly religious purposes. Again it was left to the individual Board. Hence representation to the Board was critical and elections hotly contested. The School Boards were the prime example of direct local elections and were thus potentially the most democratic bodies in the kingdom, at the time.

So as to allay the fears of interference in religious affairs, a separate Inspector from the Diocese also visited the Anglican schools annually to test the religious knowledge of the children. These inspectors were conspicuously more lenient than HMI. They usually commented on the appearance and behaviour of the children – cleanliness being next to godliness – and often recorded the tone and pleasantness of a school. Their Reports, too, are interesting as they also indicate a gradual shift in focus: from the simple *knowledge* of Scripture and Church teaching, as assessed through direct oral questioning or, by 'recitations', to (not until 1900s) the ability to *apply* the moral lessons to be derived from these scriptures to their own lives, assessed by a more discursive approach.

It was the Diocesan Inspector who recorded greater understanding of the children's development. Monteclefe Log (1933) contained a detailed reflection: '*Std I+II bright and promising, Std III+IV disappointing, but at a notoriously difficult stage in school life when the body grows faster than the mind. They were at a loss when asked to apply the knowledge to themselves. Std V+ a good sound grounding. The teaching has reached their thoughts and feelings.* Two years later, he noted, '*Group 2 have a remarkable vocabulary and freedom of expression. Group 3 as usual the progress slows down… they are too much taken with growing up... but the teaching gets there, especially when they try to say what they think about relating their Christian duties to their own lives. Group 4 a readiness to think. Excellent throughout*'.

It was also for Religious Instruction that most of the earliest examples of wall pictures and even a flannel board were suggested. Further, it was the missionary speakers, giving occasional talks on travels to Africa, who might introduce illustrations with a 'magic lantern', and it was the Churches and Chapels which often gave children their first experience of a film show with inspiring stories of the likes of Livingstone. Certainly Religious Instruction was often made lively and vivid through the latest equipment and technology to support its educational message.

a. Behaviour: Playgrounds and 'Having a lark'

Even if the children were cooped up inside the school they did, weather permitting, have the chance for some exuberant activity on the playground. A chase game called *Hare and Hounds* was popular at Blagdon, while respondents recall *Leap Frog*, or *Grandmother's Footsteps* and, if anyone had a ball (made from a pig's bladder after a recent slaughtering), 'catch' or maybe cricket was possible [it was only mentioned between the wars after a sudden official interest in sport led to improvements to playgrounds which made more sports possible]. *Lampey* was another popular game, at Kingston Seymour. This was a chase game, when the 'catcher' held hands with an already touched and caught 'prisoner' who together caught others till there was a long and unwieldy line of 'catchers' who (still with a free hand only at either end) tried to encircle and touch (catch) the remaining 'free' children. *Hoops and marbles* were only possible if the playground surface was flat: rutted cart tracks were not suitable and macadamised roads only gradually spread to outlying areas in the inter- and post-war years. *Skipping* was popular and many rhymes (noted in the Opie's Oxford Book of Nursery Rhymes) were adapted and chanted in the children's play. [Incidentally, no accidents from autumn conker fights were ever recorded.]

Plate 9

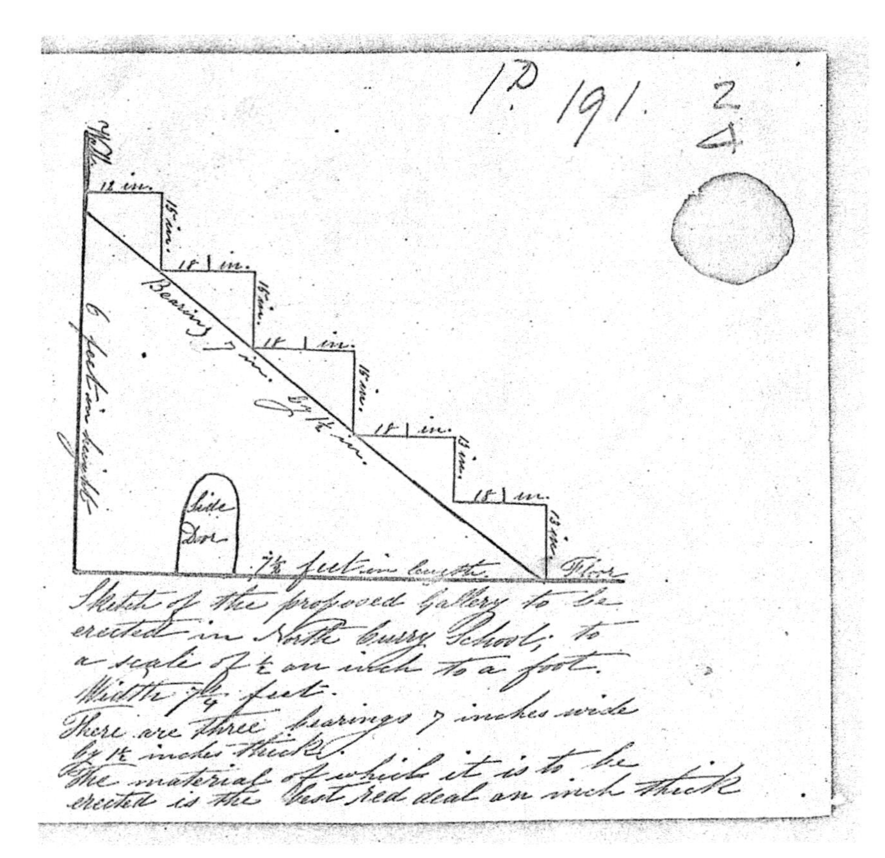

Sketch of a tiered Gallery for Infants often used in 'Object' Lessons

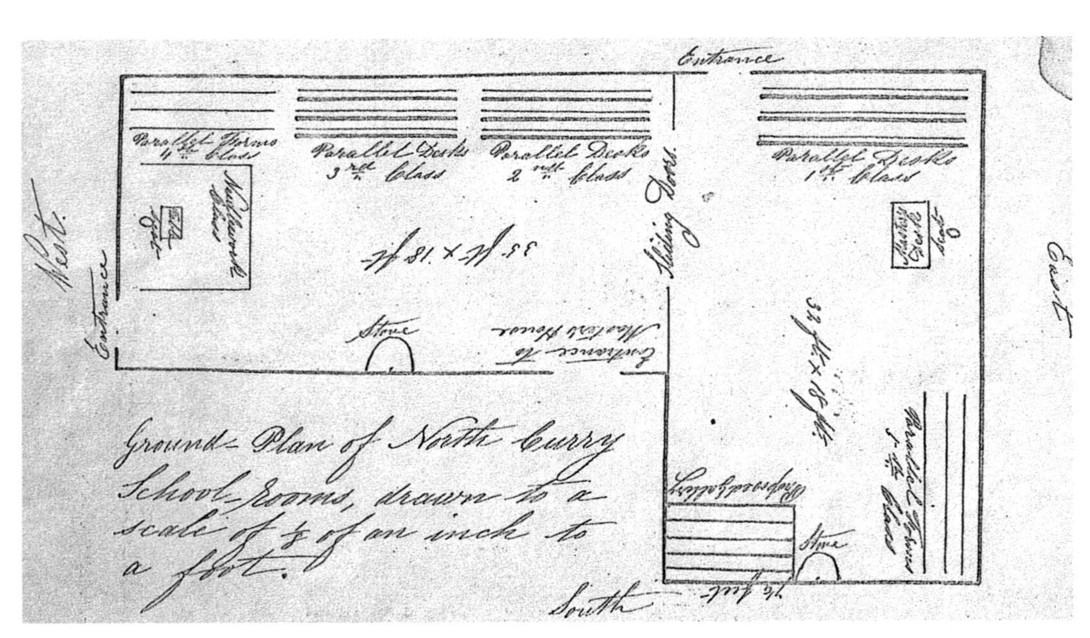

Plan of school hall showing desk layout and classroom with Gallery (left)

Plate 10

Schoolroom 1937

Schoolroom 1937

Plate 11

Handwriting: to copy from easel

Using slate, sand-tray, sampler at Radstock Museum

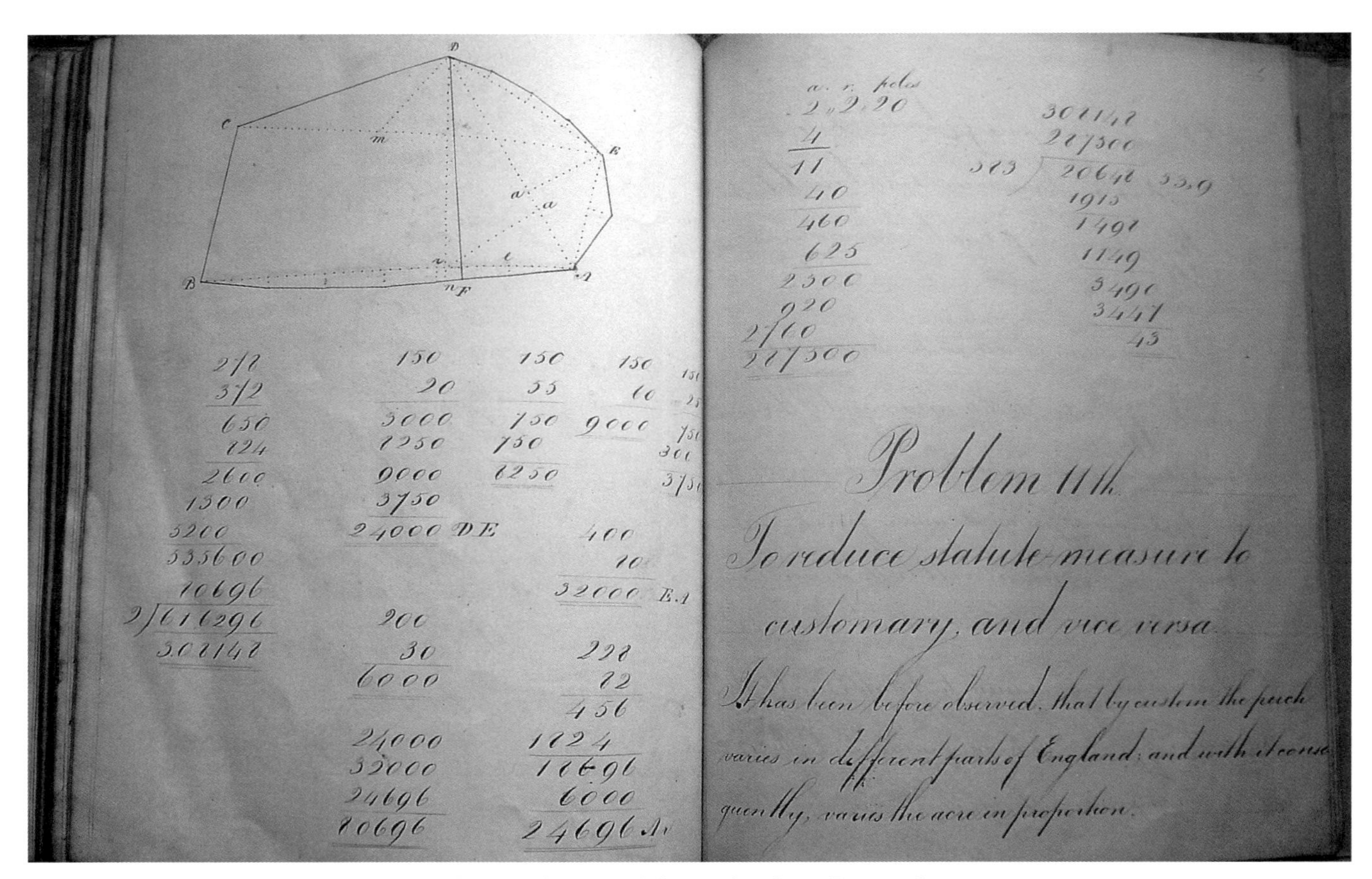

Problem 11th.

To reduce statute measure to customary, and vice versa.

It has been before observed, that by custom the perch varies in different parts of England; and with it consequently, varies the acre in proportion.

Mensuration: Land Surveying from Luccombe
Reduction from Customary measures to Statute measures.
Acres, Roods Poles (22 poles to rood; 24 poles to rood in Corn/Dev/Som/Staff/Lanc/Linc)

Plate 12

Sewing Class at E. Huntspill, 1920s

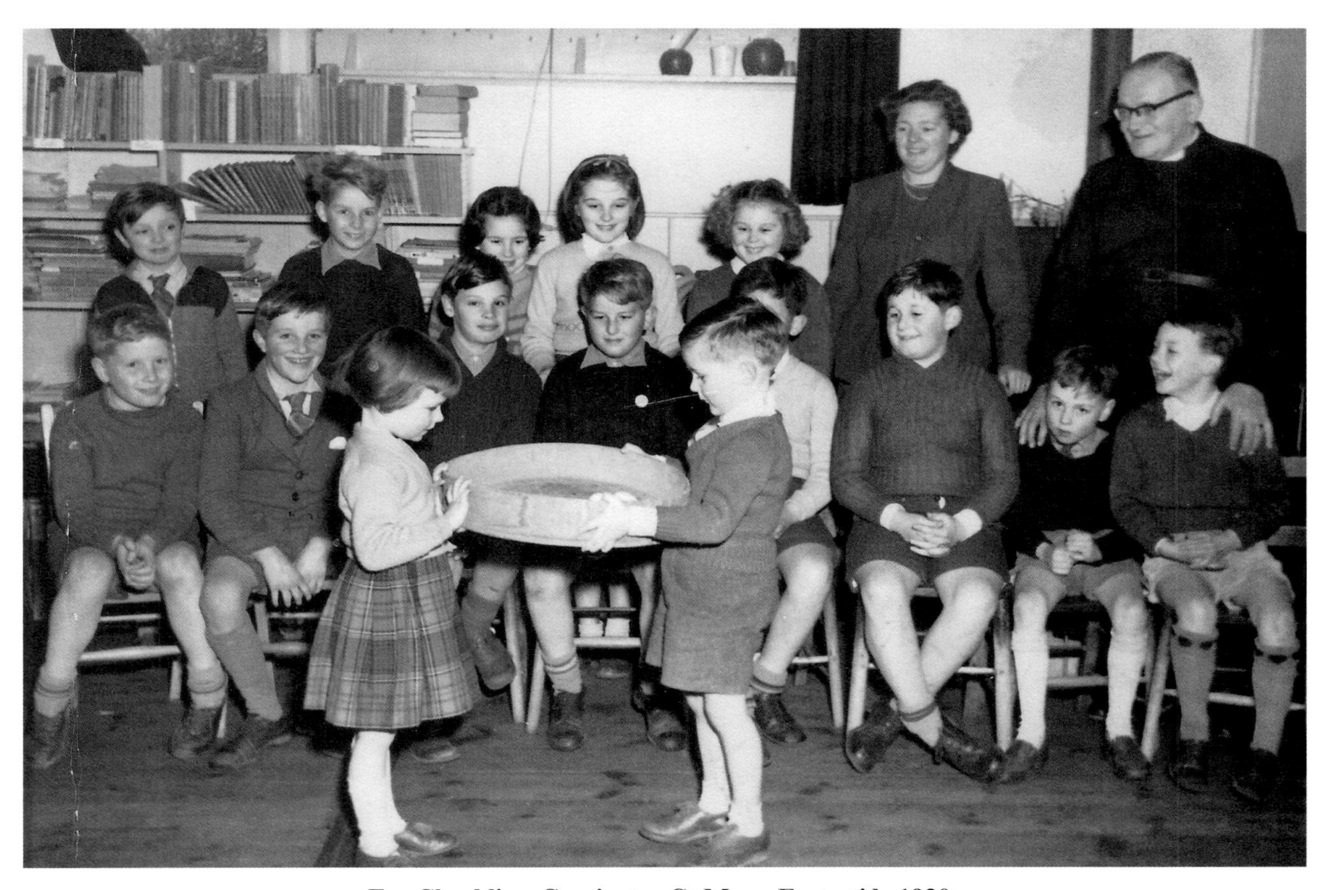

Egg Shackling, Seavington St Mary, Eastertide 1920s

Most 'fun' was obtained in ways directly related to whatever was 'at hand' during the walk to and from school: daring each other to try various exploits, such as jumping the ditches, climbing trees, scrumping for apples, or, playing *Hide and Seek* and (in winter) walking on the iced drainage-rhynes and snowballing. Many of these activities resulted in children arriving at school dirty, wet and in need of a good scrub.

Not until 1900 is there a record of money being spent on equipment for play. With the one exception of Monteclefe which received 2 swings in 1873, it was Cutcombe, in 1900, which kicked off the new century with a swing for the girls and a trapeze, climbing ropes and rings for the boys. In Keinton, some India-rubber balls and 2 skipping ropes were provided in 1928, but not until 1932 did Captain Fitzgerald conduct some ball games with the boys and, hopefully, left the equipment at the school. Only in 1954 is there a record of Kingston Seymour receiving any equipment, in this instance, climbing apparatus. However, we have already noted the gradual introduction of sports' equipment during the 1920s and 30s which would have expanded the children's opportunities for physical activities.

Death was never far away – in the songs and stories used in schools, nor in the children's lives. Yet the constant and recurring childhood diseases seem to have resulted in very few recorded deaths in the examined Logs. Several schools have at least one, but some only one over what was often a lengthy period (1860s – 1940s). However, sometimes a death is a result of a particularly horrible accident. At Isle Brewer's (1900), *'A child of only five years old met his death by falling into his father's mill and was crushed by the wheel'*. Another boy, at Skilgate (1910), had his hand *badly damaged in the chaff-cutting machine*. Yet, an incident of a very different order caused another death: this time *'from the sting of a wasp'* (Hlc 1911). More typical were the deaths from diseases still common at this time: diphtheria - one death (Skg 1908), three deaths (Wrl 1913) and also one death reported from meningitis (SmB 1906).

Accidents seem to have been rare, either in the classroom or out on the playground. Monteclefe seems to have suffered most – considered one of the more difficult schools in the county.
A child fell on the steps of the gallery and cut her lip (1870).
An infant got a pin stuck in his mouth fixed in the teeth. Sent for the doctor but he and his assistant were both out, so eventually it was removed by Mr Miles the Chemist. A few weeks ago the same Infant got a pin stuck in his ear (1889).
A little girl fell down in a fit and was taken home by a teacher. A boy threw a stone which hit Bessie Gulley on the head. The doctor was called. Her head is still not well (1895).
Vera Parker fell and hurt her face badly. It was washed with boracic lotion before she went home. Last Friday Flossie Sweet fell and hurt her knee. The playground is in a very bad condition. Repeated complaints have been made to Managers and HMI (1927).

Other accidents occurred elsewhere:
A leg was broken at Blagdon (1880)
And another at Coleford (1882)

Two serious accidents are reported at Oakhill after school medical services and insurance had been offered to schools and parents became more aware of 'responsibilities':
A boy fell and broke his leg on the football ground. Very regrettable (1925).
A boy fractured his arm and the family sent the receipt to the school (1930).
However, he was not on the school premises, although it was during the play period and he should have been and, therefore, the school was not liable. It resulted in the

Managers reviewing the level of supervision during such periods, and quickly taking out an Insurance policy, paying 10s pa to cover a maximum claim of £500. [The blame game had already started].

Rivalries between pupils from different schools (possibly relating to religious differences) were also recorded. On-going rivalry erupted between the Wesleyan and Anglican schools in Coleford (1904). Stones were thrown between Wesleyan Holcombe and Catholic Downside (1909). In Oakhill, it was not the children who were at fault, but the Anglican Vicar, who was said to be spreading rumours and accusations against the British school!

Only one instance of bullying on the school premises was recorded and two interesting examples of particularly positive behaviour. Two boys were caned for bullying (Ctc 1945), one of whom then complained to the Vicar! One positive instance comes from Kingsdon, in 1901, where the Vicar came to talk with some boys who had started a little society. The Head noted, *'There are 4 boys who are trying to put down the habit of swearing amongst the children. To these 4 boys, the Rector gave cards and the society named The King's Messengers'.* Sadly no more is mentioned about this society. Another instance is from Somerton. It is the only example of a prize 'For being Kind' which came from Monteclefe Girls' School (1915). The Head recorded, *'A girl was voted, by her peers, as being kind, gentle, friendly and honest. She was awarded the Honours Prize and given a beautiful satin-lined work-basket'.*

Involvement by the children was not unheard of in some other schools. One Head regularly noted how the prizes were distributed according to the children's votes (OkBr 1932, 36). This very democratic tradition also occurs in the Sunday School Minutes, of the Wesleyan and Methodist Schools in the mining areas.

b. Punishments: Bad Boys (and Girls)

Bad behaviour in school and outside: Children can also get frustrated with their teachers, their lot, their peers and so bad behaviour was not infrequent. We have already seen the anger that erupted against certain Heads at the troubled Kingsdon School, where the parents were vigorously involved as well. Common occurrences ranged from *spitting at the girls*, *getting into the girls' playground*, *cutting the woodwork*, *being obstinate*, *disobedient*, *impudent*, *throwing stones* (ChM, Kgd, SmB), *theft*, (Kgd, SmM), and *gross indecency/outrage* (ChM, SmB, SmWE). Horsington seemed to have had a considerable problem with 'indecency' and numerous incidents over several years (1896-1900) are recorded: *'indecency, interfering with the girls on their way home, hair-pulling* (Hsg), *exhibiting indecent drawings to the girls* (Hsg*), behaviour of a filthy character in the closet, indecent behaviour towards EC (girl).* Finally, a note arrived from a parent complaining that, *'HK repeatedly interferes with her daughter during her progress to school and he is in the habit of taking a knife to her. I hope you will be good enough to admonish him so that he does not repeat it'.* Yet none of this appears to have gone to the police or Managers.

The girls, however, were not above reproach. Kingsdon girls were reprimanded for throwing stones and sometimes for rudeness. At this school, playtime for Girls and for Boys had to be held at different times for a period in 1898, as behaviour got so out of hand. Other, lesser, instances include girls being kept in at the end of the day for talking too noisily in Sewing class (SmM 1870). Sometimes the very visitors, who so often came as friends of the schools, were asked to use their status and authority to hold the miscreants to account. This was particularly so with delicate matters of cleanliness with the girls. Thus, at Monteclefe, Lady Smith was called to speak to a child who repeatedly came to school very dirty and would not wash when facilities were provided. She subsequently arrived clean and with her hair tied with a ribbon – perhaps provided as good psychology on the part of Lady Smith. The boys also needed a firm hand as at Kingsdon (1898), where the Rector was called in to admonish some boys for bad behaviour such as throwing stones at telegraph wires and, similarly, at Somerton Boys, Captain Pinney, *'Spoke to the Boys and made them aware of the dangers of throwing stones at telegraph wires and trains'*. The police were sometimes called to the school premises – often to deal with threatening parents – but also to warn children of the dangers of continuing to play in the road, after the advent of the motor car.

The following lists from Cutcombe and Blagdon show a wide range of reasons for canings:

	Cutcombe		**Blagdon**
Feb '77	eating another's diner (G)	June 1912	impudence after correction
Nov '77	bad language	Dec 1918	rude conduct
Feb '78	obscene writing on a slate	Sept 1919	disobedience in eating apples in class
July '78	pilfering (G)	Apr 1920	kicking a girl in the head
Sep '79	bad language	Jan 1921	impertinence
May '80	bad language (second warning)	1922 - 26	4 occasions of stone throwing
July '85	filthy ways on the playground	1926 - 29	65 occasions to 31 pupils
Oct '89	stole a biscuit from another (G)		for lateness, careless work, constant
Feb '89	impudence and bad language		chatter, laughing in class, copying,
			'cooking' answers, scrumping apples

Two different schools, two different time periods, a different frequency of canings and for rather different reasons. Punishment was a very subjective matter. Heads were free to impose their own codes, though a maximum guide was 10 stripes or 600 lines. Canings at this remote Exmoor **Cutcombe** School were not very frequent. The only items which were a-typical were the cases of stealing food. This, perhaps, tells us more about the family conditions and maybe the long walk to school than the character of the child. Later, at the same school there was a period of theft which was solved by laying a trap of marked coins. A boy was discovered, the father informed and it was he who undertook the punishment (not recorded).

Blagdon is a larger village on the northern slopes of the Mendips, where there seems to have been a high level of poverty. The level of caning rose dramatically just after World War I. Was this a measure of social dislocation, the individual 'style of the Head' who was in charge from 1918-1926, and another from 1926-33, or, a result of the type of Head preferred by the appointing body? Also at Blagdon, an earlier Head recorded in 1886, *'Having punished a boy for disorderly conduct he then used foul language. Thereupon I gave him 3 stripes on the most fleshy part of his body'*. Another Head must have been at his wits' end: he reports caning a boy (1907), *'as hard as I was able'*. Punishment policy changed after World War II – even in Blagdon – evidenced by the Logs which report the use of the slipper: *6 on seat for breaking furniture* (1955), *12 on seat for playing truant* (1964), *6 on seat for lying and throwing stones* (1965). Despite all that went on in schools, it was often the caning which seems to be such a vividly remembered part of school life. Some soft-hearted female contributors report always hiding under their desk-lids when this happened.

Minor offences were dealt with by keeping children behind and delaying their home-going, as for girls who were noisy during sewing (SmM 1882), for carelessness in arithmetic (Hsg 1896), to merely 'giving lines' – as in the cases of an understanding teacher who sympathised with the truants' urge to look at a crashed plane in 1942 and so gave only a mild punishment (KM). In Keinton boys were frequently punished for stealing apples, once for riding a farmer's pig and, once for killing a cockerel 'in self-defence'!

Other mis-demeanours were of a different nature. Parents had to supply basic equipment themselves, but clearly the financial strain was often too much. A letter sets this out (Hsg 1889),

Sir I hear you intends to punishing my boy for not bringing a copy book. I give you to understand it is not in my power to buy copybooks as our income is but 11s 6d a week to keep ten of us.
From yours truly, E B.

And a year later (Hsg 1890),

Sir, Will you kindly let Walter out a quarter to four to keep up with the cows from Mr Perrot and sir I must tell you that I cant ford to bye coppy books for the children as I have anough to pay the school money with our large family Will you kindly oblige, E H.

Such insights are heartbreaking. Hopefully, the ending of fees which came later in that very year, 1890, will have helped precisely families like this. Other parents show a willingness to challenge:

I have wrote this note to tell you that I shall see Mr Ballwood [Manager] *to ask if you are allowed to let your little dog run and for the big girls to set it at the little ones to make them cry and then for the school Mrs to have them in and punish them. From Mrs H.*
– a parent who had regular run-ins with the Head (Hsg 1896).

Punishments were sometimes specifically related to schoolwork such as, '*Slovenly writing*' or '*Wilful disobedience in working their multiplication sums contrary to the way they have been taught*' (Hsg 1896), '*For having their books open on the desk shelf during dictation*' (Hsg 1899).

c. Police and Village controls.
A conspicuous feature of rural life was the way in which it 'took the whole village to bring up a child'. Parents were legally responsible for the attendance of their child (as we shall see in the section below), but 'significant others' were also involved in the cleanliness and behaviour of the children (as we have seen above).

Criminal acts did occur, both on and off the school premises, in which school children were involved. A series of thefts was reported concerning small amounts of money and of clothing (SmM 1876). Serious arson seems to have occurred on two occasions (Hsg 1897 and 1904), once when fire broke out in the stables. 'S*everal boys were seen prowling around the Manor House stables, which burnt down in the night*' (1897), and later, '*A rick caught fire, and a girl was taken to the Magistate's Court' (1902).* The outcome is not reported. The Police were sometimes called to the school to investigate more serious matters: A boy, who was found to have stolen 4d and was also '*taken for house-breaking and stealing*', and then sent to an Industrial School (Chl 1915). Ten years later, a troubled family had one son cautioned who was, at a later date, found hiding from the Police in connection with another offence, and the following year three siblings were also in trouble with the Police for minor problems (Chl 1924-26).

Of a very different nature, more than one instance of 'indecent behaviour' is reported. In one case the Head noted, '*A parent complained of gross outrage against her son committed by two boys at the instigation of an older one from a neighbouring school. Police were instructed to watch the neighbourhood during the evening hours'* (SmWE 1885). Other reports of 'indecent behaviour' seem to have referred to 'hair-pulling' – whether more was involved but, out of delicacy, was not identified is impossible to tell.

In the remote villages justice had to be administered very locally and often immediately. It took a long time for a Bobby to cycle out to make his proverbial "*Allo, 'allo, 'allo, What's all this then*?" approach. However, as policing became more widespread and more officers or Special (volunteer) Constables were 'on the ground', the arm of the law did sometimes play a part.

Keinton's Special Constable reports several occasions when he clipped loitering lads around the ear, or engaged boys (with their hands thrust in pockets) in a casual, lengthy and seemingly friendly chat, before saying, "*And put out that cigarette before it burns holes in yer pockets*", or, putting a large boot on a miscreant's foot before commanding, "*Be off wi' 'ee or I'll have yer Dad ont' 'ee*". Contributors reported that villagers who witnessed bad behaviour at the weekend would warn the perpetrators that they would "*tell the Master on the Monday*". When everyone knew everybody, they all kept a watchful eye, but equally they would look out for each other in times of need.

Lesser offences were just reported to the Managers or directly to the Head. One such complaint about the children shouting too much was received (OkBr 1904). The Head noted, *'I took no notice as noise is a child's prerogative'.* [One wonders who made the complaint and how often it had been made before.]

iv. Attendance Record: the battle against Absences.

Given the typical state of rural schooling, it is hardly surprising that a child might be seen *'creeping like snail unwillingly to school'* (even from Shakespeare's time). But children did not, yet, expect much of a 'childhood'. There were many other pressures to keep them away from school. Girls were in constant demand at home to help with wash-day, look after the little ones, or carry father's lunch to the fields during harvest time. Boys too were under pressure to take small jobs to add a few pence to the family pot. The typical tasks were seasonal:

Spring: bird-scaring, picking snowdrops, primroses or daffodils for sale,
April: helping parents in *the garden*
May + June: carrying bark on the Moors, hay-making,
July: whortleberry-picking on the Moors,
Harvest: gathering each crop as it ripened throughout the summer,
Autumn: fruit-picking in certain areas – especially for cider-making, as well as potato and mangel-picking, or, being *'busy among the swedes'*,
Winter: stone-picking before ploughing, hedging, and helping to 'beat' for the Lord of the Manor's shooting parties.

Referring to the last, *'They are paid 1d a day, so how can one stop it?'* bemoaned one Head. So many absences occurred around the end of September for blackberry picking that many schools gave in and took a week off as Blackberry Week.

There were other particular cases: one child said he had to deliver letters, so the Head told him to do it in the afternoon (Hsg 1875). On one occasion the Head noted, *'High winds have resulted in a substantial fall of acorns. Only 8 children attend today'* (Chf 1887) – presumably these were collected for the pigs and, again, *'Meteorological conditions satisfy the requirements of the annual acorn gathering so attendance suffers'* (Hsg 1896).

The summer Harvest Holiday still deserved that name. It is clear that each school decided its own holiday dates each year according to when the harvest was ready. Thus dates vary between the west and east of the county and from year to year. For example: in the west below Exmoor, Skilgate tended to have early holidays to catch the whortleberry-picking time (though there were also many children in the fields in October for potato-picking) so, in the 1880s holidays were taken from the beginning of July, though weather changes led to holidays in 1876 and 1909 both starting in the third week of July. In the south, Chaffcombe, Chillington, Horsington all had later holidays starting at the end of the first week of August (in 1876 holidays started so late in August, that Horsington only took 2 weeks that summer). The eastern areas were fairly similar to those of the south.

Attendance mostly depended on the willingness of the parents to send their children. Even from the clergy there was not always support for education. A Rector in Walton 1867 said, *'It was unjust to make boys attend day school as their parents needed their earnings'*. Such sentiments were echoed by a Kingsdon farmer (1867) who preferred to employ boys who had not gone to school, though *'I don't mind a little reading and writing',* while at Westenzoyland (1868) the Head soulfully declared, *'The uneducated parents were indifferent to their children's education'*. Kingston Seymour (1874) reported, *'The Attendance Cane does not appear to have improved attendance. A large proportion of the parents are unconcerned about the education of their children and do not care a snuff'*. This concern was echoed by HMI (IsB 1888) who noted, *'There is little or nothing to praise nor are the results likely to improve as long as attendance is so disgracefully irregular'* (Boys at this school were often in the fields and the girls at home sewing shirts or buttons). Right into the C20th there were still pockets of resisting parents: the West Pennard Head 1923 reported, *'The attendance is shocking. The parents are quite indifferent'.*

From the time of the 1862 Revised Code, recording and checking attendances became a prime task for the Head and Managers. This was because it was one of the criteria to qualify for a grant. Many different techniques were introduced to try to boost attendance: money prizes, medals, tickets or cards were distributed and the child's attendance record marked. Blagdon started such a scheme in June 1882, with Red Tickets for 10 consecutive attendances, Blue for 9 and White for 8, but *the value not yet decided* (by September the Managers decided that the 'value' was to be the honour of receiving it!). Good attendance sometimes merited the waiving of fees for the next term or year (ChM 1887): when one boy achieved full attendance for 6 years it resulted in a prize in the form of clothes such as a shirt or chemise (Hsg 1872), or a cash prize (Kgd 1877). These were given out, with some ceremony, by a local notable at an annual event. Some children, even whole families, were constant winners, while others were permanent losers. One child had a complete attendance record over the full 9 years of his school life (Luc 1913) while two more children at the same school (Luc 1915) also achieved a perfect record for 7 and 10 years respectively [think how young they must have started!, but note that these children gained from having an education free from the School Penny fee].

Legislation does not seem to have made much impact on most of the schools. Only one Head noted an increase after attendance was compulsory in 1876 (Hsg), while several mention attendance *'much bigger than last year'* after fees were abolished in 1890. The Act of that year gave managers the option of abolishing fees in return for a per capita grant. It sometimes took a year before Managers agreed to apply the policy to their particular school. In several schools abolishing fees made little difference, while in others there was a marked change in the numbers recorded, as in the examples overleaf:

Coleford:	1891 on Roll 78,	**48 attend,**	yet in 1895 on Roll 78, **68 attend;**
Horsington	1890 on Roll 141,	**74 attend May; 94 attend Oct;**	1893 on Roll 137, **104 attend**
West End Inf	1891 on Roll 73,	**65 attend May, 81 attend Nov.**	
Monteclefe G	1890	**112 attend**	yet in 1891 **145 attend**

Attendance Officers were appointed by the School Boards in the 1880s and in 1884 parents could be prosecuted and fined for their child's non-attendance. The Cutcombe Head reported absences to the Attendance Officer in June and July 1880. In 1884 the Managers gave prizes for good attendance, and visited lax parents with warnings and again the next year. The only recorded prosecution, at this school, was when a father was fined for his son's non-attendance (Cte 1914). In other schools the practice of summoning and fining parents was much more frequent. Kingsdon in 1884 had 14 prosecution cases: 8 parents were fined 5s, 3 fined 3s 6d, 3 only 2s 6d. In 1901 another was fined 10s, and 4 were fined 5s each *'before the Magistrate at Petty Sessions'*. Monteclefe also regularly served summonses on reluctant parents. Many other schools, such as Brewham, never brought summonses – perhaps they knew parents did not have the money to pay. Sometimes Heads and even HMI bewailed the fact that the Attendance Officer did not prosecute, but, he was an elected officer from amongst his fellow villagers and often seemed loathe to do so.

Another headache when marking the School Registers stemmed from the children who attended more intermittently. No Log mentioned travellers and only one refered to gypsies. Perhaps the seasonal fruit-pickers and farm-workers did not send their children to school for they, too, were needed to earn extra pennies. At the turn of the century, however, a different kind of migration hit some villages: the railway navvies (KM and ChM) and reservoir workers (Bgd). They were viewed with great suspicion during the few years when they were encamped nearby before moving on, and were frequently blamed for disease and theft. Yet little space was devoted to these children – perhaps the numbers admitted to school were small.

A further feature relating to transient populations was the custom of hiring and firing on the farms. In March, around **Lady-Day**, a number of Logs note several families leaving, or 'changing houses' – a custom still mentioned in 1907. (Ctc, Skg, Chf, Chl, Hsg and OkBr). It appears that the more peripheral farm-hands only had a year's contract and could then be turned out of house and home, lose their job and garden, up sticks and move out. The number and occasions of admission and re-admission of children around this time of year is noticeable.

The movement of families also occurred in the mining areas as pits closed and strikes bit deep into the social fabric of the communities. The 1890s were very bad years for the Coleford schools. Many families left the area and looked for work in Bristol, South Wales, even as far away as Canada.

a. Cleaniness

At West End Infants, in July 1875, the Rev Strong sent home two children to be washed and have their hair combed. In November 1877, he sent a boy home who came to school very dirty. In June, 1891 two girls were sent home because of dirty pinafores. Much later, in September 1903, George Cornick wrote, "*A big boy who has never been to school arrives in a very dirty state and needs to be washed every morning before he can sit with other children. I have sent a message home to his grandmother with whom he lives. She is too infirm to attend to him.* (By 1904, he was removed to another home.)

Monteclefe Girls were frequently sent home to wash. In 1883 a new Head started a campaign for cleanliness, punctuality and regularity. Examples of her campaign include:

November 1883, Lily H came to school very dirty. *'She was washed by an older girl, but this gave offence to her sister who was very saucy. She and her brother were sent home on Friday to wash.'*
October 1884 *'Louisa S was sent to wash herself. She stood in front of the water one hour, then ran away to her mother in the factory, who returned in a white passion and made a dreadful scene. She would not go away till she thought the policeman was coming, then she climbed over a wall.'*
December *'E R came to school very dirty and objected to the use of cold water. Her grandmother came on Wednesday not at all pleased that she was required to wash. She was taken to Lady Smith and, finding cleanliness is considered necessary, the girl comes cleaner now with her hair tied up.'*
November 1890, *'Rose G kept at home as her father objects to her washing with the school soap'* (the family used Pears at home!).

In May 1914, the school was still battling for cleanliness, this time in the form of 'dirty heads'. Offending parents were fined 5s each for sending their child to school in a 'verminous condition'. This frequently caused real offence. We have a reported case in Blagdon, 1909, *'A relative of one of the children has just been into school and assaulted me. He has received a card saying his son's head is dirty. He laid hands on me and swore. I called the policeman. Next day he apologised'*. In the same year, in a different vein, the Head reports, *'I sent home one boy who was too strong smelling for anybody to sit near'*. The doctors of this era sometimes reported that children had not changed their clothes for 6 months. It is little wonder that teachers often sewed bags of sulphur into their skirt-hems to ward off 'vermin' and 'disease' (Horn 1989).

b. Illnesses. One of the chief reasons for non-attendance was medical: illness was rife, school closures not infrequent as epidemics of now preventable diseases took their toll. During winter coughs and colds were commonplace, but it was outbreaks of scarlet fever, diphtheria, as well as measles, mumps and chicken-pox which caused real fear. It seems possible that the more remote schools fared better in this respect, or maybe they were not always acknowledged before the days when health officials came to identify the occurences. It may relate to different expectations in different areas, or simply Heads recording events using different criteria. In the new century several diseases, had to be reported, by law, to the new Schools' Medical Officer. Thus:

1883 Kingsdon was closed for 2 weeks with chickenpox
1892,'99 West End closed for 4 weeks for scarlet fever and scarlatina
1905 West End was again closed, for diphtheria; in 1908 for whooping cough, and 1913 for mumps
1905 Blagdon closed for 18 weeks during the year, for outbreaks of diphtheria
1912 Montclefe was closed for measles and whooping cough, in 1916 for diphtheria (when the school had to be scrubbed and disinfected with Izal), and again in 1920 for measles.

Some schools were closed more than once in a year, as series of illnesses attacked already weakened children. Most schools experienced some closures, though there does appear to have been rather more such epidemics in the three Somerton schools (Boys, Girls and Infants) than in many of the smaller rural settlements. Again, reporting was not always consistent, so omission of closure does not necessarily mean absence of illness.

The Weather, too, was closely allied to illness. Reporting this aspect was very variable amongst the Heads. Maybe it depended how used you were to the local 'wet and rough' weather of the Moors, or the 'inundations' on the Levels. Obviously, the more remote schools suffered more: children in Isle Brewer's were sent home early if the river was rising owing to heavy rains, or, in Cutcombe, if the snow was becoming heavier. Several times children could not get to school because of deep drifts along the field paths or iced roads. If they did manage to get through, they arrived soaked and had to change and hang their clothes to dry by the fire. Many younger children regularly did not attend during winter – the way being difficult. The summer was often as bad. A despairing, but poetic, Head (Hsg 1890) wrote at the end of May, '*Nature so wept at this lovely month's exit that only 22 children put in an appearance. Nature has been having a rather watery time of it*'. Recently he had recorded 74 attendances and 67 absences.

c. Ages for school admission and completion

School Leaving Age: There was a considerable difference between expectation and reality: the pressure to start earning was strong. Far from official eyes, the implementation of regulations was often lax. In the 1860s children were nominally expected to attend from 5-11 years, but there was no requirement. However, after the Factory Acts and Mines Acts from the 1830s the numbers of hours worked had gradually been lowered and the starting age for such work raised, making schooling more possible. The acts also had an impact in Somerset for, although predominantly agricultural, there were many related factories (tanneries, glove-making, spinning, weaving, straw-hat making and other out-worker tasks).

The school-leaving age was attacked by employers wanting young cheap labour and by the parents who wanted their children to start earning. After compulsory schooling was introduced from 1876, children could be exempted and allowed to leave early if the required number of days of attendance, or the minimum pass at Standard IV before the appropriate birthday had been reached. This system of 'exemptions' was complex and often circumnavigated. From 1880 there was the added minimum age limitation on exemptions set at 10 years, rising to 11 years in 1893, to 12 years in 1899. Further, there were frequent arguments over children wanting to leave on their birthday, rather than wait till the end of that term. In fact there were plenty of contentious aspects. Many children took *part-time* and *temporary* jobs, as at harvest. Each of these terms was (deliberately) misunderstood. There was also an attempt to make all work illegal for people outside the family and not on family land, but with so much village inter-marriage what counts as family? By 1891 managers could opt for free elementary schooling in exchange for a per capita grant. Again exemptions were added, the bar raised to Std V and changes made over the next decade. Finally, in 1902 elementary schooling was compulsory and free from 5-13 years, but with no exemptions – but, as ever, implementation was varied. The School Leaving Age continued to rise: 14 (1918), 15 in 1936 (though not implemented till 1944) and raised to age 16 in 1972.

Half-timers: Finally, with exemptions for young leavers came the requirement to attend for two hours of education each day until the required leaving age had been reached. This was often resented by the employer and young employee and was inconvenient for the teacher. It must often have been a dispiriting experience for all concerned. In rare circumstances a Factory might have its own school, as at Silk Mills in Evercreech. Half-timers who worked in the factories in Chard are recorded at Chaffcombe (1879) and at Isle Brewer's (1888, 1903). Other examples include a child from the Langport Union Poor House who attended Charlton Mackrell. In Monteclefe half-timers were admitted in 1880 and 1885 from a local factory, some of whom were boarded out by the Langport Union (workhouse). Such children were frequently torn between employers' demands to do extra and the requirement to attend school. Another example of split loyalties comes in 1902 when young Albert was absent owing to the funeral of his employer. No other such mentions are made.

Towards the end of the century, when a child left, or entered, details were supposed to be added to the Registers (age of entry, previous school experience, age at leaving and reason for leaving). Examining the existing Logs at Cutcombe for these years, it is possible to find occasional children who are 14 years old but have only reached Std III. Conversely a few bright children had completed Std IV, but not yet reached the minimum age: these applied for a Labour Certificate. Detailed records show interesting features of school leavers in the years immediately before WWI: JP from Std II and GF from Std III both left when aged 14; ten years later, amongst the leavers one left from Std II, one from Std III, 5 from Std IV and the rest from Std V. Clearly, there were wide ability differences with which both staff and students had to contend.

In the 1920s, it is estimated that 80% of children didn't attend any place of schooling after completing Elementary School. Leaving restrictions were relaxed during the labour shortages in the World Wars. At the other end of the time-scale we find from an analysis of 1851 census records of the western sector, that there was considerable variation in the percentage of eligible scholars attending: from Exton (21%) and Brompton Regis (30%), to Cutcombe (67%) and Luccombe (71%). The chief landowner of Luccombe was the Acland family which was known to have paid for several children to attend and to have helped in the building of a purpose-built school several decades later. This may account for the high percentage from this small settlement. Hence we find the picture of schooling is anything but consistent across Somerset at this time.

School Admission Age. Children living near the school would regularly be sent to attend at 4, at 3 and very occasionally at 2 years old. Their names can be seen on the 10-yearly census returns, marked as 'scholar' - when the next baby arrived the penultimate one was sent to school. Recurrent comments were made by HMI and sometimes by Heads if severe overcrowding was experienced. But often it was a 'community service' which the school provided to meet the needs of hard-pressed mothers. In the decade between 1899 and 1909 Isle Brewer's admitted nine children of 3 years and two of 4 years old. Kingsdon recorded admitting a 3-year old in 1884, 1891, 1892 and 1899. Cutcombe also had several 'babies'. Frequently these were younger siblings of children already attending the school. Conversely, there were also several families living at almost 3 miles' distance which reduced their likelihood of attending. The number of young entrants seems to have changed dramatically at the beginning of the century, so that HMI note, *'Many of the children attending this school do not begin until they are at least 6 or 7 years old. It is not to be expected that they will achieve the same results as elsewhere'.*

In Isle Brewer's, another isolated school, 'babies' often seem to have been admitted: one 3-year old a year (1888, '99, '00, 01), two 3-year olds (1903), three 3-year olds (190), a single 3-year old each year between 1906 and '09). In West End Somerton, 1903 there were 5 children under 3 years old, in 1908 15 were under 5 and 19 under 4, all on the Gallery, *'confined to desks for want of space'.* At adjacent Monteclefe, HMI commented, *'The classroom for the Infants is quite unsuitable for three classes. There are 46 children of five years and more, and 23 of less than 5 years'.* In 1909, the school decided that under 5s were to be excluded – although this was relaxed during the war years, if accommodation allowed. The same exclusion was reinforced in 1923 and also recorded in Coleford in the same year.

v. Welfare Reforms

An even stronger concern for the child (though for political reasons it still had to be couched in terms of national need) was expressed by ex-Prime Minister Lord Roseberry, in 1906, in support of the Liberal government's educational welfare reforms: he urged the House to realise that *'It is not rank socialism but first-class imperialism, for Imperialism cannot be built on the rickerty shoulders of existing elementary pupils'.* Following this, a major break though came when school medical services commenced as a result of the Medical Inspections which were introduced for children over 12 (and possibly likely to leave soon) and all new infant entries. A school Doctor or Nurse began annual inspections to check the children – the first check at Isle Brewer's was in 1908. Some parents however, refused to allow their children to be examined (IsB 1914, Chf 1923). Some Doctors worked alongside the Attendance Officer to check on stay-at-homes. They also gave permission for when a sick child could return. One Doctor allowed a child to return just half-time on the condition that *'His mind should not be unduly taxed with Arithmetic or any other mental subject'* (OkBr 1906).

The Nurses usually checked for 'dirty heads': cards were given to parents of children who suffered from 'verminous conditions' – sometimes resulting in an abusive response, as it was considered a slur on the family to be found 'with lice'. (Even in the 1970s school nurses came to inform parents with some trepidation as to what reception they would get.) Dental inspections soon followed – Luccombe in Exmoor being the first to be noted in 1913 (treatments had to be paid for, but cheap toothbrushes were offered at 3d each in the 1930s). Again, some children, even if their parents allowed it, screamed so much the dentist could not examine them (Chf 1931). To access the Occulist's skills, children were invited to attend at the specialist's premises. Transportation sometimes made this difficult, and follow-up treatment was also not free. During the 1920s and 30s all schools were recording access to specialist medical facilities. Parents seemed to have been ambivalent about the new medical services. Glasses had to be paid for and, again, not all parents accepted the invitation to attend. One child was almost blind, yet her parents would not allow her to wear glasses (KSy 1923). One child was stone deaf: *his* parents, however, accepted a place at a special school where he could receive the support he needed. He was recorded (SmB 1916) as *'an intelligent child who draws well'*. There was some very visible support for children with severe problems who were lucky enough to get it. Special aids were offered: an eye-patch is mentioned (Skg 1929) which has to be worn for 2 hours each day, and another child was *'Not to read ordinary books and to use his arm-blackboard for writing* (Chl 1930).

Another worry was the poor food that children often had, as well as the long journeys. Children were usually expected to return home for dinners. But in every school there were children from the boundaries of the catchment area where this was impracticable. Those for whom the distance was too far, were sent with food, often a hot potato – frequently eaten on the way to school. Perhaps this was the cause of the few noted cases of pilfering of biscuits and the like. Some children may well have 'picnic-ed' with relatives or friends who lived closer to school, or snacked in a corner of the playground. Heads did sometimes heat milk for the children and once the Lady of the Manor sent round some soup on a particularly cold day (Chf 1890). A mention of dinners being formally allowed in school occured during WWI. Clearly schools did not then have cooking or heating-up facilities and such equipment came later in the 1930s.

Hunger was a real worry during periods when there were stoppages and lock-outs as in the mining area in 1921 and 1926. Dr Weaver came to examine children who might be suffering from lack of food, but he felt that the Somerset Coalfield Relief Fund had saved many already. It was a time when children were often absent picking coal to try and sell. Nevertheless, some were fed at school from local donations over the summer months and, in 1926, many were again fed at school, while others were sent to temporary homes elsewhere (Clf).

It was not only hunger and sickness which affected some of the children, but their general poverty was also evidenced in their poor clothing. Log books from particularly poor areas reveal the extent of rural poverty in the last quarter of the C19th, which does not continue to be mentioned after the turn of the century –

perhaps as a result of the growing impact of the general welfare reforms. Pockets of extreme poverty can be seen on the Lowlands around Isle Brewer's and in the east at Brewham and Horsington. In some areas the local Lords of the Manors even subsidised families to help them emigrate to Australia and New Zealand, as there was such devastation in the rural neighbourhoods.

Welfare also stretched to cover wider problems of care. We find only a few instances of the NSPCC visiting schools regarding children about whom concerns had been raised (Skg 1913). Decades later, there was still a need for vigilance: the NSPCC came to check two children *'who were found to eat excessively at dinner and dress very poorly'* (Chf 1964).

Special medical campaigns also began between the wars. Ionized chocolates were given, in 1924 and 1926, to children in Blagdon and Keinton as part of an experimental programme against thyroid problems. An annual **Health Week** began in 1930 during which special competition essays were written and events held: in 1932 boys in Cutcombe made a healthy soup from vegatables grown in the school garden. Several incidents of warm **milk** being prescribed for children suffering from anaemia are mentioned. Also, **malt and codliver oil** were frequently prescribed from 1930s. Milk came to be offered to anyone who wished to join the scheme at ½d per 1/3 pint, though later it was provided free (till 1972). One respondent admitted, *"We often took the milk because of the straw!"* Another favourite supplement was **codliver oil and malt** which was offered to children who needed to be strengthened. They were often required to be weighed weekly on the new school scales, to check their progress. A further development was in 1934 when children's posture was examined: several children were prescribed a daily half-hour of lying on a board.

In a parallel campaign some schools joined a **Horlicks** campaign whereby malted milk was given free, while the **Anglo-Swiss Condensed Milk Company** offered to provide milk in the schools, and **Lever Bros** promoted a **Clean Hands Campaign**, while encouraging the use of their soaps. The1930s saw many other campaigns for pupils' welfare. **RoSPA** gave Road Safety talks in schools: motorised traffic was becoming more common and the children were not adapting their behaviour. The days when a man would walk in front of a car with a red warning flag as it drove through built-up streets were over! Also, the **RSPCA** came into schools to give talks about animal welfare.

The 'strugglers' and the 'stars'

Not only was the variable academic quality of the pupils a difficulty, but the lack of resources and support further compounded the problems for the teacher. In small rural schools, a teacher may have had small classes but they included children from a wide range of ability. At Cutcombe the Head, on his arrival in 1877, noted a backward child in the school. Already in 1880 we saw the Head at Blagdon, who took the older pupils, record in the Log, *'The labour of teaching what they ought to have learned at five is immense'*. He struggled on and commented on one child in 1888, *'The boy seems incapable of learning anything. His sister failed three times. I have spent much time trying to teach the backward children'*. Elsewhere, West End (1885) was more fortunate and records progress in this area, *'Several backward children are coming along fairly'*.

Instances showing concern about what to do with children with learning or behavioural difficulties recur. Violence was sometimes involved and this required action, but what? A young boy of 4½ screamed, kicked and bit: he was caned and had his boots taken away (SmM 1898). In 1904 at Keinton, 'representations' were made to the County Secretary for Education which came to nothing, and again in 1925, a child was examined but *'with no result'*. Further, at Kingsdon, the Head noted, *'An imbecile boy attending Infants, aged 12 yrs'*. Another instance occurred in 1914: *'In March a child, certified MD* [mentally deficient] *hurt two other children today. One was struck on the nose causing it to bleed, another one struck on the ear causing temporary deafness'*. In May, the child was excluded.

Although an Inspector had been appointed in 1921 by the County Education Committee to oversee the working of the Mental Deficiency Act of that same year, there is little evidence from the Logs that there was either the knowledge or the provision necessary to help either the child, the teachers, much less the parents. It is the local Doctor who was the first to be consulted. So we find, *'The Doctor was invited to see a 'special' case* (Skg 1924) and again two years later. This resulted in a child being sent to a special school at Yatton, a considerable distance away, so presumably residential, but not allowing easy family access. Another Doctor made a school visit to examine a child and recommend a special school, but the mother was reluctant (1923). Dr Weaver also came to Coleford in 1925. *'To examine five children of weak intellect'*. Testing was eventually mentioned rather than just examination, though what this involved the Log does not record. In 1930 the Blagdon Head notes, *'A child was tested: age 8 yrs 3 mths, mental age 5 yrs 4 mths'*. No mention of any follow-up was given. The problem relating to another child was noted (Ctc 1931, 1932), *'A boy cannot do any of the work because of mental weakness'*.

The difficulties such children experienced were immense. Teachers recognised that a child might have a problem but may not have been able to identify its different manifestations and did not know enough about the various causes to be able to respond with anything other than frustration or kindness. Many such children were left to ruminate in a corner as the proverbial 'village idiot' and while they did not disrupt the rest of the class they were abandoned. Other teachers tried hard to support them but, without specialised knowledge, it was difficult to meet their needs.

The first instance of the involvement of a School Psychologist was in 1935 when a meeting was arranged, to which a mother was invited. However, on the appointed day, neither the child nor the mother appeared - such appears to have been the fear of *'Them what interfere'*. Two decades later, a Psychologist was again asked to attend a child and mother at school. This time the meeting took place and the child was later transferred to a Home for Maladjusted Children. It was this kind of 'stigma' that many families sought to avoid. As the role of the Psychologist evolved we hear of extended support from the Psychologist who even visited a sibling of a child who had been taken into a Residential School at Monkton Priors (Chl 1935).

In 1957 we read of a 'peripatetic' teacher for backward children visiting Coleford and in 1967 such a teacher was referred to 'a Remedial'. Labels change but not much else. Only in 1975 was an opportunity noted to disseminate information about particular conditions affecting learning: a Lecture on Dyslexia. Not till 1980 when the Warnock Report was published was there a serious attempt to identify and support all children with 'special needs' at both ends of the spectrum.

Scholarships: At the opposite end of the achievement spectrum were the bright students. In some schools these were formally appointed as monitors to teach the others, or informally became 'helpers'. Later when Diocesan Scholarship Exams and County Special Places Scheme made access to secondary education possible, for these few children, new opportunities arose. From the 1930s some schools made special arrangements for star pupils, and were proud of the numbers who were accepted for the next level of education (SmB, SmM, KM).

Somerton Boys' seems to have had a good track record in sending boys to secondary education on scholarships and bursaries: to illustrate the variety of mechanisms by which pupils could access further education we can note four boys who won Junior County Scholarships in 1899, two more who passed directly to a specific school, Langport Grammar in 1909, and two more who were successful in the Free Places examination. Keinton was also successful in gaining admissions to particular schools: St Hilda's for Girls (1916), Sunny Hill for Girls (1920), as well as Sexey's and Langport Grammar. The inter-war years were fruitful for Monteclefe too: a girl won a grant from the British Legion to attend Bishop Fox's School, Taunton, in 1926, and another passed to Bishop Fox's two years later, while in the same year yet another girl was admitted to Bridgwater High School. So, despite the claims that this was a difficult school, and thanks to some of the battling Heads, some children – both boys and girls – were able to take advantage of the opportunities.

Sadly, some of those who could have made it were sometimes denied the chance: at Cutcombe, (1931) the Head recorded, *'A girl passed Part I of the scholarship exam, but her guardian refuses to allow her to sit for the second part'*. Perhaps her earning potential was more important to the family during those difficult slump-times. Generally, the school strongly supported children entering for the exams and provided extra teaching-time and tuition: a positive result was sometimes the occasion of a half-holiday for the children, as when places were won at Minehead (1928), Exton and Winsford (1929) and, from Enmore a child went to Dr Morgan's Bridgwater (1945).

In the eastern mining area, vocational scholarships seem to have predominated: two Technical Scholarships to Frome were won (Clf 1892); one child won a place for 3 years at a Devon County School with a £10 annual grant (OkBr 1905); one girl won a scholarship to the School of Housewifery in Street, with free board and fees paid (Wrl 1912), another gained a Junior County Scholarship (Wrl 1916) and several scholarships to Cannington College Bath were won between 1928 and 31; two scholarships were won to Bath School of Art, and one to Bath Technical College and places were gained at Sunny Hill Bruton (Hlc 1936, 1946, 1944).

In the lowlands and southern areas few scholarships seem to have been won or even attempted. However, after a new Head arrived achievements rose in Horsington: a girl entered Sunny Hill, Bruton and another went to Lord Digby's School, Sherborne (1907), another to Sexey's (1908), another to Lord Digby's (1911) and one entry to Ilchester grammar was recorded (Hsg 1937).

Travel and Transport

In rural areas, children often had very long journeys to school each day. Shank's pony was the only method of transport. Where possible most walked home for lunch too. It was not only the distances which would need to be travelled, but the nature of the terrain: up hill and down dale, across muddy fields, over ditches and stiles, rutted tracks and slippery roads. Children often travelled between 2 and 3 miles to school, each way. No wonder they loitered around the grounds at lunchtime while other children went home for some food.

Not until the 1930s was much in the way of school transport offered to children: bus companies providing the travel – not very reliably at first. Children coming from Babcary to Keinton were frequently late. There were a mixture of reasons: delays owing to waiting for a late child, mechanical breakdowns and burst tyres – these were early days for motor vehicles and neither vehicles nor roads were always suitable – and then there were drivers' strikes as well.

Staff suffered too. The unfortunate Miss Yelverton at Kingston Seymour had serious difficulties in getting to work. The Head reports,

In Mar 1914 Miss Y is frequently late… by train.
May 22nd late because of puncture to bicycle tyre
Sept 7th late because of tyre burst
Sept 23rd Puncture
Sept 24th Accident with bicycle
Oct 1st Miss Y gave notice. She has found a position closer to her home.

In Westhay, the Infant teachers seem to have had a bad time of it: one fell from her *bicycle* (WhM 1929) and another had two accidents on her *auto-cycle* (1937, 1941). Elsewhere, teachers arrived by train which was sometimes late, others even owned a *mot-a-car* which invariably caused problems too. Some teachers gave up, resigned and took a post nearer to their homes.

vi. Treats

Yet it wasn't all misery. After all, schooldays are the happiest of your life, aren't they? In fact some schools seem to have had so many opportunities for a day off, especially during June and July, that it is a wonder any work was completed at all.

After the strictures of the 1862 Revised Code, Heads had to seek permission to set aside the timetable, even for half a day – for example when attendances were very low due to extreme weather, or significant amounts of illness.

There are very rare accounts of famous or important visitors arriving at school. Luccombe Managers noted that local Sir CTW Acland visited the school (he was ex-officio Chairman and then a minister for education in Lord Roseberry's government) and he also brought with him Lord Salisbury, then Prime Minister (1895, 1903). He had earlier visited Skilgate as well (1892). Clearly he liked to keep in touch with the 'chalk-face' and was keen to show the PM what real village school conditions were like. This was at the beginning of the sweeping reforms that followed, notably in medical, insurance and welfare services for schools.

Another famous person, of a very different kind – was also recorded as a visitor. Miss Enid Blyton called at Writhlington in 1958 though, sadly, there are no details of what transpired. Another mention of this author is at Chillington in 1939 when children sent off knitted squares to Miss Blyton as a contribution towards blankets for the war effort which she seems to have been encouraging among her thousands of devoted fans: an early example of harnessing fame to support those less fortunate.

Customary Treats. Occasional days, or half days, were given as bounty by a patron of the school. Sometimes this was after a pleasing visit to a school when the children had sung particularly nicely or after the annual Inspection as a reward for a *good showing*, or – of necessity – in preparation for a forthcoming school concert. There were also occasional tea-parties held at the Manor House or Vicarage, when a magic-lantern show might be given and a good tea was served. This was sometimes in the summer or after Christmas. The pre-Christmas concert did not often occur till the beginning of the century and the first Nativity Play mentioned is not till 1945.

In some parts of the county, where the Autumn **Carnival** tradition was particularly strong, a holiday would be granted on the principle *'if you can't beat 'em, join 'em'*. When the railways and later charabancs came on the scene between the wars, then each church or chapel, as well as the Band of Hope and the Temperance Society and, in addition, local Clubs (welfare organisations), each had their full-day trips. Local farmers sometimes lent wagons for an outing and sweet-makers Messrs Fry and Sons even lent motor coaches for a school outing to Bath (OkBr 1935). June became a very sociable month. The larger the village the more treats there were. Somerton, for example, had both Church and Chapel outings, also a Women's Day arranged by the local organisations.

There were the tradition-based events relating to the Church calendar such as **egg-shackling** at Easter, mentioned in the area around Seavington St Michael and North Curry. Each child put an egg (with their name on it) into a large sieve which was then shaken till only one whole egg remained – the winner. **Gooding** on December 21st (in one log, referred to as 'begging') seems to have been a West Country alternative to collecting money on Boxing Day (or, more recently at Halloween or Guy Fawkes) but one in which the children were heavily involved. There were also events closely tied to the agricultural year such as **Fairs** associated with Cattle, Sheep or Poultry, as near Cutcombe and Frome. As the holidays were arranged around the Church (or agricultural) calendar many of the festivities happened when school was already out. Nevertheless, these customs provided plenty of opportunities for extra holidays as well.

There were also local events when many children regularly played truant such as the Horse Racing near Keinton, or the local Hunt. Very rarely a Circus might come to the nearby town, so a holiday was granted – the Head predicting that attendance would be low anyway. Other specific events were very occasional: Horsington Head, in the late 1870s, had to close the school on St Thomas' Day (Dec 21st) as the school Hall was needed for the distribution of money for 'the second poor' according to the terms of a local charity. At the same time, Isle Brewer's closed for one day in April and October for the **collection of tithes**. Elsewhere there was a joyful occasion, *'The whole village rejoiced at the return of Capt and Mrs Sherston from their Wedding Tour'* (OkBR 1894). A different wedding was celebrated with a half-holiday and a bun for each child given by Manager Mr Paget on the occasion of his wedding in 1897. Another turnout witnessed the return of the daughter of Manager Mr Spencer, after her marriage (OkBr 1905), for which the school was given an extra holiday. In fact many schools found plenty of opportunities for frequent half-day holidays – though this declined considerably after the turn of the century, when County Councils took over.

There were other reasons for closing the school. These included royal events such as weddings, coronations and funerals. A very sad reason is noted in North Curry in 1866, for the Day of Humiliation before God *'for the staying of the Cattle Plague'*.

Another kind of treat came with the coming of the School Photographer, first noted at Kingsdon (1877) and Skilgate in (1879). Others followed: 1891 (Clf), 1911 (IsB), 1926 (SmB), 1930 (Blg), 1932 (Wrl) when the photo showed long school desks still in use, very stoney-faced children and staff holding a lengthy pose for the longer exposures then in use and, finally, in colour in 1955 (ChM)!

Curriculum Treats: The inter-war years at last witnessed a more active element to the curriculum which emerged particularly in the form of sport, music and crafts. These years saw a flowering of festivals of many types, all of which must have added to the enjoyment of schooling, allowing a wider range of skills to be valued and introducing some creativity. How much and how quickly such opportunities were grasped depended very much on the personal interest and energy of the Head. The lists of events below give some idea of the variety and distribution of such developments:

b. **Music** also received particular attention
   Choral: in Winsford 1878, Yeovil 1891, Midsomer Norton 1907, Frome, Minehead 1949, or, run by organisations such as the Diocesan Festival in Wells (mentioned in 1893, 1930s;
   Dance: Country and Folk Dancing in Wells (mentioned in 1927, 1929).

Enthusiasm for music in many forms seems to have grown. By the 1930s Festivals and Competitions became widespread, and children would be entered to win prizes for their school. Country Dancing also grew in popularity: Chillington entered a Festival with a Ribbon Dance 1929, Writhlington put on a Dance show for the British Legion 1933. The Wells Country Dance Festival still survives today.

b. **Sport** took off in a big way between the wars: area or district events were organised so that small schools could combine and compete in a more challenging context.

Inter-school competition (1926 KM),
Olympia Sports (Ctc 1931)
Watchet Area Sports (1950s)

Larger schools also started to hold their own individual sports and entertainment days, so long as a local farmer would lend a field.

c. **Handicrafts** became ever more popular and local Flower and Craft Shows were held in many villages at which the children's work was displayed and often won prizes. It meant a wider audience and a positive incentive to try and produce something worthy of entering the show. Girls won a prize for *Mending and re-Making a Garment* (Luc 1916) and for *Hemming a Duster and Darning* (Hlc 1922). More unusual crafts were sometimes undertaken: lace-making at Writhlington (1911), and pewter-relief work at Chaffcombe (1932) which was '*much praised and for which a letter of thanks from the organisers was received*'.

Within individual schools, an increasing range of activities can sometimes be found where there was a particularly active Head. This was the case at Keinton when Mr Newstead took charge. Many other events also started to take off:

School Magazine	(KM 1922)
School Debates	(KM 1928)
Spelling-Bee competitions	(KM 1930, Ctc 1939)
Draughts Competitions	(KM 1930)

The opportunities for all such activities were clearly greater in less remote areas and their spread was uneven over time and area.

The inter-war period seemed one of positive changes, despite the real hardships following the Slump of 1929. New ideas and new practices were being implemented. Yet, in the next chapter we need to turn to the impact of two World Wars on the school and village, and to the difficulties in recovering from this.

Part V
Forwards or Backwards – Recent Years

From World War I
to the Swinging Sixties

The new century began so positively with many important reforms for children's schooling and welfare, but the final part of this story also has to record the impact of two world wars. While the interwar period saw significant developments in ideas about elementary education, and the spread of secondary, it also saw their implementation hindered by the economic disasters of the era. Again, after the Second World War, new hopes were raised, frustrated and, at last, begun to be implemented by the time our story ends.

Fig. v

Key National Dates	Somerset Examples
1902 Con **Balfour Act** County Councils took responsibility from elected School Boards; empowered to provide Elementary and Secondary School. 55% of teachers still no college training	**New Elementary Council School buildings** e.g. Writhlington, Westonzoyland, Keinton Mandeville, **Secondary buildings** e.g. Cannington Evening Technical School, Huish Episcopi... **Area Teacher Training** e.g. Minehead, Bridgewater, Weston, Bruton, Langport.
1906 Lib **School Meals Act** provided 'for necessitous children' – often the only hot meal of day: new kitchens installed	
1907 **School Medical inspections begin**	Doctors examined children annually, Nurse visits 'to check heads' regularly.
1908 **School Insurance available**	To protect schools e.g. when playground accidents occur, as at Oakhill 1930.
1914 **School Leaving Age** raised to **14 years**	**Scholarship exams** sat by more candidates (County/Diocesan) for secondary places
1918 **Fisher Education Act** Finally abolished ALL fees for Elementary Education *School Certificate Exam* and *Highers* introduced for School Leavers	**Teacher Training**: several schools host students from local Colleges: Fishponds, Cheltenham, Salisbury, Exeter etc. Teachers' courses + visits increase.
1921 Free milk to needy children (1946-1971 for ALL)	**Spread of Sports** facilities and local competitions to improve health.
1926 Hadow Report: promoted Tripartite Secondary Education 1929 Wood Report on **Mental Deficiency**	Debates regarding new secondary schools: feared loss of top scholars and effects on rolls e.g. Coleford, Writhlington, Westonzoyland
1931 Hadow Report on **Primary** Education 1933 Hadow Report on **Nursery and Infant** Education	Debates on **closures** of smaller schools e.g. Cudworth, Chillington though some postponed on account of outbreak of war and arrival of...
1939 SLA raised to **15 years** (implemented *after* the war)	**...Evacuees** arrive from Bristol, Birmingham, Southampton, Dagenham etc
1944 Lab **Butler Education :** Universal + Free education for 5-15 years 1951 *O and A level* exams begin for School Leavers (+*CSE* 1965)	
1960s **Teacher Training Certificate** increased to 3 yrs	**Curriculum Experiments**: *i t a* method to teach reading e.g. Keinton, Coleford; Nuffield Science and French tried in larger schools.
1970s **Teaching: all graduate profession 4yr B.Ed / 3+1 PGCE**	End of *All-Age* Primary Schools.
1965 Circular 10/65 requiring plans for Comprehensive Education 1972 **James** Report on **Teacher Education** 1972 SLA raised to **16 years** 1974 Comprehensive Education introduced	Period of **clustering** for small schools and campaigns against **closures**
1978 **Warnock** Report on **Special Needs**	
1988 Con **Baker Education Act:** Local Management of Schools. SATs	*SATs*: national tests at 7,11,14, 16 yrs
1989 **National Curriculum** – English, Science + Maths; other subjects followed. Further professional training: 3 'Baker Days' per annum	*GCSE* for Sch Leavers Leaving age effectively raised to 18 yrs (all *not* in employment to be *in* education)
1990s Lab 'League Tables' begin (likened to Payment-by-Results?)	
2000s Selective Ed re-introduced - Academies, Foundation Schools established	**Rev Poole's Enmore School** becomes a Foundation School. More **closures**

Chapter 10
From World Wars to the Swinging Sixties: Hadow 1926 and '31, to Plowden 1967.

We often forget that the period covered by the school Log Books included three major wars: 200,000 British soldiers were sent to South Africa during the Boer War1899-1902; followed by the millions engaged in the Great War 1914-18, and in the second World War 1939-1945. Few Log books refer to any events outside the life of the school – after all, the guidelines regarding what should be recorded were very limiting and prescribed. Nevertheless several Logs note the relief of Mafeking and of Ladysmith and the end of hostilities in 1902: half-day holidays were given.

However, many Logs make no mention of the Great War at all; some only to record if a member of staff joined the Forces, or, a local event - such as a plane brought down nearby (Clf), though more mention food campaigns. In contrast, every Log mentions the Second World War. This begins of course, with the order for immediate closure of the schools on September 1st at the declaration of War, in order to implement plans for the mass evacuation of children from London, Southampton, Bristol and Birmingham. This is followed by several official campaigns encouraging children to participate in a number of ways and appealing for engagement in the War Effort.

i. Years of World War: How the schools were involved: ***a. 1914-1918***
Given the numbers of fathers, brothers and uncles who joined up, and given the close-knit character of the villages, there must have been few children who were not touched by the toll taken by the years of fighting.

In some schools, the children were quickly engaged in knitting for the Forces. Already, in October 1914, girls at Kingsdon were busy: soon 6 pairs of stockings, 9 pairs of socks, and 5 pairs of mittens were sent off. In November of that same year girls at Chillington started to '*make comforts for soldiers, the material being bought by the children themselves*'. By the following year both '*boys and girls were knitting comforts, during the Scripture Lesson'*. They switched to knitting socks the next year and we then hear of several pairs being sent to Taunton, which was presumably a collecting point. In contrast, it seems Writhlington was slow to get involved. The first reference to the war comes in December 1917 when it is recorded that '*four pairs of socks are sent to Lady Hylton'* and again, a year later, '*a parcel of socks, bags and lavender sachets* (?) *are sent*'. Their efforts were more considerable than these entries seem to imply since, in March 1919, the Somerset Volunteer Help Association presented ten girls with Certificates for 100 socks and 200 hospital bags.

Other ways of supporting the Forces can be seen at Chillington, where children were asked twice asked to **bring eggs** from their home chickens to take to the local hospital for the wounded soldiers (1916 Feb and July). Boys became more heavily involved in growing produce in the School Gardens, many of which were enlarged. Extra time was allowed for Gardening in place of Drawing lessons, Cardboard Modelling and Scripture (Chl 1916, '17,'18).

Labour exemptions: The usual Labour Certificates giving exemption from school continued to be granted to those who had passed Standard IV before reaching 14 years of age, added to which it was also possible to get War Exemptions to provide extra labour for the war effort – often working on the land (SomB 1916). From the outbreak children were directly recruited into the war effort through being asked to undertake tasks as their patriotic duty and thus were given further opportunities to support 'our boys': This included the older boys working in the fields at harvest-time so, two boys aged 12 and 13 years were exempt '*as they are needed to replace the men while at war*' (Luc 1914) and again as '*so many of the men have left for the war*' (SomM 1915). By September 1918 girls were being used to help bring in the harvest which, the Head notes, '*is always late in the hills*' up at Cutcombe, Exmoor.

School contributions made by the younger children as well began in the autumn of 1918 when children were officially asked to pick **blackberries** for jam making (Chl, Okh, Blg, SomB) – in after school hours. From Somerton, 847lbs or 7½ cwt were collected over a two week period at the end of September! In tiny Luccombe, 100 lbs of tomatoes, marrows, beetroot, cabbage and spinach were grown in the school garden in 1917. A more unusual request can be found at Charlton Mackrell: Lady Thring arrived at school in September 1917 and '*spoke on the value of* **conkers** [which contain acetone used in the production of cordite for explosives]. *The children seemed deeply interested and promised to collect them*'. This request is also noted in Radstock where, in October of that year, the Head noted in his matter-of-fact manner, '*Boys collecting horse-chestnuts which I then store and send away for the making of munitions. The Rector taught Scripture on Wednesday*'.

Several schools noted an increase in the marking of Empire Day with Patriotic songs, including Kipling's *Children's Song*. From 1915, Chillington added flag-saluting ceremonies on several other days such as St George's Day, the Queen's and King's birthdays and on Trafalgar Day. In Somerton, Empire Day was the occasion for an address '*on the meaning of the Union Jack*' (SomM 1916), and another '*by several gentlemen on the privileges, duties and responsibilities of citizens of the British Empire*' (SomM 1915), while collections were made and £3 16s 0d raised for the Overseas Club (SomM Dec 1918). Money was raised in other schools too: on 21st October, Trafalgar day, 11s was raised for the *Red Cross* (SomB 1915), carols were sung and a collection made for *St Dunstan's Home for Blind Sailors* (SomM 1916) and, in January 1919, money was collected in Coleford for the *King's Fund for Disabled Soldiers*. This was followed on July 19th, on the Official Day of Celebration of Peace, by singing Patriotic Songs and performing Repetitions. The Head added that '*As the day was wet tea was offered inside the school and Returned Servicemen gave a Concert*'. All these actions must have put severe strains on the Heads trying to cope with the difficulties and, from 1916-19 (Luc) a War Bonus of an additional £8 15s was paid to Heads.

In Blagdon, on the Mendips, the Head noted, 'S*oldiers were manoeuvring in the hills. Their presence has made much difference to attendance*' (1915). Evidence of war in a different form also caused a distraction in Coleford. In February 1917 and again in September 1918, a plane came down nearby. Boys were given permission to visit the wreck and instructed to make mental notes on what they saw in preparation for a report. On the second occasion the Head added that the best three reports would earn a prize. No idle afternoon off for these lads! Only one school (SomB 1918) noted a funeral which the whole school attended, as it was that of an ex-pupil, Percy Norris, who died of wounds: boys were asked to line the street for the cortège. Another death is noted by the Head at Kingsdon who recorded that he was absent for a week owing to *'the illness of his wife from shock of learning that our son had fallen in action in May 1916'*.

Pupil Population: A final way in which the Logs noted how the war impacted on the children was in terms of changes in the number on roll and in the staff. During the first World War, evacuees were not a major concern, but in Somerton the Logs noted, *'A refugee Belgian boy, who knows some English and can make himself understood is admitted. He appears fairly sharp for his age (9 years)'.* And in the sister-school two further Belgian children were admitted *'who only speak a few words in English'* - perhaps younger siblings (SomM 1915). Similarly, in Radstock two Belgian boys are recorded from among the refugees received there. *'They are intelligent but as yet only speak Flemish.'* By October of the following year, the Head regretfully noted that, *'One of them has been transferred to London: He has made excellent progress and I shall be sorry to lose him'.*

In Cutcombe the school population changed for a different reason. Several families moved down the valley to farms which were offering higher wages. The Head noted (1916 and 1917) that 'many homes stand empty'. This must have caused a considerable reduction in numbers. In two schools 4-year old children were again admitted, perhaps to relieve pressure at home. Conversely, by 1918, the policy was reversed in Somerton Montclefe as the Infant section was full *'because of the number of children who are not residents but have come to escape the Air Raids.'* This was the only reference found to any evacuation, but it was an 'unofficial' movement, often of children coming to stay with relatives in a 'safer' environment.

Call-up: There was some movement amongst the male staff owing to volunteering or to call-up. Chillington saw young pupil-teacher Frederick Salter leave immediately, on September 7th 1914. He was replaced by two Monitresses. Somerton schools seem to have been considerably affected: pupil-teacher Mr Sweet enrolled in the Navy, while his colleague Mr Stone was passed fit for military service in 1915 (SomB). This gap in the teaching force was filled by the Head's wife, Mrs Strong, stepping into the breach, until a new Head arrived in June of that year. Another member of staff from the same school, student-teacher Mr Burroughs, left for the Forces in 1917. At Oakhill British School, Headmaster Mr Bright, 'joined the Forces' (Oct 1916), and in March 1918 the Vicar of Cutcombe left to become Chaplain to the Forces. Mr Bright returned after the war and remained as Head for some 26 years.

One report is made of an ex-pupil returning to visit his school, bringing a German helmet and pieces of shell from the battle-field (Skg 1917). One can imagine the wide-eyed boys listening to the tales: did he tell of comradery, bravery and glory, or of mud, rats and gore?

A very mixed story comes from Radstock where several old boys' involvement was recorded in detail. Headmaster Lewin, recorded the following in 1914 for the week ending Sept 11th:

> *Events of stupendous national importance have taken place. The great European War has broken out and our school has been effected. The materials for our improvements have been delayed. We were unable to re-open till 7th. Mr Stephens is in Camp on Salisbury Plain and the Managers have appointed Mr Clifford Gregory, who has recently left Bristol Day Training College, as temporary teacher in his place. Edgar Bolwell began work as pupil-teacher. He is apprenticed for one year* [sister to teacher at neighbouring Writhlington?].

However, sad news came in October 1915, reported in a most muted fashion:

> *The War Office telegrammed me that Capt RR Lewin* [Head's son] *had been killed in action. He was one of our old boys with a most promising career before him.*

And on July 2nd 1917 came different news concerning another son:

Lieutenant CJ Lewin Somerset LI has been awarded the Military Cross. He won it on or about his 19th birthday. The official record reads as follows:

For conspicuous gallantry and devotion to duty. When in command of a raid upon an enemy trench he led his men with the greatest dash and determination, turning the enemy out with the bayonet in spite of all the wire being uncut in front of the trench. He afterwards showed great coolness in collecting his men and bringing them back to lines. This young officer is now Aug 20th in hospital at Newcastle-upon-Tyne suffering from wounds in the upper right arm, severe.

The down beat tone continued when Mr Lewin noted in 1917, Sept 7th news that *'Capt. Stephens has been retired from the army on account of ill-health and has resumed school duties. Gardening continued on Wednesday'.*

By the time the war had finally ended another Head was in post who noted, on hearing that Cecil Lewin MC (who had previously recovered from an earlier wound) had then died in action on 2.11.18. *'This is the third son of the late Headmaster to make the 'Supreme'.'* There follows a list of other 'old boys':

A scholarship winner and Pupil Teacher GH Woodland, 2nd Lt RAF, has died at Newcastle on 5.11.18. His remains were buried with military honours in Radstock churchyard.
Driver E Radford, an old boy has won the Military medal
Sgt Carpenter DCM has been awarded the Military Medal
2nd Lt H Hockey who won a Military Medal has been awarded the Military Cross. This is the 12th honour to have been won by an old boy of this school.

There is great contrast between schools as to whether the war is mentioned at all. According to the guidelines only events which effect the school – in particular, its staff, accommodation, timetable, attendance should be mentioned. Some schools make several entries, as in Radstock where the Head Lewin had personal experience through his sons who were in the Forces.

Yet, given the prolonged horrors of this war and the overwhelming numbers of people involved, it was remarkable how smoothly life went on in the world of village schools. The Logs continued to note problems with the stoves, with 'the offices', with absentees, with the day-to-day running of the school. Was this 'stiff-upper-lip', a deliberate attempt to try to retain normalcy in the school, or merely because of the constraints on what was expected to be the proper content of School Log Books? However, the memorials in every village churchyard tell a very different story. In Somerset, there are perhaps ten **'Thankful Villages'** across the county (out of the possible 52 such villages across England and Wales), being those where all the serving men returned alive – though this calculation is problematic, depending on the cut-off date selected (whether 11.11.18, or extended to include all uniformed personnel who may have died later of wounds or of the great post-war flu epidemic to which many, weakened by fighting, succumbed). Sadly, none of the villages and schools which form the focus of this project was one of these Thankful Villages.

The declining inter-war world situation seems to have penetrated the classroom, in just a few schools, where the Head was so motivated. One Head arranged for the school to listen to the King's Address to the Five-Power Naval Conference on the wireless (1930). Another Head noted, *'Today I read the Board of Education pamphlet on the* Disarmament Conference *to Std V+VI+VII'* (SmB Feb 1932). Elsewhere a Head wrote, *'Work has sometimes been difficult owing to the world condition and consequent interruptions. I have however insisted on keeping the school quite as normal'* and, later, *'Read a message from the* League of Nations *on Armistice Day and talked about how we can bring about peace'* (Wrl 1938). Yet, despite these early concerns the conduct of the war goes unmentioned at this particular school, although the Armistice is recorded.

b. 1939-1945

The second World War affected the schools much more directly. On the very first day of the September term all schools were closed to discuss evacuation plans and soon afterwards the evacuees started to arrive.

Evacuation: In September 1939 Chillington received its first group of just 4 while in nearby Cudworth the school, having closed in 1926, was re-opened to order to accommodate evacuees. In October Coleford had already received some evacuees and the Head asked for repairs to the partition which separated the evacuee children from the locals, until they were moved into the Parish Rooms six months later. Segregation was often the response: larger groups of evacuees had separate teachers who came down with their charges and separate Registers had to be kept for what amounted to a parallel school.

In Blagdon we can again see the policy of separation at work: a few Infants arrived in September 1939, then 36 from London and Liverpool, which was followed by 40 from Dagenham in June 1940 together with their two teachers who set up in the Parish Rooms. The next year more children came down from Bristol, though it is not clear whether they were merged with the more local children or with the Dagenham children. Still more arrived at Cutcombe, in 1939, and an additional group of 40 with only one teacher came from Bristol in 1940. Accommodation became a real problem: 10 children had no seats or desks. Not too far away more children came from Bristol to Nettlecombe in 1941. Where the numbers were smaller or distances greater teachers came down regularly to see how the evacuated children were doing (Cutcombe 1930, 1940).

Schools in other areas were also destinations for the evacuees. Westhay received several in Sept 1940 and also had to borrow desks. In May 1941 Kingsdon received 12 more from Bristol and, in December of that year, 71 evacuees were sent to Oakhill British School. More must have been sent to the Church of England school just across the main road, for in February 1944 the British School sent 3 barrow loads of coal and later they lent two dozen Readers and one dozen History books to the enlarged school.

Not only did desks, coal and books need to be lent to support all these new children but their welfare needed to be checked as well. In the schools, after each new wave, the Doctor came to check the children and to inoculate them if necessary (diphtheria is mentioned). There were also specifically war-related checks to be made: Wardens came to check the gas masks which had been issued. Air Raid Wardens quickly came to discuss a suitable shelter for Oakhill children, windows in the Refuge Room were wired to reduce shattering (Ntc 1940), blackout was installed (Clf July 1941, and Ctc 1942) and a stirrup pump was demonstrated (OkBr and Ctc Jan 1941). The police were also detailed to give talks to the children on the dangers of unexploded bombs (Chf 1944) and of picking up strange objects (KgS 1944).

All this upheaval must surely have been very disturbing for both the local children as well as the trauma of relocation itself for those evacuated. Moving from city to village, from family to strangers, much has been written about the varying experiences of these children. Memories sometimes recall evacuees being blamed for bringing nits, for stealing, in fact for trouble in general: they became scapegoats. The Logs recorded little. There was an occasional entry - concerning a caning of evacuee children. No names. Were they that anonymous, or was it the delicacy of confidentiality? Sometimes rivalries broke out: children were hurt in the playground and the Doctor sent for (OkBr Sept 1942). In June, in the same school, an evacuee (again no name) got his finger stuck in a small bottle so the Doctor was called. By December of that year there were 31 local children and 20 evacuees, but, by June 1945 we hear *'Mrs Whitock and the evacuees return home'*. Sighs of relief all round.

For some schools, however, the evacuees resulted in schools re-opening (Cudworth), for others it gave a stay of execution. Chillington, which had sunk well below the critical enrolment of 30, suddenly found numbers boosted: in 1942 it had 19 local children on Roll plus 14 evacuees. Writhlington, which had been threatened with closure with only 33 on Roll in 1939, was almost overwhelmed by 159 evacuees in June 1940, though the vast majority returned within a few months: by December numbers had fallen back to 103, and two years later to just 58. Later, with adjacent housing developments the school grew and thrived.

Incidents: A disturbing story was recorded in one of the mining areas. 1940 had seen a massive intake of evacuees which had proved hard to accommodate, physically, never mind the social adjustments necessary. The number of children on the school roll had been 33, but this rocketed to 103 when, in June, a group of 159 children from West Ham were billeted in one village with three of their teachers to accompany them: 49 Infants were added to the village class, with some juniors, while the older ones were accommodated in a nearby Miner's Welfare Hall and a Primitive Methodist Chapel. The older boys were housed in a Hostel, where they slept. In order to stagger the holidays taken by local and London staffs, it was decided that over the summer holiday the evacuees were to continue attending in the Welfare Hall under the supervision of their own Head who had accompanied them.

In 1941 a serious incident occurred. We find that on July 1st - 2nd the *'Head attended Bristol Assizes during the trial of the Rector, who was acquitted'*. This was followed by the statement, *'Five boys from the Hostel are absent because of gossip in connection with the case'*. Again, in July 27-28th the Head was at Winchester Assizes for a second charge against the Rector, who was again acquitted. The Head recorded, *'The judge decided that the story told by the bomb-shocked boy of 10 years was unreliable and unsupported by any evidence'*. We can only surmise the nature of the charges, but it is interesting to note that it even came to court. Subsequently, the boys were taught in the Hostel where they slept, by one of their own (male) teachers, which resulted in total segregation.

The problems experienced by the evacuees in the Hostel did not end there. On October 1st a teacher reported the loss of £3 notes. It was discovered that a £1 note had been changed at the Post Office by a hostel boy, which was reported to police. After 3 hrs of questioning by the Constable, WB confessed to taking £3 from the teacher's bag. The following day the Constable showed the Head knives (for cardboard-modelling and stencilling) and string found in the hostel, also 12 pencils and 6s from the milk money tin. The Chairman was asked if he wished to prosecute. By November WB was tried for theft and sent to a remand home for 3 years. Even this was not the end.

Later that month the Head recorded, *'Six boys were found smoking cigarettes in the school lavatories. Also, twice this week the gate has been lifted from its hinges. Once it was found several yards up the road. I was told the name of a Council School boy and two others who had helped him.... I wrote a letter – to the Police – in the boys' presence as a deterrent (not intending to post it). However, I dropped it on the way home and it got posted... I immediately rang the police to explain, but the Constable thought it wise to visit the homes of those concerned.... One father came to school and was abusive, another came and threatened me, and the mother of a third similarly...* Further, in February 1943, the Head reported, *'On going home I found several pieces of broken inkwell. Various boys said they had smashed them. I caned them all for wilful damage. It seems it would be better for the whole school if LS, who starts these acts through bad temper, be sent to school at the Hostel for evacuees'*. This was a rare instance where the evacuees so spectacularly failed to integrate and where they developed such a negative reputation. The Hostel was in danger of becoming a general sin-bin, with even the local 'bad boys' threatened with being sent there.

Nevertheless, many of the children settled comfortably and achieved well in school. Kingsdon noted an evacuee who gained a special place at secondary school and, at Charlton Mackrell, another boy won a Metropolitan Scholarship for a secondary place which he was soon able to take up. His leaving was considered a loss to the school. There were also warm memories: several children kept in contact with their host families and returned to visit. One child evacuated to Somerton, returned years later to teach and later became a manager.

Campaigns for the War Effort: Apart from the disruption to the composition of the school, there was also disruption to the curriculum during these war years. Many of these, however, were probably welcomed by the children. Often the first change was greater time and prominence given by the girls to making items for the Forces: added to the knitting and sewing of items to be sent to the Forces, was the Sale of Items for local purchase and home use, the proceeds of which were then donated to one of the numerous available funds contributing to the War Effort (KM, Kgd 1940).

In November 1939 children started knitting **6" wool-squares for blankets**: within a month 30 such squares were sent to a campaign led by the children's author Enid Blyton (Chl Nov 1939). The **Dig for Victory** campaign extended to the school gardens which therefore moved up the curriculum ladder of importance: for example, 220 yards of land were given by Mr and Mrs Hobhouse for the boys to dig over (OkBr Feb 1940). This was the province of the boys who, in addition, were sometimes set the task of making toys which were also sold to raise money (KM 1941). Down on the Levels, Westhay boys were given leave from school to help on the farms during harvest to make up the depleted workforce (June 1941).

Many specific campaigns were introduced throughout the war as needs changed and the focus of effort shifted. These were much more extensive than during the 1914-18 war and engaged people in many different ways. As far as the school children were concerned it meant a return to **blackberrying** and, in addition, to picking **rosehips** for vitamin C. This was recorded from 1942 and continued annually: the canteen at Oakhill school made 80lbs of blackberry jam using 41lbs of preserving sugar in September 1944 – a champion achievement. Interestingly, on Exmoor, Cutcombe children were asked to pick **sphagnum moss** in June 1942 [perhaps as insulation in the transportation of explosives, also to dress wounds as its acidity reduced bacteria], and also **foxgloves** [for medicinal purposes]. Writhlington School must have been champion at **egg-collecting**. The tradition of sending eggs to the local Paulton Hospital began before the war (1936) and lasted until well after (into the 1970s). In May 1936, 100 fresh eggs were collected after an appeal from Paulton Hospital, together with 11lbs of **silver foil** from around 60 children, then 143, and 112 but, in 1940, it dropped to 86, rising to 103, then falling to 62 – perhaps wartime scarcities were eked out by more home consumption but, in 1970, they achieved the marvellous total of 444 eggs from a school of about 70 children!

Collections of **waste paper** were frequently made: as suggested, old school Registers were sent from Oakhill (1940) – a possible reason why many school records fail to survive to the present day and, in the same year, three boys from Cutcombe were allowed to travel to Blagdon to *'fetch iron for the Collection'*. Seventeen bags of paper were collected for the Albion Paper Works (Chl 1940) and the nearby Chard Company was recorded as sending lorries to collect iron, bottles and rags from the same area a month later. Cutcombe girls seem to have been very active, for we find Mrs Luttrell coming to thank the girls for the jumpers knitted for the Liberate Europe Campaign (1943). Westhay school were given the target of collecting 600 books for the paper campaign, but they achieved 953 (1943)!

There was also **fund-raising**. Money was sent to Mrs Churchill's *Russian Aid Fund* (Ctc 1941). Children collected 30s which provided 1500 cigarettes sent to France (Chl 1940). A concert raised £13 for the *Red Cross Prisoners of War Fund* (Okh 1944) and two years later the children received a letter from the Forces in Burma and Malaya thanking them for the cigarettes bought with their donation (OkBr 1946).

The whole community was also involved in fundraising for the annual War Effort Campaigns: 1941 saw **War Weapons Week**, in which school children were invited to contribute to what became known as ***'The Children's Tank'*** (KM 1941); in 1942 it was **Wings for Victory Week**, for which Cutcombe raised the staggering amount of £401 18s 2d; 1943 was **Warship Week**; and 1944 **Salute the Soldier Week.** For each of these campaigns the average school managed to raise about £20 – still a considerable sum in small, rural communities.[The timing and naming of these campaigns seems to have varied slightly across the county.]

A further detail would have affected all communities. For the first two years of the war, all bells were silenced, by order of Churchill. This included church bells, bells in Town Halls, clocks and, of course, the school bell. Bells were reserved to signal the expected German invasion: when the danger was deemed to have passed, the school bell again rang out to hurry the laggards to school.

While the children were doing their bit for their country, the local authorities were mindful of their duty of care towards the children. In 1940 Circular E285 was received at Oakhill, which required a half-hour afternoon rest-period for the youngest children. Organised schools games were supported and several inter-school Area Sports were arranged throughout these years, as part of the campaign to keep healthy. Equipment was sometimes in short supply, but a farmer donated two bladders for footballs (OkBr 1940). One major development was a programme of hot dinners for all children who wanted them. This resulted in a widespread move to create canteens and employ dinner-staff to distribute and supervise the meals, which often came from central kitchens (OkBr 1940, Ctc 1942, Clf 1943, Blg and IsB 1944). Clothes were also distributed: 1943 and 1944 saw clothing coupons delivered to Oakhill School, while several pairs of Wellington boots arrived at the school from the Women's Voluntary Service the following year. Finally, aid was a two-way affair: American Red Cross Boxes arrived at Cutcombe in March 1943, for which the children sent letters of thanks.

The adults, both staff and parents, were also involved – as supervisors of these efforts and also directly through Dances and Whist Drives which are mentioned in Manager's Minutes. Schools were also encouraged to buy War Savings Bonds and special school savings schemes were started.

ii. Changes in the inter-war and post-world war period

Village populations underwent considerable change during these wars. For some villages it hastened what was already a quickening rural decline, a few experienced a brief reprieve with the temporary swelling of numbers owing to the evacuees' stay, while others experienced a population explosion as a village ear-marked for expansion in the post-war housing boom.

However, while 1945 may have seen the end of two world wars, new wars continued to rage and upheavals reverberated worldwide. Neither did the end of hostilities witness the last evacuation groups. Immediately after the second war, groups of Poles are remembered as being settled for a time in some local areas (KM 1945) and, in 1957, refugees are noted in the Logs relating to those who had fled the Hungarian Uprising in the previous year: some children were admitted at Blagdon and Cutcombe, but nothing more was mentioned. However, rural Somerset seems little affected by the Vietnamese Boat Children or the Ugandan refugees from Idi Amin's regime, in the 1970s.

In general, the Logs continue to show the slow return to normality in the schools and then, to show some of the developments which normality could make possible. However, others were not so lucky.

Amalgamation and Closures

The population had declined severely in many villages, beginning with the Agricultural Depression of the 1880s. It continued to decline further at the turn of the century and then be devastated from the inter-war financial collapse, the Slump and the general de-population owing to mechanisation and urbanisation. Inevitably this impacted on small village schools.

In the mining areas, which had suffered population decline during pit-closures, there were many reappraisals of school provision. In the whole period prior to WWII, discussions about LEA-led amalgamation of the two Oakhill schools were very acrimonious – the Anglican school refusing to give up its denominational status. Discussions took place from 1922 to 1924 and again from 1926 to 1928, when it was noted that schools with more than 30 children on roll could not automatically be closed. As their numbers were over 40 they were safe for the moment. By 1935 there were only 21 on roll at the British School but in July 1939 numbers were back up to 41. The evacuation certainly helped to postpone closure for, in 1940, admissions were over 50, swelled by children from Dagenham and, by 1941, they were over 90. When the danger abated post-1944 and evacuees began to drift away, numbers dropped to 44 local and 25 evacuee children. The school was eventually closed after hostilities ended.

Nearby, in Coleford, further discussions took place between1935 and 1939 but were postponed till after the war. The situation was eventually resolved by building on a new site and combining the Wesleyan and Anglican schools as a County Council School. Pre-war Writhlington was also threatened with closure as numbers were low. But, having had a stay of execution owing to the war, the school proceeded to flourish and expand successfully in the post-war years to meet the demands of a new housing estate. Meanwhile, Holcombe was closed in 1930.

On the western side of the county there were similar reviews of school provision. Isle Brewer's closed in 1914, Skilgate in 1938, Luccombe in 1945, Nettlecombe in 1945, Cudworth in 1945, Goathurst in 1953, Fiddington in 1954 and Chillington in 1971. Periodic waves of closures have continued, especially coinciding with Beecham railway cuts in the late 1960s, and have since turned many schools into village halls or private residences. Around 3% of village schools in Somerset closed in 1905, a further 5% by 1920. Nearly a further 20% closed in the years after the Great War and the economic crisis following the Slump, and almost 30% after the Second World War.

The lives of some were prolonged if there was no alternative within easy reach. Thus, in the west, tiny Oare with only 10 pupils in 1905 continued till pupils fell to 8 in 1933; Hawkridge, already dangerously small in 1905, fell from 23 to 13 in the same period. Both then closed. Exmoor, however, with only 30 pupils in 1905, fell to 15 in 1933 and 19 in 1957 but was saved for development and would take in pupils from surrounding schools which were later closed. Similarly, on the Poldens, Bawdrip, although falling from 51, to 24 and then 22 (between 1905, 1933 and 1957), was also destined to absorb pupils from surrounding areas and then expand to its current healthy numbers. In the east, Yarlington fell from 24 to 7 (between 1905 and 1933), and then closed, and Lamyatt fell from 27 to 22 and even 18 in 1957 and was then merged and closed during the 1960s shake-out. This was the fate of many of the smaller schools – the majority of which were kept alive by Council funding, rather than as Voluntary Aided, or Controlled schools. Location was not the key criteria: proximity, funding (church support or endowed) and 'success' also played a part: it is noticeable that once the Head had been downgraded to an 'uncertificated female', in the inter-war years, it often signaled that the end was nigh!

Staff left throughout the period and it is curious to note the changing fashions in presents for leaving teachers. Many schools seem to have had a generous tradition, particularly Writhlington, which changed over the years indexing changes in life style: a cut-glass powder bowl and scent-spray (SmM 1929), a leather travelling writing-case (1931), to an electric flat-iron (1934), electric alarm clock (1935) a revolving desk chair for the Head, male, (1936), a cruet and book shelf (1959), electric kettle, tea-set and electric toaster (1966).

Re-organisation and Internal re-structuring

Once secondary education became more widespread in the 1930s after the first Hadow Report (1926), 're-organisation' became the watch word. This Report was the first of three significant landmarks in the development of education policy. The first Report strongly argued for the tripartite separation of secondary schooling into equal-status sectors: an existing grammar, new secondary modern and the heralded technical schools (very few of these last were built causing long-term shortage and loss of status of much needed skills). This attempted to address the growing demands for wider access to secondary education following the swelling numbers attending elementary schools: the desire was there but the form was disputed.

By 1920 an estimated 80% of children still had no 'secondary' education, though LEAs were encouraged to offer 40% of available places on scholarships (in fact only 25% of places were in this category). Re-organisation also spelt the end of the all-age school for pupils from 5-14 yrs in a single school: in 1926, 91% of 5-13 year-old children were in all-age schools, by 1949 only 36% and by 1965 just 1% (Plowden 1967). Then, as now, the communities fought to 'save our school'. In 1930 discussions began in Coleford, and again in 1932, when meetings were held to '*protest the building of a Senior School for those over 11 years*' though, as elsewhere, plans eventually agreed for 1939 were postponed till after the war.

The inter-war years also saw major changes in expectations of the new Primary Schools. Hadow, in 1931, famously declared that education should be based '*on the curiosity of the child*' (shades of Rousseau), and that the curriculum should be '*thought of in terms of activity and experience rather than as knowledge to be acquired and facts to be stored*'. This signalled what became known as the child-centred approach and was echoed in the 1967 Plowden Report which stressed that '*at the heart of the educational process is the child*'. (This was later reversed in the 1981 DES document which stated '*The school curriculum is at the heart of education*'.) Plowden went on to underline the importance of '*individual discovery, first-hand experience and opportunities for creative work*' and that '*knowledge does not fall into separate compartments*'.

In response to these newer ideas re-organisation became an evolving concept – both internal and external. Experiments were made to arrange children according to age rather than exam results (Ctc 1934) which helped to end the anomalous position of over-age children. We find children being arranged in groups, working together (KgS 1934). Later, in 1967, Coleford was discussing internal re-organisation in the form of vertically arranged Family Groups, where children of different ages were in the same class - something which had always existed in smaller village schools by force of circumstances but was now given a new label. In addition, we find discussions about transforming Coleford to a 'First School' for younger children only in the 1970s, while the concept of 'open-plan' rooms was raised while the new building at Farley Dell was in progress.

Kingsdon became a Junior-only school from 1929 when the seniors were sent to Somerton: closure was first discussed in 1971 but it was not until 2011 that it was finally closed. Charlton Mackrell lost its seniors in 1940 to Huish Secondary School and continues to thrive today. At the same time seniors from Somerton Boys' and Monteclefe Girls' were also lost to Huish: these two schools later merged in 1963, survived and thrived. Nettlecombe had been sending seniors to Washford or Watchet from the 1930s, before closing in 1945. Cutcombe began sending its seniors to Minehead from 1948 and then gradually began to expand in the post-war period while surrounding schools closed. Blagdon initially reverted to the same size after the war but, when the seniors were removed to Churchill School, it became a 2-Teacher school of 60 pupils, yet successfully expanded to 159 on Roll by 1956. Few of these changes took place without the mobilization of local opinion, particularly that of the parents, who now, more than ever, felt involved with their local school.

Parental involvement.

From the end of the C19th there was a considerable tradition of holding concerts and dances, but these were mainly in order to help to raise funds for the school. However, opening the school to demonstrate what went on inside, in order to help parents understand (and win their support) was a new idea. Early examples of this came in the form of an *'Open Hour, or Exhibition'* (Skg 1878, Chl from 1920s). An *Entertainment with coffee* (SmM 1895) also gave a chance to show-case the children's skills of Recitation and Singing, as did a performance of *Folk Songs, Kindergarten Games, Recitations* (SmWE 1906) where the Head specifically noted that it was held as an opportunity *'to view occupations in order to rouse interest'*. Other schools began traditions such as *Annual Mother's Day,* held in December (Skg from 1924) when Mothers were invited to come and sing carols and to see exhibitions of their children's work.

All of this amounted to a seismic-change in relations between the school and the village. Parents did not only come to school to complain, explain an absence, or upbraid the Head on the treatment of their child. Now they came to feel proud of their child. It was a chance to feel proprietorial about 'our school'. Teachers wanted to get the parents 'on-side' in the newly expressed knowledge that home support was important to the child's success in school. It was the beginning of the idea of a new partnership in education.

However, parents can be a feisty lot! In 1950 a group went on strike (KM) and refused to send their children to school for six weeks, until better transport had been arranged for those children from surrounding villages which had lost their schools. It is doubtful they were placard-wavers, but they could certainly dig in their heels.

To avoid closures, a range of strategies was tried. Small schools sometimes 'clustered' to share resources and staff. Outreach facilities from Libraries and Museums helped to bolster materials for teaching, just as the judicious use of School's Radio and Television services helped in a resource-scarce environment.

With regard to many of these changes, parents became an immensely powerful force, not only when campaigning against closures, but in being harnessed to help in a variety of ways. This could be inside the classrooms – to hear children read, or to help with cookery and, also, outside – when accompanying school trips. Parents became an essential part of the management through organising fund-raising events to help 'keep the show on the road', and sitting on committees which helped to plan the development of the school. All of this was just beginning as our story finishes: within the time-span of this project only two formal Parent-Teacher Associations are mentioned – Somerton Monteclefe 1948 and Kingsdon 1972 (since closed).

Finally, schooling is forever evolving – sometimes revolving – in its fashions and fads, its objectives and assessments, its methods and materials, its structure and procedures. These will continue to change as society's expectations alter and politicians' decisions re-shape the enormous and complex process of educating our children and young people, and continuing to educate our adults too.

Perhaps this opportunity to reflect on the village schooling of one county has shown us how far schools have changed but also what has been retained. While each county is different, most schools have now been drawn into a national system and thus share many features with other counties. Yet Somerset is interesting as it is geographically and economically so varied, but it also balances areas of agriculture and industry, ports and inland waterways. Its villages illustrate a diversity of livelihoods and range of characteristics which give a fair overview of the state of education over this period for much of the rest of England.
But the story never ends…

Epilogue and Appendices

This story has led us a long way in time, in conditions and also in expectations of schooling. We have seen enormous changes in all aspects: changes which are still ongoing. The lives of children have perhaps changed the most. 'Childhood' has been accepted: a period of labour-free years where education is intended as a focus of the child's life – an education not only to fit us for society but to develop the potential of each individual. Few of the ideals are new: we can return to Comenius, Locke, or Rousseau to select the now current ideas of school as a means of promoting child-centred learning, enhancing individual potential, developing life enrichment. Yet we are still struggling to find ways of individualising an essentially collective endeavour whereby we put large numbers of young people in a common institution for a set number of hours per year, all following a centralised programme which is nationally monitored.

Below are several appendices which give further details to information in the related chapters.

Appendices:

App. 1.1 Key details of Parishes and target Schools

Parish	Sponsor	Population details	Open Build Enlargement	Closure
1. Blagdon	Thomas Baynard 1687	1801 797; 1851 1128; 1871 975; 1901 1131; 1951 1053; 2001 1172	C17th 1842 for 120, enlg '95 for 170 1909 for 183, adds in C20th	
2. Enmore	Rev J Poole Earl Egremont	1801 254; 1851 343; 1871 293 1901 271; 1851 249; 2001 233	1810 1847 for 80? + **THo** ->1963 1888 enlg at rear, adds C20th	
3. Cutcombe	Richard Ellsworth 1714 *SchRm blt '20*	1801 594; 1851 860; 1871 689; 1901 446; 1951 419; 2001 403	1820 1875 for 200 + **T Ho**	
Nettlecombe		1801 329; 1851 353; 1871 344; 1901 260; 1951 259; 2001 199	1819 for 120, enlg '25 for 130	1945
Skilgate	Earl of Carnarvon	1801 226; 1851 266; 1881 219; 1901 161; 1951 133, 2001 96	1860 1861 for 50, enlg '83 for 65	1938
4. Isle Brewer	*(Duchy of Cornwall)*	1801 181; 1851 328; 1871 371 1901 258; 1951 224; 1981 185; 2001 155	1861 1869 for 60 chdn	1919
Meare / Westhay		1801 753; 1851 1605; 1901 1305; 1951 922; 2001 1238	{1840 for 87, '80 +66 Inf {1903 for 70B, 57G, 67Inf	1945
5. Chaffcombe	Earl Poulett	1801 1851 265; 1871 280; 1901 228; 1931 210	1878 for 60 chdn	1959
Chillington	Earl Poulett	1801 216; 1851 320; 1881 228, 1901 163; 1951 126; 1981 88; 2001 104	1861 1882 for 60	1971
6. Charlton Mackrell	Brymer Trust Bld cost *£2,500*	1801 268; 1851 381; 1871 419; (1881 259) 1901 610; 1951 591; 1971 655;	1830 1853 for 108, adds in C 20th	
Kingsdon		1801 455; 1851 523; 1871 431; 1901 252; 1951 313; 2001 353	1846 1872 for 60, enlg '78 Clsrm	2011
Keinton M	*£950*	1801 206; 1851 584; 1871 523 1901 508; 1951 421; 1971 569, 2001 1000	1861 1875 for 100 1902 new build for 135	
Som W. End Inf	Pinney	}	1750 barn conv 1875 for 90	1960s
Som Free B	1635 endw	merged }	1891 120	1963
Som Monteclefe G	Pinney	1801 1145; 1851 2140; 1871 2302 } 1901 1797; 1951 2076; ? 2001 5000	1851 for 200, enlg'88 +80 Inf adds in C 20th	B+G+I merge 1963
7. Horsington	Martha Wickham 1734 endw	1801 883; 1851 834; 1871 734 1901 619; 1951 611; 2001 571	1833; 1857 for 100, enlg '03 +98	
8. West Pennard		1801 727; 1851 874; 1871 794; 1901 662; 1951 634; 2001 662	1856 Nat for 150 1878 Wes for 60	
9. Holcombe (Wes)		1801 581; 1851 464; 1871 780 1901 487; 1951 612; 2001 936	1857 Wes for 90 1868 for 100, enlg '83	1970
Ashwick (British) Oakhill		1801 776; 1851 848; 1871 819; 1901 976; 1951 950; 2001 1291	1857 Br for 130 1867 Nat for 80, enlg'94<140	1950
Coleford		1801 ; 1851 1400; 1871 1766; 1901 1210; 1931 1269;	1829, 1834 Inf 100, '47 B+G +150 1960s new build	
Writhlington		1801 108; 1851 292; 1871 401; 1901 496; 1931 551;	1854 for 85 chdn 1901 new build for 140	

App. 1.2 i: Distribution of Anglican Sunday Schools x Regions

Area/ Year	01 Mendip	02 Quantock		03 Exmoor	04 Taunton + Levels	05 South	06 Central		07 S East		08 East		09 N East	Totals
		W	E				W	E	S	E	W	E		
No of Parishes	*21*	*16*	*15*	*28*	*33*	*21*	*08*	*16*	*17*	*21*	*09*	*15*	*23*	***215***
No. SnSc 1870+														***00***
1846-69	*02*	*02*	*04*	*04*	*12*	*09*	*02*	*05*	*01*		*04*	*02*	*04*	***51***
1833-45		*04*	*07*		*03*	*01*		*03*	*01*		*02*	*02*	*01*	***24***
1800-32	*01*	*06*	*20*				*04*	*08*	*11*			*05*		***55***
Pre-1800	*03*	*03*			*01*	*01*		*01*	*01*					***10***
Total Sn Schs	***06***	***15***	***31***	***04***	***16***	***11***	***06***	***17***	***14***		***06***	***09***	***05***	***140***

App. 1.2 ii: Distribution of Dissident Sunday Schools x Regions

Area/ Year	01 Mendip	02 Quantock		03 Exmoor	04 Taunton + Levels	05 South	06 Central		07 S East		08 East		09 N East	Totals
		W	E				W	E	S	E	W	E		
No of Chapels	*08*	*02*	*10*	*18*	*24*	*09*	*04*	*04*	*12*		*13*		*17*	***121***
No. SnSc 1870+				*02*							*01*		*04*	***07***
1846-69			*01*	*02*	*01*		*02*	*02*					*02*	***10***
1833-45			*06*	*01*				*01*						***08***
1800-32	*02*	*02*	*01*				*01*	*02*	*05*		*01*			***14***
Pre-1800				*01*										***01***
Total Sn Schs	***02***	***02***	***08***	***06***	***01***	***09***	***03***	***05***	***05***			***02***	***06***	***40***

These tables show a similar distribution as that of the Day schools (Chapter 1).
In all cases, area 2 (Quantocks and Poldens),
area 6 (Central, around Martock and Somerton),
area 7 (South east, around Milborne Port and Wincanton)
are each higher in numbers of Sunday Schools (as they are in Day Schools) than other areas

Also, areas 3 and 9 (Exmoor, including the western ports of Minehead, Porlock, Watchet and the north east mining area around Radstock) are, in the later periods, higher in 'dissenter chapels' and Sunday Schools, than some other areas.

The arc of lands reaching from the Quantocks, Poldens, centre and down to Milborne links west and east being lands which are higher and drier than the surrounding flooded lowlands. This arc also carries the ancient Pilgrim route from the coast to Glastonbury, and includes parts of the old Roman road too. It seems to have been a route by which goods and ideas could spread and where minds were receptive to 'new ways'.

App. 4.1: Main Benefactors and examples of their Schools

Lord Egremont ***west*** Nether Stowey 1813 *w Th Poole* Enmore 1847 *w Rev Poole*	Over Stowey SnSc 1819 1883 enlg £100 for *E J Stanley* MP Quantock Lodge
Earl of Carnarvon ***west*** Chipstable 1876 *w Ld Portman*	Brompton Regis 1861 *Ldy Carnarvon* Bury 1870s *Lady Carnarvon*
Acland ***west*** Allerford +Selworthy 1861 Stogursey 1861, enlg'89 Newton,M Petherton 1867	Withycombe 1866 Porlock Port 1876 Luccombe 1881 Winsford 1881 *w Ld Carnarvon*
Lord Egremont ***central*** Ashill 1842	Ilton 1861 (1875) Williton?
Sir Alexander Hood ***central***	Sampford Brett 1867 *w Ld Egremont*
Luttrell ***west*** Minehead 1840 Kilve/QuantoxheadW 1875	Dunster 1872 Luxborough 1872
Sir Richard / John Slade SheptonMallett 1627 *Sch+THo* NPeth ***BluecoatSch*** C18th in 2-str ChHo	St Michael Church *Lady Slade* 1770s Brdgw Buncombe *Lady Slade* 1836
Lord Poulet ***south*** Wrington 1857 *£1500* **pointed style** Misterton 1874 (w Ld Portman) Chudworth 1876 Chillington 1882	Lopen 1878 Knowle St Giles 1883 Seavington St Michael 1889 Hinton St George *Lady Poulett*
Lord Portman ***south+east*** Sutton Montis 1841 Haslebury Plunknett 1858 Barrow N, Barrow S 1861, 1875 Broadway 1870 Hardington Mandeville 1875 *w Wadham Coll*	Corton Denham+AbbasTempeC '45 Coker E 1851 Chinnock E 1877 Thurlbare 1872 Pennard E 1876 + Pylle 1875/6 Corfe 1883
Lee of Dillington ***south*** Whitelackington 1875	Bickenhall 1889 *w Ld Portman*
Strangways/Earl of Ilchester ***south*** ChinnockW 1833 *w Wadham Coll*	**Lord Digby, Sherborne** Limington 1834 *w Wadham Coll*
Local notables: Poole family Nether Stowey Thomas 1813 Enmore Rev John 1847 Batcombe " "	Rode Pooll family 1860 *suptWesSc* St Decumans 1872 Rev *Robert* Poole

The table gives examples, as reported in the Trade Directories, which are not always fulsome in the detail given. Many additional villages were under the sway of such Lords of the Manor but their involvement with the school was not always made clear. Further, several livings were held by Oxbridge Colleges. There does not appear to be any noticeable link between their Church responsibilities and any educational ones – which is unsurprising given the Colleges distaste for 'popular education'.

App. 4.2: Main Architects and examples of their Schools

R Carver Nether Stowey (advisor) 1813	Nettlecombe 1919 (architect) Milverton 1835
James Thompson Norton St Phillip 1827	
G T Williams Limington 1834	
C E Giles Charlton Mackrell 1853 Stoke St Gregory 1857	West Hatch 1858
George Reed ? **TH Wyatt**	Burnham 1856 Lullington 1862
Charles Bond *blr of Barrington* Puckington 1862	
W Clarke Brewham S 1863	
John Norton Charlton E? 1853	Stogursey 1860 High Ham 1865 (demolished)
Henry Hall Horsington 1857 West Camel *T Ho* 1869 Ansford 1876	Milborne Port 1864 *£2000* Henstridge 1872 *£1300* Cadbury N 1875 *£1100* Langport 1876/7
JH Spencer Norton Fitzwarren 1872	Creech St Michael 1873 Trull 1875
JM Allen Coombe St Nicholas Curry Rivel 1876 Ilminster 1877 Brd Sc	Shepton Beauchamp 1865 Crewkerne W St 1871, N St 1877 Clapton 1878
Benjamin Ferry Dowlish Wake?	**Diocesan Architect** Buckland St Mary 1876
FB Bond Chilcompton 1897 *alts*	
AB Cottam Bridgwater 1896	Langport Grammar 1896 W Huntspill 1897

Given that 'architects' as a profession only began to emerge in the mid-C19th – and their services cost additional money – it is not surprising that we do not often know the names of the architects, if indeed they were employed at all. Many buildings, in the domestic 'Tudor' style would have been erected by local builders using time-honoured methods. Individual architects used different ideas or responded to different client demands at each build. It is difficult to identify 'their' style. By the C20th this had changed, particularly when the LEA took over and used local authority architects and issued often conforming guidelines.

App. 5.1 i School Distribution: % of schools *built* in each period x region

	1 Mend	*2* Qntk*	*3 Exm*	*4 Lvl*	*5 Sth*	*6 Som*	*7* SE*	*8 East*	*9* MinN*	100%
1902 1944										
1901 1870	6	**15**	12	**22**	**15**	**13**	1	10	4	*98*
1869 1846	10	10	**15**	9	11	8	**12**	11	10	*96*
1845 1833	8	**27**	3	3	5	5	**19**	**10**	**19**	*100*
Pre - 1833	18	9+	13	4	18	4	9	9	13	*97*

+many schools existed in *other* buildings, only purpose-built in 1870s

Above we find that other regions (1,3,5) started early and then seem to pause before reviving later, as grants became more widespread. As before, we see that almost the same regions (2,7,8 and 9) are the ones in which building was soon established.

App. 5.1 ii School Distribution: % of schools *built* within each region x period

	1 Mend	*2* Qntk*	*3 Exm*	*4 Lvl*	*5 Sth*	*6 Som*	*7* SE*	*8 East*	*9* MinN*	
1944 1902										
1902 1870	20	32	30	**56**	37	47	3	27	11	
1869 1846	**52**	**35**	**57**	37	**43**	43	**61**	**55**	**50**	
1845 1833	12	27	3	3	6	8	26	12	27	
%	*84*	*94*	*90*	*96*	*86*	*98*	*90*	*94*	*87*	

By analysing the figures to focus on each region we can see that areas 2,7,9 show a high percentage of schools built before grants were directly available. The general interest in education seems common to all these areas in the 1846-69 period where building grew apace – funded from private and community support as well as from the more available grants. The Levels area (and central), particularly seemed to need the additional help offered by the provision for School Boards to set up new schools where there were insufficient facilities.

App. 5.2 i Distribution of schools by size (where known) x region

No. of pupils	*1 Mend*	*2* Qntk*	*3 Exm*	*4 Lvl*	*5 Sth*	*6 Som*	*7* SE*	*8 East*	*9* MinN*	Totals
230+	4	1	(4)	(3)	6	2	3	1	3	*27*
120-230	4	2	6	9	**13***	7	6	**10***	**10***	*67*
80-120	**7**	**14**	9	10	10	**9**	**11**	9	4	*83*
40-80	3	**14**	**22**	**17**	**13**	8	**11**	**10**	5	*103*

We can see the majority of Somerset village schools are very small: these figures give numbers on Roll, but the numbers attending were much smaller.

Increase in larger schools relates to proximity to manufacture/mining centres
5. near Chard, Crewkerne, Yeovil
8. near Wookey/Westbury (Mendip lead), and Doulting/Pilton (quarrying)
9. around the Radstock coalfield

App. 5.2 ii Distribution of nonconformist schools (where given) x region

	1 Mend	*2* Qntk*	*3 Exm*	*4 Lvl*	*5 Sth*	*6 Som*	*7* SE*	*8 East*	*9* MinN*	
1870-1901	1		3*				1		1	
1846-1869	4*	3	1	1			1		6*	
1833-1845		3					2			
Pre - 1833	1	1					1	1		
Total	6	*7*	***4***	***1***			***5***	***1***	*7*	

Each of the main towns in each region had a nonconformist school, and
1. includes manufacturing centres of Axbridge and Cheddar
3. includes port centres of Watchet and Williton;
6. includes Radstock coalfields

6a. Teachers and their Qualifications

Figures for school staff before 1870 are haphazard. These below are national, not Somerset – quoted from Tropp (1957), in the Plowden Report (HMSO, 1967) and figures (^) from Horn (1989) – but they help to gauge the spread of schooling

App. 6.1 i: Numbers of teachers in State Schools by qualification and gender

	1847*-59	1870	1880	1899	1914^	1947	1965
Cert M **Teachers F**		6,395 6,072	21,223 31,718	24,253+ 37,832+	13% trained + cert	Total PrimT 115,000	Total PrimT 140,000
Uncert/Assist M **Teachers F**		487 775	5,047 22,914	4,750 25,500	27% untrained +cert		
Trainee M **Pupil- Teachers F**	7,343 5,261	6,384 8,228	7,246 26,757	6,081 24,702			
Supplementary M **(Art 68) F**			11,678	16,717	41% untrained no cert		

* The Pupil-teacher scheme began in 1846

+Of the certificated males 69.3% had been trained for 2 years
2.6% 1 year
28.1% had had no training

+Of the certified females 46.5% had been trained for 2 years
2.6% 1 year
50.9% had had no training

Training Facilities: App. 6.1 ii: Changing Training Facilities + numbers of students

	1846	1861	1890	1900	1914	1965
No of Colleges	2	35				
Day Centres			3,000	4,000		
LEA Colleges					22	120
No of students		2,100				70,000

6b. Numbers of Schools and Pupils

App. 6.2 i: Growth in Numbers of schools + pupils: [post 1870 schools merged + enlarged]

1729	1,419 'Charity' Schools	22,303 pupils	
1780	1,000 Sunday Schools	69,000 pupils	
1800	18,000 all Elem Schools	500,000 pupils	25% of parishes had no kind of school
1861	59,000 Elem Schools	2.5 mill pupils	4% of parishes had no kind of school

	1800	**1861**	**1870**	**1899**	**1947**	**1965**
No of Schs **Board Sch**	18,000	59,000+	13,000 300	20,000* 2,500	21,000^	21,000^
No of Pupils **in Board Sch**	500,000	2.5mill	1.5mill .5mill	 2.0mill	3,5mill	4.0mill

+ of which 25,000 received grants (20,000 for National, 1,000 British, 1,600 other denominations) for 1.5million pupils

* Nos of schools receiving grants of which 11,00 National and 5,500 British Schools
^ Date from Plowden para 1081, and from para 1185f

Selected References

Background Sources

Bradley JJ *The State and Education in England and Wales* Macmillan 1969

Cressy D *Education in Tudor and Stuart England: Documents* Arnold 1975

Lawson G & Silver H *Social History of Education in England* Methuen 1973

May T *The Victorian Schoolroom* Shire 1996

Midwinter E *Education in the Nineteenth Century: Documents* Longmans 1970

Philosophers, Philanthropists, Pioneers

Hopkins M *Hannah More and her Circle* London 1933

Page J *Sarah Comer and her Cheddar Charity* Charity Trustees 2002

Poole Rev J *The Village School Improved* London 1812

Sandford Mrs *Thomas Poole and his Friends* 1888, 1996

Stewart WEAC *The Educational Innovators: 1881-1967* London 1968

Specific Aspects of Education: Teachers and Buildings

Dent H C *The Training of Teachers in England and Wales 1800-1975* Hodder 1977

Rich RW *The Training of Teachers in England and Wales During C19th* CUP 1933,'72

Sandford F ed. *Reports on Elementary Schools 1852-82 by Matthew Arnold* London 1889

Tropp A *The School Teacher: from 1800 to the present day* London 1957

Seaborne M *The English School: architecture and organization 1370-1870* London 1971

Harwood E *England's schools: history, architecture and conservation* Eng Heritage 2010

Books on Individual Village Schools: Child's Experience

Bushell HWD *School's Cool* North Curry Society 2002

Davies K *Fiddington Village School* History Circle 1989

Day A *A History of E. Harptree School* private publication

Fryer JA *Penny to go to School* (Churchill) Woodspring Centre 2011

Laver S *The Story of Enmore School* for 175th Anniversary, 1985

Mansfield P *History of a Somerset Parish*, 2005 Enmore School archive

Nye L *A Village School* (Brewham) priv publication 2010

Ward S *Don't Learn my Son no Sums* (Bishop Sutton) Yardstick pub. 2009

130 years of Othery Village School Local History Group 2010

For Comparison

Horn P *The Victorian and Edwardian Schoolchild* Alan Sutton 1989

Horn P *Education in Rural England 1800-1914* Alan Sutton 1978

Sellman RR *Devon Village Schools in the C19th* Newton Abbot 1967

Simon B ed. *Education in Leicestershire1540-1940* Leicester University Press 1968

Swinborne AJ *Memoires of an School Inspector [Yorks] held at* Durham Univ, c 1912

Local Data (General education references held at C/E/4/.....)
Victoria County History, Somerset [some volumes online]
Parish Packs, local reports etc available in **Somerset Heritage Centre**, Taunton
Trade Directories Morris 1840, Kelly from 1861-1933
Education Returns 1902, made to the new Local Education Authorities

Noble Woman's Work in Cheddar [re Hannah More] D/P/ched/17/7/7
Hannah More The Blagdon Controversy DD/SAS/C795/FA/12
Subscription Books D/D/Bs 39, 41, 44
Nomination for Licenses (Schoolmasters) D/D/Rn

Account of Church Education among the Poor in the Diocese of Bath and Wells, 1834
Rev JBB Clarke *Diocesan Inspector of Schools*, Report 1847
Rev W Mitchell *Diocesan Inspector of Schools*, Report 1869

Index of Key People and Places

i. Key People significant to the story of village schooling in Somerset

ii. Key Places and Schools used in the study

Pages listed below indicate where school Logs are quoted, or school is cited to illustrate a shared characteristic.

Brief reference is made to several other schools as well, in passing, which may illustrate a particular point but are not part of the focus study.